A MIND AT SEA

A MIND AT SEA

Henry Fry and the Glorious Era of
Quebec's Sailing Ships

JOHN FRY

DUNDURN
TORONTO

Editor: Allison Hirst
Design: Jesse Hooper
Printer: Webcom

Library and Archives Canada Cataloguing in Publication

Fry, John, 1930-, author
  A mind at sea : Henry Fry and the glorious era of Quebec's sailing ships / John Fry.

Includes bibliographical references and index.
Issued in print and electronic formats.
ISBN 978-1-4597-1929-3 (pbk.).--ISBN 978-1-4597-1930-9 (pdf).--ISBN 978-1-4597-1931-6 (epub)

  1. Fry, Henry. 2. Merchants--Québec (Province)--Québec--Biography. 3. Shipowners--Québec (Province)--Québec--Biography. 4. Ship brokers--Québec (Province)--Québec--Biography. 5. Reformers--Québec (Province)--Québec--Biography. 6. Shipbuilding industry--Québec (Province)--Québec--History--19th century. 7. Sailing ships--Québec (Province)--Québec--History--19th century. 8. Québec (Québec)--History--19th century.

  I. Title.

HE769.F79 2013   382.092   C2013-905483-9
                                         C2013-905484-7

1   2   3   4   5   17   16   15   14   13

We acknowledge the support of the **Canada Council for the Arts** and the **Ontario Arts Council** for our publishing program. We also acknowledge the financial support of the **Government of Canada** through the **Canada Book Fund** and **Livres Canada Books**, and the **Government of Ontario** through the **Ontario Book Publishing Tax Credit** and the **Ontario Media Development Corporation**.

Care has been taken to trace the ownership of copyright material used in this book. The author and the publisher welcome any information enabling them to rectify any references or credits in subsequent editions.

J. Kirk Howard, President

The publisher is not responsible for websites or their content unless they are owned by the publisher.

Printed and bound in Canada.

VISIT US AT
Dundurn.com | @dundurnpress | Facebook.com/dundurnpress | Pinterest.com/dundurnpress

Dundurn	Gazelle Book Services Limited	Dundurn
3 Church Street, Suite 500	White Cross Mills	2250 Military Road
Toronto, Ontario, Canada	High Town, Lancaster, England	Tonawanda, NY
M5E 1M2	L41 4XS	U.S.A. 14150

"*The beautiful St. Lawrence sparkling and flashing in the sunlight, and the tiny ships below the Rock ... whose distant rigging looks like spiders' webs against the light ... form one of the brightest and most enchanting pictures the eye can rest upon.*"
— CHARLES DICKENS

"*Industry is the enemy of melancholy.*"
— WILLIAM F. BUCKLEY JR.

Contents

RIGGING CONFIGURATIONS OF WOODEN SHIPS CONSTRUCTED IN EASTERN CANADA IN THE NINETEENTH CENTURY

SQUARE-RIGGED

Ship   Barque   Barquentine

Brig   Brigantine   Snow

FORE AND AFT RIGGED

Schooner   Three-Masted Schooner   Sloop

Illustration from *The Charley-Man*, adapted by Doug Abdelnour.

Preface

By 1855, Canada ranked among the world's great ship-owning and ship-building nations. A vast dispersed flotilla of 7,196 Canadian-constructed wooden ships sailed the oceans of both hemispheres.[1] Quebec was the business centre of it all, one of the world's most important trading ports, and it was here that twenty-seven-year-old Henry Fry settled about a century after British soldiers ended France's failed North American empire.[2]

At the time of two decisive battles that took place on the Plains of Abraham,[3] Quebec was overwhelmingly French-speaking, and it would become so again. But for a few years in the middle of the nineteenth century, two of every five residents of the port city used the everyday language of English, and even more did so in business.[4] Shipbuilding and owning, and timber commerce — largely conducted by men like Henry through their British contacts — dominated the economic life of Lower Canada, while the city served off and on as its capital.

At the time, shipping agents and brokers were not generally admired for their business ethics. Many were known for charging usurious fees in advancing money to shipbuilders. They overloaded unseaworthy ships with timber to enlarge their profits, endangering the lives of seamen. Henry Fry was a notable exception.[5] Scrupulous, honest, and generous, he fought against human rights abuses, such as excessive deck loading and crimping. "He was an outstanding figure in the maritime history of Canada," wrote Basil Greenhill, former director of the National Maritime Museum in Greenwich, England.

Canada's maritime record was enriched by Fry's achievements, says Eileen Marcil, author of *The Charley Man*, the most complete and authoritative history of Quebec's great shipbuilding era. Marcil provided much of the research for this biography.

As Lloyd's agent for the St. Lawrence River, Fry was a fountain of information about cargo rates, tariffs, ship insurance, hull and deck design, and the details of sails and rigging. "No man had a better knowledge of Quebec shipping and shipbuilding," wrote the maritime historian Frederick William Wallace.[6]

Canadian shipbuilders and owners like Fry captured a huge share of the world's carrying trade, "building up a reputation for smart ships that was a legend in nautical history," Wallace wrote. But then the industry "vanished utterly into the mists of oblivion."

Replaced by steam-powered iron vessels, the great wooden square-riggers sailed off over the horizon. No museum exists to commemorate the vanished work of the men — French, British, and Irish — who built Quebec's million tons of sailing ships. After the industry collapsed, hundreds of skilled carpenters, smithies, block and mast makers, riggers, and rope and sail makers left the Quebec shipbuilding yards to seek manufacturing jobs in New England. Many in the English business class returned to England, or fled for Montreal, in an exodus comparable to that of a hundred years later when fears of the economic consequences of Separatism drove much of the anglophone business class out of Montreal.

That the author should be the great-grandson of the subject of this biography may raise suspicion that it is one of those whitewashed family hagiographies. I freely admit my admiration of Henry Fry. Yet I've not failed to describe his blemishes — for example, the racial superiority that he occasionally vented. He suffered from mental depression for a period in his life. It was not pleasant for me to describe with factual accuracy his episodic mental illness, previously concealed from our family.

In a few places in the biography, notably chapter 1, I have resorted to imaginary scenes. I've done this with judicious care, fictionalizing for the reader only what I already know is likely to have been the true case of what happened. At worst, you can call it informed speculation.

My descriptions of Quebec are an unapologetically written anglo-phone perspective of nineteenth-century Canadian life. Admirers of

Fernand Ouellet's *Economic and Social History of Quebec* will find little to disagree with in my account of the dominant role played by the British merchant class in shaping Quebec's economy. Scholarly francophones, however ardent their biases, will nevertheless want to add my account to the historical record.

Henry Fry was a Victorian of bristling courage. He fought injustice strenuously. He gave copiously to the poor and defended the disenfranchised. He battled his illness with persistent courage, and against all odds overcame it and went on to write essays and reminiscences, and in 1896 the definitive *History of North Atlantic Steam Navigation*, a reference book employed by maritime historians to this day. His life is a window into a forgotten time of Canadian enterprise.

Persons of Interest

Belleau, Sir Narcisse-Fortunat (1808–94): politician, lawyer, business-man, lieutenant-governor of Quebec (1867–73).

Cauchon, Joseph-Edouard (1816–85): Quebec journalist, politician.

Cook, John (1805–92): first moderator of the General Assembly of the Presbyterian Church in Canada.

Dawson, Mary Jane: wife of Henry Fry. Born 1836, Halifax; died 1932, Montreal.

Dawson, Samuel Edward: brother of Mary Dawson Fry, close friend of Henry, publisher, historian, Queen's Printer of Canada, 1891–1908.

Dinning, Henry (1830–84): Quebec shipbuilder.

Dufferin, Lord (1826–1902): governor general of Canada (1872–78), and his wife, the **Marchioness of Dufferin and Ava.**

Fry, Christopher (1907–2005): playwright and author. Born Arthur Hammond Harris; author of *The Lady's Not for Burning.*

Fry, George: father of Henry Fry. Bristol, England, 1783–1868.

Fry, Henry: Quebec merchant; ship-owner; president of the Dominion Board of Trade and Quebec Board of Trade; Lloyd's agent for the St. Lawrence River; author. Born 1826, Bristol, England; died 1896, Sweetsburg, Quebec.

Siblings of Henry Fry: Alfred, Charlotte, Charles, Samuel Holmes, Elizabeth, Lucy, Frederick Morley, Edward Carey, Emma.

Children of Henry and Mary Dawson Fry: Mary "Mame" Dawson (only daughter), Henry Jr., William Marsh, Arthur Dawson, Alfred Gardner, Frederick Morley, Ernest John.

Hallock, Dr. Winthrop: pioneer of *The Cottage System for the Insane Cromwell, Connecticut.*

Hamilton, Reverend Charles (1834–1919): first Anglican bishop of Ottawa.

Laurier, Wilfrid: head of the Liberal Party, 1896.

Macdonald, Sir John A.: first prime minister of Canada.

Marsh, David: Baptist minister, Quebec. Died 1889.

Ross, James Gibb: Quebec merchant, investor, and politician.

Slack, Dr. George F.: physician, Farnham, Quebec.

Stearns, Dr. Henry: superintendent of the Hartford Retreat, Connecticut.

Stevenson, James (1813–94): general manager, Bank of Quebec, father-in-law of Henry Fry Jr.

Whitwill, Mark (1838–1918): shipbroker, Bristol, England, employer of Henry.

Yeo, William: merchant, ship-owner, Devon. Son of James Yeo (Prince Edward Island merchant and politician). Early financial backer of Henry Fry. Died 1872.

**Please note: Quebec, in this book, refers to the city of Quebec. The province of Quebec came into being in 1867 with Confederation, when Lower Canada ceased to exist.

1

1877
Launch

Success can be a hair's breadth from ruin. One day in a man's life can begin exultantly, yet end ruinously before the sun has set.

For Henry Fry, the long northern day of June 27, 1877, contained lustrous promise. The glittering surface of the St. Lawrence River mirrored the slivers of cloud drifting across the sky. Under the cliff rising to Quebec's Plains of Abraham, Henry and a group of smiling, festively dressed people were gathered beside the two-hundred-foot-long, fully masted and rigged sailing ship *Cosmo*, which rested on its launching ways in Cape Cove.

"Hurrah!" shouted Henry, standing next to his close friend, shipbuilder Henry Dinning. The men were on a platform under the *Cosmo*'s iron bowsprit. Ahead of them a slender, elegant woman wearing a black full-length bustled dress, gaily smiling, had just raised her hand holding a bottle of port, which she cracked vigorously against the bow.

"God bless the *Cosmo* and all who sail in her!" she cried.

"*Maintenant,*" shouted the yard foreman. "*Faites sauter la clef.*"

Down at the stern, a workman sledgehammered away the last block holding the 1,220-ton ship in its sloping cradle. There was a loud creak. The ship quivered, and the tamarack frame moved an inch, then another, before picking up speed on the greased ways and sliding down into the cove, sending a grey-blue wave into the St. Lawrence.[1]

"Hourra, Hurrah," cried the mixed crowd of carpenters, caulkers, ironsmiths, joiners, painters, and riggers standing around. It was a day of celebration for the men — French-Canadians, Irish, Scots, English, and a few craftsmen recently arrived from Europe. They'd just enjoyed a free whiskey, a tradition at ship launchings, when they were paid, though not required to work. They'd axed and sawed and hammered in the frigid outdoors through the winter of 1876–77 in order to build the magnificent square-rigger, and they were grateful to the two men who'd given them employment. Some of their families would have suffered desperately were it not for Dinning, the shipyard's owner, and for Fry, the Quebec shipping merchant who'd designed and financed the iron-masted *Cosmo*, and whose wife, Mary Dawson Fry, has just smashed a bottle of fine Portuguese port wine against her bow.

Mary was not only godmother to the new *Cosmo*, but co-signer on a $48,000 loan to build her[2] — the equivalent of nearly a million dollars today. Even though her husband assured her that the money from the *Cosmo*'s first cargo would be enough to satisfy the banks, the borrowing worried her. Mary Fry, however, was a woman who readily displayed neither weakness nor worry. She perpetually bore herself bravely. Mary had been the bulwark of Henry's existence in their two decades of marriage, the ruler of his family during his frequent absences in England.

Beside Mary at the launch were her six sons. The youngest, less than a year old, was cradled in the arms of their only daughter, seventeen-year-old Mame. The boys appeared tense, warily searching their father's eyes for a hint of approbation. Behind the family stood Henry's clerks, who'd walked to the launching from their office on St. Peter Street. Also present was Mary's brother, the smart and scholarly Samuel Edward Dawson, book-seller, future Queen's Printer of Canada, historian, and bosom pal of Henry.

Pacing among the cast of characters was shipbuilder Dinning — good-tempered, always optimistic, sporting a tall stovepipe hat and bow tie and gushing with pride. The *Cosmo* and the hull of the *Lorenzo*, resting on the stocks nearby, would be Dinning's last wooden sailing ships — indeed, the two were among the last forty built in the Port of Quebec, concluding a 130-year era that saw the construction of 1,633 sailing ships, two-thirds of them launched in the stupendous period of shipbuilding from 1840 to 1870.[3]

On the day of the *Cosmo*'s launching, in coves all up and down the shores of the St. Lawrence, an uncountable number of squared lengths of timber bobbed in the water, ready to be loaded onto vessels sailing to Europe. Upstream from the *Cosmo*'s launch site, down to the St. Charles River and across to the Île d'Orléans, rafts the size of small islands held thousands of tons of wood.

Before the launch, Henry had spoken briefly to the crowd, and then asked David Marsh, the pastor of Quebec's Baptist Church, to say a few words. Marsh and Henry were close. Henry once described their friendship, outside of his own family, as "the warmest and tenderest I ever knew."[4]

"Reverend Marsh, please grace us with your benediction."

"I shall, Henry," responded Marsh. Hatless and wearing a thread-bare, short-tailed frock coat, the pastor bowed his head and proceeded to intone the words of Psalm 107 to the crowd: "They that go down to the sea in ships, that do business on great waters; these see the works of the Lord, and his wonders in the deep."

A brisk breeze had begun to blow in from the river, stirring the water so that Pastor Marsh had to raise his voice to be heard. He possessed the gift of speaking simply and fervently. A sophisticated scholar and lecturer on astronomy and chemistry, Marsh had been chosen to tutor the daughter of Lord Elgin when the latter was governor general. Now, against the backdrop of the St. Lawrence River, Marsh lauded the work that the construction of the *Cosmo* had provided to needy men and praised his friend Henry Fry's willingness to risk his business fortunes.

It was perhaps enough that every Sunday Fry absorbed his friend's sometimes diffuse homilies. So, as Marsh spoke, Fry found that his mind drifted to thoughts of the hectic hours that lay ahead, crammed as they would be with obligatory meetings — sessions with his banker, notary, a sail-maker demanding money, the harbour commissioners, the Young Men's Christian Association. Henry didn't resent the burden of the work. When he suffered a tinge of melancholy, he sensed that the cure was industriousness, an acknowledged virtue of the Victorian age.

Henry was more imposing in appearance than one might expect of a man of medium height, his torso disproportionately long in relation to his legs. He wore a black wide-lapelled topcoat over a cutaway morning coat suited to the occasion. His face was chiseled, forthright, with comprehending eyes and firm, compressed lips. His bronze hair, thinning on top, receded from a broad forehead. It was thick and curled at the sides of his head and over his ears. A polka dot ascot tie was partly concealed by a beard, which formed a collar around his neck, a style fashionable at the time, one that left the chin and mouth clean-shaven. His fifty-first birthday was only a few weeks off. A portrait of Henry, taken five years earlier by the celebrated Montreal photographer William Notman,[5] reveals a man with a slight paunch, nourished by a fondness for sweets. But there was no other hint of softness. Notman's portrait is one of a determined, defiant character. Henry's face bore no visible hint of vulnerability or failure. "He was a bold business man," wrote the maritime historian Frederick William Wallace, "not afraid to risk his capital when others held back. In any walk of life he would be characterized as a man of resolution and daring."[6]

The *Cosmo*, with its three iron masts and bowsprit, was Henry's triumph. Though it was the last ship he commissioned, it was his best. An act induced by the charitable goal of providing the unemployed with work and wages had resulted in "the finest ship ever constructed at Quebec," according to Lloyd's of London. High praise, considering

Notman Collection, McCord Museum, 1-70328.1.

Notman Collection, McCord Museum, 1-4235.1.

A mind at work: *Henry Fry was president of Canada's Dominion Board of Trade in 1872. A year later, in London, he convinced Parliament to ban wintertime deck loading of ships, which was costing the lives of hundreds of seamen on the North Atlantic. Montreal's renowned photographer William Notman made several portraits of Fry over the years, including the two above.*

that in the previous seventy years Quebec yards had launched almost a million tons of sailing ships of one hundred tons burden or burthen — ships capable of carrying cargoes of more than a hundred tons.[7]

The *Cosmo*'s bottom was made of prized rock elm, the frame, beams, and most of the planking of tamarack. The master's cabin was beautifully walled in ash and black walnut panelling. With her two-hundred-foot length on a thirty-six-foot beam, *Cosmo* would prove fast in the water. In just six days she would depart on her maiden voyage, carrying a cargo of wood from Quebec to Liverpool.

Cosmo was a ship that deserved to be memorialized, and yesterday Henry had commissioned the building of a nine-foot-long wooden model.[8] He had written a letter to an artist in London commissioning a painting as well. He was unconscious of the fact that his pleasure and pride would soon dissolve.

Wooden shipbuilding, nineteenth century: *The planking stage of a sailing ship's construction, on the St. Lawrence River shoreline around Quebec.*

Henry named the *Cosmo* after the barque on which he'd first sailed to North America in 1853, twenty-four years earlier. Ships had infatuated him ever since he was a boy in Bristol, which at one time in the eighteenth century had been Britain's second most important city. "The love of ships and everything connected with them seemed to be innate," he wrote. "As soon as I could toddle around the Quay of Bristol, I began to study the models and rigs of vessels."[9]

Yet by the time Henry began purchasing his own ships in 1855, the future lay with iron hulls and steam. Passenger service from Quebec to Liverpool by sail could take less than three weeks; westward, and in bad weather, more than two months. Steam, by contrast, reliably cut travel time to fewer than nine days. Nevertheless, Henry had persisted in owning freight-carrying sailing ships, for reasons not only of sentiment but of economic reality. Quebec was blessed with a seemingly limitless supply of wood, and wooden square-riggers before 1870 were still the most cost-efficient means of trans-ocean transport.

Back on the dock, Henry glanced at Marsh. His religious mentor and treasured friend was still delivering his homily, eyes frequently closed in reverence as he spoke. Henry was reminded of the Baptist Church's critical role in his own decision to leave England, and his eventual settlement in Quebec. He'd originally departed, he told everyone, because he was suffering from overwork. But had another difficulty consumed him? To his Baptist minister in Bristol, the twenty-nine-year-old Henry had confessed that he was wracked by doubt. "A painful conflict ensued which robbed me of all peace," he recalled about his state of mind. He had left the church, but was about to return to the fold, "when from mental over-exertion and late hours of business, my health suddenly gave way, and both body and mind became prostrated."[10]

His breakdown could have been triggered by the speculative, nerve-wracking career that he'd chosen. The shipbuilding business was tough and physical, and financial danger lurked everywhere. Ships all too often were driven ashore or broke apart in violent seas, and loss of lives was common. The value of cargoes rose and fell as they crossed the ocean. Shipping was not a business conducive to tranquility or spiritual calm.

Henry's bout of depression lasted a year. Yet almost immediately after crossing the Atlantic he was brokering cargoes and making deals.

As the years progressed, he commissioned dozens of sailing ships and loaded them with grain, wood, rails, hemp, nitrate, and other cargo. They were then shipped out to the farthest corners of the world.

Shipbuilders and maritime scholars admired Fry's encyclopedic knowledge of ships — both sail and steam. His knowledge was reflected in exquisite pen-and-ink drawings that he made of the ships in which he owned a share, with accurate detailing of every square foot of sail and inch of rigging.

Marsh, still orating beside him, reminded Henry of himself. *We both dislike pretentiousness and intolerance,* he reflected. *Injustices readily anger us.* Henry had partly inherited his acute ethical sensibilities from the Bristol Baptist church, Broadmead, where he was a member. Broadmead's congregants had courageously favoured emancipation in a city that had only recently designed and built ships for the express purpose of transporting African slaves to the Americas.

Henry sniffed out injustice as keenly as some men do opportunity. He was an early conservationist, saying that Canada should focus on preserving its forests, rather than stripping them indiscriminately to satisfy markets for cheap raw wood.[11] He publicly attempted to persuade the government to suppress the scandal of crimping, in which Quebec criminals haunted the port, bribing or forcing sailors to leave their ships, conniving with tavern owners to make them drunk, then delivering them to another skipper for a fee. In 1874 he had helped to persuade the British Parliament to pass a bill prohibiting the greedy practice of loading additional cargo on decks in the winter months. It made ships top-heavy and vulnerable to capsizing in the storm-ridden North Atlantic seas, causing the deaths of hundreds of helpless men who enjoyed no supportive political constituency other than that furnished by men like Henry Fry and Samuel Plimsoll, creator of the Plimsoll line, who, like Henry, had been born in Bristol.

Just four years earlier, in Ottawa, Henry had been elected president of the recently founded Dominion Board of Trade, Canada's leading business organization made up of regional boards of trade with delegates from twenty-two industries. In London, he told the Associated Chambers of Commerce of the United Kingdom about Canada's pride in its equal laws, "under which English and French, Protestants and Catholics, can live together in peace and harmony," while praising Canada's ineradicable ties to Britain.[12]

Canada's nineteenth-century successes, like Henry's, were profoundly affected by the young country's economic and political bonds with Britain, and ultimate governance originated in Albion. True, Henry was no longer wholly British, but he could not be Canadian without being British. He was repelled by proposals for political or commercial union with the United States and openly expressed dislike for "Yankees" who wanted access to Canadian markets without lowering the protectionist duties shielding their own industries. "Are these the men to control the tariff and destinies of this free, happy country? God forbid!" he wrote in one of the anti-U.S. piques that occasionally agitated him.[13]

He took pleasure in money and savoured his successful investments, but also enjoyed the act of giving. He served on the boards of a dozen charitable and business organizations. He donated today's equivalent of almost $100,000 to repair the monument to Wolfe and Montcalm next to his home, a few hundred yards from the battlefield where troops under the two generals had settled the political fate of British North America in 1759.

As the time of *Cosmo*'s launching, the sun was beating down on the crowd, and Henry felt compelled to interrupt the Reverend Marsh,

Bibliothèque Nationale, Quebec.

Learned man of spirit: *Quebec Baptist Church pastor Rev. David Marsh, intimate friend of shipowning merchant Henry Fry, tutored a governor general's daughter.*

whispering in his ear: "Dear Mr. Marsh, you are speaking well, but the men want their food and drink." Rev. Marsh tactfully rounded out his thoughts about ships going to sea. The outdoor sermon ended, and the *Cosmo*, having slid down the ways, sat rocking gently in the river. The crowd turned to a table on an adjacent wharf, laid out with sandwiches, cheese, biscuits, ale, and spruce beer.

Henry gazed at the docks where the first ships since the breakup of the ice had arrived from Europe and were discharging their cargoes. As Lloyd's agent, he was at the epicentre of the hyperactive world of marine commerce, tracking ships as they sailed up the St. Lawrence to North America's heartland. To fill them with profitable cargo — typically squared timbers pulled out of giant rafts floated down the St. Lawrence from Ottawa and farther away — he spent at least two months in England, drumming up business in London and his home town of Bristol. He crossed the Atlantic thirty-seven times in twenty-five years, usually in winter.[14] In 1877, though, Henry had sent his youngest brother, business pupil, and partner, Edward, to negotiate the sale of wood.

The Frys were a family of difficult individuals, often in need of help from eldest son Henry. He gave the command of one of his ships to his surly, queer-tempered brother Samuel Holmes Fry, who later so insulted him in his home that Henry discharged him. He rescued another brother from destitution in Africa. A cousin, whom he made master of the wonderful Massachusetts-built, oak-framed sailing ship *Sunbeam*, accidentally ran it aground. Against Henry's best judgment, his youngest brother Edward had bought an interest in a narrow iron ship whose masts had to be cut away in a storm when it was in danger of foundering. Then Edward became his partner in Henry Fry & Co. of Quebec City.[15] Henry was counting on Edward to have found buyers in England for the pine, oak, and elm to be carried by *Cosmo* across to Liverpool.

When the launching ceremony was over, the celebrants gave way as Henry, Mary, and their children boarded a tiny steamboat back to the city. On the short trip down the river they passed many ships at anchor or tied up at wharves. Behind them rose the cliffs of knobby brown and grey limestone veined with grass, bramble, and willow — excellent hand- and footholds for a nocturnal climb. A floating dock in L'Anse des Mères held a ship whose hull was being repaired. Past Près de Ville, the water taxi headed toward the heart of the Lower Town, dropping its passengers off at the Napoleon Wharf, near Henry Fry & Co., located on St. Peter Street.

And suddenly, there he was. Out of the corner of his eye, Henry spotted Edward, just arrived from England. Edward was a handsome man, athletic and fierce-looking. The thirty-five-year-old had a shock of curly hair, a strong nose, and piercing eyes.

Henry shook his brother's hand heartily: "I trust you have good news."

"I'm not certain what to say," stuttered Edward, not usually reticent or inclined to stammer.

"You're aware, Edward, that I borrowed forty-eight thousand dollars to build *Cosmo*, counting on the fact that I will be able to pay back the banks with the wood that is to be loaded onto her in the next few days. I instructed you to sell it in England."

"Dear brother, as I say, I am not sure about what I can tell you." Edward averted his eyes from Henry's steady gaze. "I met with lumber merchants in Bristol. Business is at an ebb, they advised me. The prices I was offered were ridiculously low."

"What are you saying?" demanded Henry harshly, his voice cracking. Mary inched closer to the two men, anxious to hear. "Have you sold the pine deals and square tamarack as I arranged, or not?"

"I was able to sell nothing, I'm afraid."

Henry's face flushed in anger, his eyes blazed. "You have failed to carry out my instructions!" he choked out.[16] "How could you have let such a lamentable thing happen?" Then, just as suddenly, Henry's face paled and his cheeks became ashen. His shoulders slumped. Mary, fearing he would fall, grabbed hold of one arm to steady him.

"We must leave now … go home," whispered Henry.

2

1826-38
A Love of Sail

Henry Fry was born and grew up in Bristol, England. Those who knew him weren't allowed to forget that fact. He would remind them that sailors from his home town, not Christopher Columbus, had discovered North America, most especially Canada.

If Brittany's St. Malo represented for French Canadians the European end of the umbilical cord that nurtured Canada's birth, Bristol held a similar claim on the minds of Anglo-Canadians like Henry. One hundred miles distant from St. Malo as the crow flies, northward across the English Channel, Bristol was the port from which John Cabot (or Giovanni Caboto; he was a Venetian) sailed in 1497, thirty-seven years before Jacques Cartier set out from St. Malo on the first of his voyages. Cabot planted the English flag on a shore of Newfoundland in June of 1497,[1] establishing Britain's claim to North America over that of Spain. By Henry's reasoning, New York's annual October holiday march down Fifth Avenue should be called the Cabot Day Parade.

The exact route and time of Cabot's expedition, and the role of his son Sebastian, were subjects of intense interest to Henry (see chapter 26). He carefully described it as a "re-discovery" of North America. Viking explorers had visited the continent's shores in 1000 A.D., he wrote, to say nothing of the Indians and Inuit who were already there. Cabot, having made landfall, and believing he'd discovered the outer shore of Cathay and the infinite wealth of the East, promptly turned his eighty-foot-long, three-masted sailing ship *Matthew* around and sailed with his eighteen-man crew back to Bristol.

The port city to which Cabot returned from his voyage in August 1497, to the acclaim of the king and people of England, was, in Henry's mind, not greatly different from the Bristol of his own childhood.[2] "The street in which the Cabots lived (Cathay) and quays from which he embarked may still be seen," wrote Henry. "The lovely, tortuous little Avon, down which he sailed in his memorable voyages, still winds its way to 'Kingroad', and the Bristol Channel. Most of the streets are narrow and crooked ... full of lanes, alleys, and ancient houses. Bristol was once the second city in the Empire when Liverpool was only a fishing village, and it furnished the King with many ships of war and seamen. Ships from India, America, and all parts of the world now crowd its quays."

Henry grew up less than a city block away from the quays.

The Frys are an ancient Somersetshire family, not to be confused with the Quaker Frys of eastern England. In the seventeenth and eighteenth centuries, they tilled the soil and raised sheep in the countryside around Winscombe, a village southeast of Bristol. Nearby, some of the land is scarcely fifty feet above sea level and, though far inland from the ocean, it was sometimes inundated with saline tidal water during storms.

The topography of the area is unusual in another way. Immediately next to where the Fry family farmed, the most prominent of the Mendip Hills rise abruptly out of the flats, six hundred feet high, a southern wall a couple of miles in length resembling a Sphinx stretched out on Somerset's verdant fields. The hills' lower flanks are forested today, but as you climb, the upland becomes treeless. Here, where the land merges with the sky, flocks of sheep graze, and in the distance you can hear the herders' dogs yapping as they work.[3]

The highest of these downs form a broad, undulating east–west ridge running from the south end of Winscombe, up Wavering Down to Crooked Peak, and steeply down today to the four-lane M5 motorway headed to the southern coast of the English Channel. Back to the east, all remains pastoral beauty. On a clear day, you can view the Severn estuary and the southern coast of Wales to the north. To the south, green as a lustrous garden, all of rural Somerset spreads down to Devon and Dorset. To the west is the vast watery Atlantic, and for a moment it's not hard to imagine a shepherd in 1497 atop the ridge spotting the topsails of Cabot's little *Matthew* as it sailed toward the setting sun. To the east, across a deep cut in the mountains — for centuries a key north–south transportation route — you can see Fry's Hill, a continuation of the mountainous terrain that extends to Cheddar and its tourist-clogged gorge.

Two or three hundred years ago, immediately at the northern foot of these Mendips, in the hamlet of Barton, could be found many acres of fertile freehold held by various Frys,[4] whose sheep furnished wool used to make socks and other textile products in the Somersetshire mills of Shepton Mallet and Bath. The family held on to some of the land barely into the twentieth century. Today in Barton, Fry's Home Farm offers lodging and trailer parking to summer tourists.

Henry Fry's father, George, was born in Barton in 1783. George's great-grandfather had a brother from whom the late British playwright Christopher Fry was descended. The author of *The Lady's Not for Burning*, although born a Harris, his father having died when he was a child, was so enamoured of his mother's family that when he was eighteen years old he changed his surname to Fry. In 1978, his professional career of play and screenwriting mostly behind him, Christopher wrote a family

Photo by the author.

Pastoral homeland: *Southwest England's Mendip Hills form a ridgelike backdrop to Fry Farm and fertile crop and pastureland barely above sea level. Playwright Christopher Fry wrote of his forbears "vigorously populating the gently hilly country in Somerset, between the Mendip Hills and the sea."*

history entitled *Can You Find Me*. He begins by recording that in 1262 the vicar of Winscombe bought from the Dean and Chapter of Wells the liberty of a man named William, the son of Roger de Barton. "He and his are free," state the Cathedral records.[5]

"There must have been something promising about William to encourage the vicar so to spend his money," wrote Christopher. "From that time forward, he and his descendants were known as le Frye, the free men. For the next six centuries they went on being born and buried in Barton, Winscombe, Compton Bishop, and Axbridge."[6]

Over the centuries, the Frys survived the Black Death, the battles of Agincourt and the War of the Roses, witnessed the divorces of Henry VIII and the reign of his formidable childless daughter Elizabeth, the defeat of the Spanish Armada, and the birth of Shakespeare. In 1557, in one of the family's first recorded testaments, Isabell of Barton, widow of Nicholas Frye, is found bequeathing to her daughter Margaret a petticoat and to her sister a black kettle. Isabell's post-mortem beneficence also included saucers, an old coat for her maidservant, and a cupboard for her son John.[7]

Between 1729 and 1734 were born three brothers Fry.[8] The first, William, was Henry Fry's great-grandfather. The second, John, was the author Christopher Fry's triple great-grandfather. The third, Peter, sired a son, Thomas Homfray Fry, in whose memory there is to this day a handsome stained glassed window in the Winscombe Anglican church, bearing the Fry coat of arms, which the family had somehow acquired.[9]

"Very strange and unexpected it is," remarked Christopher Fry about the family's coat of arms. "The nature of the Frys was steady, God-fearing, kindly, unassuming, and mildly humorous; but the coat of arms shows a mailed arm holding a sword, and on the sword is impaled the bloody head of a Moor."

Near the stained glass window in the church, Henry Fry's father, George, was baptized on October 10, 1783. George was the second of four children — two boys and two girls — born to William and Ann Shephard Fry.[10] William was a gentleman having an estate in Badgeworth, a village on the other side of the Mendip Hills from Barton. He had inherited his father's houses and lands in Winscombe. What happened next, though, materially reduced the family's fortunes. William tragically died in 1793 when George was only ten years old. He and his siblings, ranging in age from two to eleven, were left in the care of their mother. The principal trustee of William's will was his brother Peter, who owned at least a half-dozen estates around Somerset. Young George did not grow up orphaned or uneducated.

The patriarch: *George Fry, Henry's father, migrated early in the nineteenth century from the family farm to bustling Bristol, seaport and shipbuilding centre, where he operated a butcher's store and ship victualling business.*

With his father's premature death, however, the die was cast. George would not gain the family homestead. Without land or sheep of his own, young George, like hundreds of thousands of his fellow Englishmen in the nineteenth century, departed the countryside for greater opportunity in the city. He turned to a trade, apprenticing as a butcher, and got himself hired by Andrew Goss, owner of a butcher shop in Bristol.

The butcher had two daughters, Joanna and Charlotte, and it wasn't long before young George's eye strayed from the cutting block to the eldest daughter. In 1811, he married Joanna. Her father may have been a suspicious fellow, obliging George, in the event the marriage didn't take place, to pay the bishop the astronomical sum of a thousand pounds, equal to twenty years of butcher's wages. The marriage fortunately took place and was consummated. The couple had one son, George.

Joanna died in 1820 at the age of thirty-two. As occasionally happened at the time, the widower turned his affections to the deceased's sister, although marrying Charlotte was another matter. The Church typically forbade a man to wed the sister of his deceased wife. Even so, it was not uncommon for the bishop to turn a blind eye to the stricture against sister-marrying in the Old Book of Prayer. George thus married Charlotte Augusta Goss in 1825, and the couple settled down at 2 Prince's Street, close to the centre of Bristol and to the docks where George was already selling goods not only to Bristol residents but also to ships victualling for their outbound voyages. Andrew Goss had helped his son-in-law buy the property.[11] Trade went on at street level, and the family lived above, including eleven-year-old George Jr., the deceased Joanna's child. (At the age of twenty-four, George Jr. migrated to Tasmania, where numerous Frys exist to this day.)

The new family grew rapidly, beginning with Henry. He was born on June 25, 1826, as Charlotte Augusta Goss Fry gave birth to the first of nine children — five boys, and four girls — whom she would bear over the next fifteen years. Henry was the eldest, and in later life the provider.

The house on Prince's Street in which Henry was born and raised was a half-block away from the lovely park-like Queen Square, surrounded by many of Bristol's finest residences. The tranquility was brutally disturbed in 1831. Henry was only five years old when the park became a bloody battleground.

The battle arose from the political turbulence in Britain's fast-growing industrial cities, which lacked fair representation in Parliament. A major city like Bristol had only two Members of Parliament, elected by the one out of ten property owners allowed to vote. A "rotten borough" — and there were many of them in England, some with as few as fifteen inhabitants — could have its own Member of Parliament.

The situation was ripe for reform, but one of Bristol's most powerful men, its Recorder, Sir Charles Wetherell, was opposed. On October 29, 1831, as Wetherell's carriage entered Queen's Square, it was pelted with stones — all this happened near the Fry butcher shop and residence. Stupendous violence erupted, and houses were plundered and set afire, the flames visible from as far away as Wales. Rioters broke into the jail and freed prisoners. Soldiers counterattacked, cutting down the rioters with their swords. As many as ten thousand people were engaged in the fighting. Five hundred died.[12]

The rioters spared the Fry home on Prince's Street. Mother and children may have gone to the country to escape, or perhaps the family cowered in fear within the walls of their house. It would have been a terrifying experience for little Henry.

The boy, though, enjoyed many happy hours. He would stand on the quayside, a stone's throw from his home, peering at sailing ships from around the world. "The love of ships, and everything connected with them, was one of the earliest of my boyish tastes," he later wrote.[13] "As soon as I could toddle round the quays of Bristol, I began to study the various rigs and models of vessels. The first five shillings I ever had were spent in a model of a hull about 18 inches long, which I rigged as a barque and called the *Endeavour* after one of Capt. Cook's exploring ships, 'Cook's Voyages' being the first prize I won at school when only ten."

Down at the dockside, Henry watched the men as they unloaded cargo, caulked the decks and hulls, and mended the spars and rigging. Once all of the outward cargo had been stowed, they would raise the gangplank. Henry would watch until their sails disappeared over the western horizon, where he himself would one day go.

In grammar school, he received an education that was typical for nineteenth-century children whose families could afford the luxury of sending a child to school, rather than having him work. Henry was well-instructed in history and geography, about which he likely knew more than a twenty-first-century college freshman. His spelling was flawless, and he developed a fine-lined, highly legible rightward-slanting handwriting. Canada's future first prime minister, John A. Macdonald, born eleven years before Henry, had received a similar education. He had sat in a small room with children of all ages and, by the time he was twelve, was well-grounded in Latin, knew French, and had worked his way through decimals, ratios, and geometrical proportions.[14]

Education for Henry was amplified by his father, George, who entertained his eldest son and his brothers by reading aloud broadsheets, pamphlets, illustrated books, and magazines about the historic, revolutionary events that occurred in his youth.[15] The boys listened through long evenings as his father described Nelson's defeat of the French at Trafalgar, the necessity of hanging pirates, or the abolition of slavery. George instilled in his son a powerful awareness of injustice of any kind. Pirates should be hanged. The levies imposed by British landowners on their tenants were outrageous. "Fine times those were for the landlords and farmers," George told his children, "but the common people were reduced to the verge of starvation."

Henry's Uncle Holmes, skilled seaman and ship's master, carved and rigged a beautiful model of a schooner for the boy, whetting his interest in the sea. Henry's youthful enthusiasm for ships infected his brothers, too. Three of them would become ships' captains.

Henry would not. He chose, or likely was assigned, to apprentice in the business, not the navigation, of boats. In 1838, the year when the teenaged Victoria was crowned Queen of England, Scotland, and Wales, Henry, then twelve, began work as a junior clerk in a Bristol shipbroker's office. His working life thus came to coincide entirely with Victoria's reign, an extraordinary era of industrial expansion and trade that came to define his life.

3

1838-53
The Young Merchant

His formal academic schooling ended, Henry's practical training began. He started work as a junior clerk in the office of Mark Whitwill, a leading Bristol shipbroker. Whitwill would turn out to be a sharp mentor for the young man. A canny businessman, he owned parts of several ships, managing them as well. He brokered cargoes and booked passengers on sailing ships travelling the North Atlantic between Bristol and New York and Quebec.

Henry joined Whitwill's firm shortly after it began promoting travel on the new *Great Western*, the first steamship to cross the Atlantic without re-coaling.[1] Henry looked out on the Severn on April 8, 1838, as the 212-foot wonder of the new age of ocean travel headed west to New York. The *Great Western* had three masts, with sails to add wind power or as backup in case the engines or huge paddlewheels should break.[2]

"She was of unusual strength," Henry later wrote, "her bottom [of wood] being solid and her frame secured with iron diagonal bracing." On her first Atlantic crossing from Bristol, with forty passengers on board, the *Great Western* took sixteen days to reach the mouth of the Hudson River. Cabin-class passage, including wines and provisions of every kind, cost thirty guineas (roughly $3,600 today ... not cheap).[3]

Bristol ultimately failed as the *Great Western*'s homeport. The new steamship had difficulty entering the Avon, notwithstanding weirs and locks constructed at great expense to increase the river's depth. The company was forced to make Liverpool its homeport, leaving Whitwill to look elsewhere for business.

At the office, the teenager took all of this in, entering facts and figures about ship tonnages, rates, contracts and commissions in Whitwill's books. His mind became a storehouse of information that he would use in later years. When he was sixteen, Henry went to London for a week, spending most of his time "among the ships in the docks."

At the same time, another side of the boy began to emerge — a spiritual and religious one. "I can hardly remember a time when I had not some desire to please God. It was not, however, till about my 15th year yet my mind became awakened of ye awful importance of ye subject."[4] He found a mentor in the pastor of the Baptist Broadmead Church of Christ in Bristol, Caleb Evans Birt, who sensed a profound religious sensibility in the teenager, leading Henry to "deep self-examination and prayer."

"Feeling my utter helplessness as a sinner, I fled for refuge to ye Saviour," he confessed.

The God of refuge evidently didn't comfort young Henry, who failed to find total blissful peace in "ye Saviour." Doubt entered his mind.

Pen-and-ink illustration by Henry Fry, 1891.

First transatlantic passenger service: *In Bristol, twelve-year-old Henry Fry witnessed the launching of* Great Western, *the first steamship to cross the Atlantic without re-coaling. Wind power aided the paddlewheel. A one-way cabin fare, including meals and wine, cost today's equivalent of more than three thousand dollars.*

Possibly he suffered a crisis of faith arising from the growing accumulation of scientific evidence in the fossil-rich rocks of his native Somerset, suggesting that the hallowed Bible perhaps contained a less than accurate account of the world's origins. Possibly, he began to feel that the Baptist Church's most extreme practices of watery immersion were not to his taste. Doubting God's mission was not a respectable thing to do in nineteenth-century Bristol, and at an inner level it would likely have been deeply troubling.

"Of a naturally thoughtful mind," Henry reflected, "I could not remain content with a mere superficial assent to the doctrines of Christianity and finding difficulties that I could not understand, a painful conflict ensued which robbed me of all peace. I sought counsel of Mr. Birt, whose deeply affectionate solicitude on my behalf tended much to remove these feelings."[5]

Unfortunately, Reverend Birt left Broadmead for another church in 1844, and Henry found himself unable to openly make the public confession necessary for his admission to the Baptist Church. "I felt an indescribable terror at the idea of a *public* profession, and on the removal of Mr. Birt, my tie to Broadmead appeared to be scrapped asunder and I gave up my intentions."

Henry's mental energies swung back over to ships, the object of his early fascination. At age eighteen, he spent a week in Liverpool, where he "reveled in watching the large ships beat up the Mersey under sail."

Liverpool had rapidly overtaken Bristol as a more desirable deep-water port on England's west coast. Trade was booming, prodded by tariff reforms initiated by Prime Minister Robert Peel. Previously, trade had been hampered by high differential duties favouring goods from the Colonies. "Many of the duties," wrote Henry later, "were very heavy, even on the necessaries of life, such as grain, sugar, tea, coffee, meats, and lumber. Glass, soap, paper, bricks, malt, spirits, tobacco, and windows were all heavily taxed." He continued:

> In 1844 Sir Robert Peel was called to the helm. He was cold and haughty, but a man of high moral religious character. He grasped the situation and proposed heroic remedies in the shape of free trade. The success of Peel's measures was almost magical. Trade rapidly improved,

with [tariff-] free cotton, wool, hemp, flax; manufactures thrived; new mills were built, wages increased, imports and exports mounted up.[6]

With business booming, Whitwill entrusted Henry, then nineteen, to go across to Wales and charter ships. The next year, 1846, the young man began to travel to London on business, "sometimes going up once or twice a week." The new high-speed railway had opened between Bristol and London four years earlier. The nineteenth century's first TGV had been designed by the brilliant young engineer Isambard Kingdom Brunel, designer of the three-thousand-ton iron steamship *Great Britain*, successor to the *Great Western*. Brunel's rail line was a wonder of the world. Henry would leave for London at 8:05 a.m., conduct a day of business, and be back in Bristol by 7:25 p.m., the round trip covering some 240 miles.[7]

Wearing a black frock coat, waistcoat, and tight-fitting pants, he was a sophisticated young trader on the move. Scarcely twenty-one years old, he had already mastered the skill of balancing self-interest with the selfish interest of the other party to a deal. He conversed easily. His manner was serious, not jocular. He treated people as honest until they proved otherwise.[8] His knowledge of ships and his intense interest in them favourably impressed merchants, ship-owners, and captains.

The transatlantic maritime business was rapidly accelerating with the opening of canals to the Great Lakes. Henry clearly was useful to his boss. "Whitwill encouraged me," Henry remarked, and "often promised me a share in the next ship he bought."[9] In his youthful naïveté, he misjudged Whitwill's words, or Whitwill cynically misled him. The owner had no reason to promise him a major share in the business when his own son had just joined the firm.

The times were turbulent, business uncertain. Inflation and speculation were rife. With the Irish potato failure and crop failures in mainland Europe, "wheat rose dramatically in price," Henry noted.[10] "There was wild and reckless speculation in new railways, which in the fall of 1847 became a mania; clergymen, clerks, small capitalists eagerly applied for shares." Then, just as precipitately, the railway shares crashed, the financial markets did a swan dive, and the price of wheat plummeted. Henry was getting a taste of the manic nineteenth-century business cycle, whose whip end was often the price of shipping.

Economic depression and low prices were followed by a cycle of unprecedented prosperity, spurred by Britain's 1849 repeal of the Navigation Acts, which had required that all goods bound for the British colonies be shipped through England, stifling international trade. With the revocation of the acts, commerce soared and ship-owning profits rose. Steam power was still in its infancy; sail primarily propelled cargoes across the oceans. Sailing ships, barques, barquentines, brigs, snows, and schooners carried adventurers and supplies to the California gold fields and destitute Irish emigrants away from famine.

Henry was entering a booming industry. He had waited a long time for Whitwill to reward him, and it finally happened. "After long and weary waiting, when I was 23, he allowed me to have 8/64th [British ships were divided by law into sixty-four shares] of a new schooner named the *Alarm*." Built at Gloucester, the 109-ton *Alarm* was Henry's first business venture. His share was valued at about £150, on which Whitwill forced him to pay interest. Such was "the munificent reward for 11 years of faithful service," Henry remarked sarcastically. The *Alarm* ran for about seven years in the Portuguese wine trade and paid pretty well until it was "found to have the dry rot. Her repairs cost more than she was worth, so I got nothing for my shares."[11]

Henry's deteriorating relationship with Whitwill did not originate in any inability of his own to foster friendships or to inspire trust in others. At twenty-three, he already had a string of acquaintances willing to help him. One of them was William Yeo, of Appledore, to the southwest of Bristol on the Atlantic coast of north Devon. Yeo was appalled by the "petty" way Whitwill had treated Henry. He was so disgusted that one day in 1849 he wrote to his young Bristol friend, "Come down and spend a week with me."

Henry was impressed, if not awestruck, by the visit. Yeo was one of the wealthiest and most powerful men in Devonshire and the mightiest man in Appledore, dominating the village's economy. His home, Richmond House, a luxurious mansion that he'd built on the hill overlooking Appledore, was named after the dry dock he'd constructed in the port. He launched dozens of ships, often in concert with his father,

FOR

NEW YORK,

DIRECT FROM   BRISTOL.

The   And

Splendid   Copper

Clipper-Built   Fastened

Coppered   SHIP,

OSPREY

1200 TONS BURTHEN.

JOHN TOMLINSON, *Commander*.

(Formerly Chief Officer of the Try)

To Sail APRIL 3rd, 1855.

The above remarkably fine Ship is adapted in every respect for the Passenger Trade. She has peculiarly lofty and spacious 'tween Decks, with side ports fore and aft for light and ventilation, is a very fast sailer, and will be fitted up in the usual comfortable manner adopted by the undersigned and under the inspection of the Government Emigration Officer. Capt. Tomlinson has long been accustomed to the regulations of Emigrant Ships and is very kind and attentive to all who sail with him.

Parties wishing to proceed into the interior of America can book through at once to their places of destination on most reasonable terms. All provisions supplied will be of the best quality.

For further particulars apply to

MARK WHITWILL & SON,
SHIP OWNERS & BROKERS,
GROVE, BRISTOL.

JOHN WRIGHT & CO. STEAM PRESS, BRISTOL.

The advertisement, the reality: *This 1855 poster promoted passenger service from Bristol to New York on a "fast sailer." Two years earlier, Henry Fry sailed on a similar ship, the Cosmo. A crewmember was crushed to death by a jibing boom, the foremast collapsed, the barque returned to port for repairs, and the trip to New York took a total of forty-four days. Henry apprenticed at the shipbroker Mark Whitwill & Son when a teenager.*

James Yeo, renowned Prince Edward Island ship-owner, entrepreneur, and politician, who'd emigrated to P.E.I. from Appledore around 1820.[12]

Not unlike his ruthless, hard-drinking father, William Yeo was a tough, astute merchant. He had crewed on, then mastered square-rigged sailing ships, and was impressed by Henry Fry's knowledge of ship design. The two men hit it off.

"There is a fine new Brigantine here at Appledore," said Yeo. "If you like her, you shall have half of her and the sole management."

"But I have no money," replied Henry.

"Never mind that," said Yeo. "I'll give you a clean bill of sale, and you can pay me gradually as she earns it, and do what you like with her."[13] Henry jumped at the offer. The brigantine *Favourite*, freshly built in Prince Edward Island, had just crossed the Atlantic on her maiden voyage. She mounted two masts — the one aft carrying a fore-and-aft rigged sail, the one forward of it square-rigged, plus carrying two jibs. Constructed of tamarack, the *Favourite* measured 168 tons and was coppered and ready to sail any ocean. She cost about £1,400 (about $200,000 today). Henry became the half-owner. His enterprise and experience now came into full play. He hired a skipper and sent *Favourite* to Cuba with a cargo of iron rails. From Cuba she re-crossed the Atlantic back to London with a cargo of sugar and mahogany. She then carried coal to Venice and brought back wheat from the Adriatic to Donegal on the Irish northwest coast. And on it went for a couple of years.

"She paid very well," wrote Henry, "but I deemed it best to sell her when my health broke down in 1851 from over work."[14]

It was a small item of information: "My health broke down." The reason? "Over work." Over a matter of work? A failed business deal? A contract gone awry? Or a matter of overwork — work so intense, involving such interminable hours of travel and negotiation, that he "broke down?" Henry's suffering resembled that of his contemporary, Charles Darwin. "He wanted to work, and his work helped him rise above his illness, yet it was work that made him ill," notes the author of one Darwin biography.[15]

Because of what would happen to him twenty years later, Henry almost certainly suffered what modern psychiatrists would classify as a major depressive episode.[16] At the age of twenty-seven, he was at sea, mentally — stressed and incapacitated.

"Seeking rest," Henry sailed for New York in the fall of 1853. Violent gales assaulted the ship, the Bristol-built barque *Cosmo*. In the English Channel, the *Cosmo*'s boom jibed and crushed the head of the sailor at the wheel, killing him. In the Bay of Biscay, the ship lost its foremast head, its foreyard broke, and all above it collapsed. She had to return to Falmouth for repairs. With Henry still on board, she set out again across the Atlantic, this time running into heavy autumn gales, which caused the loss of a long boat and stanchions.

Henry finally reached New York on December 10, 1853. The crossing had taken forty-four days.[17] The terrible, stormy voyage remained so vivid in his mind that he would give the name *Cosmo* to a ship of his own twenty-five years later. It was his last Atlantic crossing by sail. Even though he almost exclusively owned and brokered sailing ships, for reasons of time and comfort he would cross only on steamships in the years ahead.

The *Cosmo* was just one of 4,107 vessels that arrived in 1853 in New York, by then a city of almost three-quarters of a million inhabitants. Henry's first sight of New York's harbour on December 10 filled him with awe — a thicket of masts and rigging filled the horizon. No fewer than sixty piers lined the East River, and there were another fifty on the Hudson River side of Manhattan Island, and even more on Brooklyn's shoreline.[18]

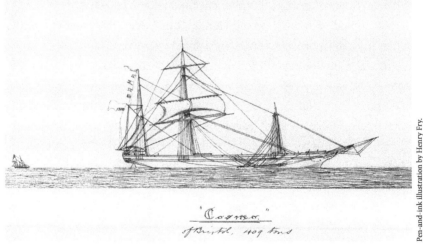

"Cosmo"
of Bristol, 409 tons

Pen-and-ink illustration by Henry Fry.

Henry Fry's pen-and-ink drawing depicts the Cosmo *after the violent storm that de-masted her in the Bay of Biscay in 1853.*

He had left England seeking rest. Perhaps the violent Atlantic crossing had shaken the burden of his depression. He headed north. By the time he reached Quebec, his burden was lifted, his spirits restored.

4

1854
Life in Quebec Begins

Although in years to come he would often visit New York City, Henry never chose to write about what he did there, whom he saw, how he was entertained, or what he purchased or enjoyed. He likely spent Christmas and New Year's of 1853 in America's largest city. Then, early in 1854, he travelled by rail via Maine to Montreal and down to Levis, making the short ferry crossing to Quebec, seeing for the first time the place that would come to define his life.

A shipbuilding boom, a frenzy of industry, greeted him. "The scene in the Quebec yards on a fine winter's day," Henry wrote, "was a very animated one ... the whirr of the saws, the blows of the mallets, the songs of the French-Canadian shipwrights raising frames or carrying planks, and the vim of the men were pleasant to the eye and ear of the onlooker."

He spent the winter making contacts with traders and ship-owners whom he'd known previously only through written correspondence. The business of building ships was booming. "Gold had been discovered in Australia," wrote Henry, "causing a heavy demand for large, fast sailing ships. There were no steamships running to Australia in those days. Everyone that could raise or borrow money rushed into ship building."[1]

As winter wound down, the days began to lengthen. In May, at last, the main elements of the port city's economy came into play — the arrival of the first ships from Europe. It was a dazzling sight. Far downstream on the surface of the broad St. Lawrence came ships from all over the world, their sails billowing and paddlewheels churning, aided in their southwest course to Quebec by favourable winds and a flowing tide that accelerated as the river narrowed. Around the mouth of the tributary Saguenay River, whales — beluga and minke — were beginning to churn the water's surface. At night, spectacular flares of the *aurora borealis* occasionally shafted the heavens. At Cap Tourmente, tens of thousands of snow geese darkened the sky on their migration north.

Where the ships reach Île d'Orléans, the St. Lawrence divides, reuniting in a wide basin at the mouth of the St. Charles River, which flows in from the north. Here the great river abruptly narrows and deepens and cliffs rise on both sides. The view from above was spectacular, with the arriving ships — "the spring fleet" — spread across the glistening water.

Charles Dickens described the scene only a dozen years before Henry Fry arrived: "It is a place not to be forgotten or mixed up in the mind with other places. The beautiful St. Lawrence sparkling and flashing in the sunlight, and the tiny ships below the Rock ... whose distant rigging looks like spiders' webs against the light ... forms one of the brightest and most enchanting pictures the eye can rest upon."[2]

Following Britain's loss of her American colonies, and before steam-powered ships and tugs made Montreal accessible, Quebec was among the world's greatest tidal ports in value of trade. For ships, it was five hundred miles closer to Liverpool than New York — during the half

Bibliothèque Nationale, Quebec/Charley-Man.

A landscape of wood: *In the nineteenth century, the north shore of the St. Lawrence River west of Quebec, Sillery, was a vast gathering place for timber to be loaded onto ships bound mostly for Britain.*

of the year when the St. Lawrence wasn't frozen, that is. It was a hub of immigration. From 1851 to 1891, a period during which 2,425,000 men, women, and children arrived in North America,[3] hundreds of thousands of them passed through Quebec, whence they proceeded by boat and rail to the American Midwest, to Ontario, and to the Prairies.

In the town, Scots and Englishmen like Henry had the business edge, enjoying commercial ties to the old country and to English-speaking North America ... cultural and economic ties to a mother country largely lost by French Canadians after their military loss and virtual abandonment by France.[4]

The city's economic lifeblood was receiving and selling wood, and building the ships to carry it. The shipbuilding had begun in the 1660s under Intendant Jean Talon. It began to accelerate around the time Henry arrived in 1854, with the demand for larger and larger ships. The hulls of the new vessels, plus older ones under repair, lined the sloping beaches and coves on both shores of the St. Lawrence, as well as the banks of the meandering St. Charles River and protected bays on the Île d'Orléans. Out in the open, even in sub-zero Fahrenheit winter temperatures, carpenters, joiners, plankers, caulkers, and riggers toiled. The crisp, frigid air pulsated with the noise of hammers, axes, adzes, and saws, and with the chanting of men hauling timber.[5] The men also bolted together huge timbers to form cages, which they filled with stone and sunk to make new wharves. With the added landfill, the lower town kept expanding.

If you were seeking a place in the world to gather massive amounts of wood, load it on sailing ships for transport abroad, and even to build ships to do the transporting, it would be hard to find a location more suitable than Quebec. The reason for the port's ascendancy in the eighteenth and nineteenth centuries is brilliantly described in Arthur Lower's landmark work *Great Britain's Woodyard*:

> Here the river first narrows to harbour proportions. Ile d'Orleans gives shelter from the hardest blows from the east, completing a natural basin: protected, yet accessible to ships of any draft and with room for any number of them. Higher up from Quebec, it was not easy for the sailing ships to go.

Along each river shore from just above the island of Orleans to where the Quebec Bridge crosses the river, there runs a narrow, flat strip of river bank under the cliffs. It slopes, and is hard. When the tide was in, timber could be moved to where it was wanted. When the tide was out, the timber could lie on the ground and be worked. At Montreal there is no tide, and the timber would have had to be removed from the water for working. It was this simple advantage that enabled Quebec to retain the [wood] trade from some time after improved transportation [steam] should have taken it to Montreal.

Along the strip were the "coves" of the timber merchants. A cove was not the natural shore indentation that we normally think of, but simply a stretch of shore where timber could be stored and worked and wooden ships built. A typical cove had a boom holding the water-borne squared timbers, a wharf running out into deep water where deals* could be piled and loaded onto ships, and an office. The coves stretched from the city's lower town all the way upriver to Sillery.[6]

The shore was one vast woodyard. Immense stocks of white and red pine, tamarack, hemlock, elm, oak, and squares of ash were culled and marked for quality — Merchantable, Second-quality, Rejected.[7] Out in the deep water or moored at piers, ships took on loads of the wood, while others rode at anchor awaiting their turn.

The shipping and timber businesses were intertwined. As an example, Henry could order a ship built in one of the coves, paying the workers with his own and with borrowed bank money. The men would construct the ship over the winter, a time when Henry was in England finding orders of wood for her to carry. In late spring the new ship was put in the water, loaded, and set sail. If opportunity presented itself, Henry could not only receive payment for the wood when it was landed in England, he might also sell the ship itself.

So lucrative was the synergy of ship and cargo that in 1823 the Scottish naval architect Charles Wood had conceived the idea of building

---

* A "deal" was a sawed plank, typically three inches thick, which came in various widths and lengths, usually seven inches wide and at least six feet long.

a cheap ship with a hull of squared timber that could carry several thousand tons of wood across the North Atlantic, then itself be disassembled and sold along with its cargo. He built two such demountable ships, or "droghers."[8] *Columbus* was one-third longer than the largest ship in the British navy at the time. Wood's even larger 5,294-ton, four-masted *Baron of Renfrew* was 362 feet long, with a 61-foot beam, at that time (1825) the largest wooden sailing ship in recorded maritime history. After crossing the Atlantic, *Baron of Renfrew* ran onto a sandbank in the English Channel. When an attempt was made to tow it, it broke apart, some of its valuable timber drifting as far away as the French coast. The ingenious idea had run aground — a spectacular speculative failure.

In Quebec harbour, as soon as the ice broke in spring, the first winter-built vessels splashed into the water, while the first timber came floating down the river amid thinning ice floes, in monstrous rafts, from as far away as the upper reaches of the Ottawa River, Lake Ontario, and Lake Champlain. Then the spring fleet from Europe would arrive and "a parade of white sails" would round Point Levi. Soon the coves on both sides of the river were a forest of masts, so close were the ships moored to one another.[9]

"Passengers and seamen streamed ashore," writes Eileen Marcil in her definitive history of Quebec's era of wooden shipbuilding.[10] "Polyglot bands of sailors shambled to the nearest tavern to join in rowdy conviviality with the timber raft crews. Groups of immigrants gazed at the unfamiliar sights, as they headed for the next stage of their journey. Old friends, long-time captains on the Quebec run, exchanged greetings."

Merchants like Henry quickened their pace as they hurried between the coffee houses, the favourite rendezvous for business deals, and their offices on St. Peter Street, where clerks perched at tall desks scratched transactions into ledgers.

The merchants typically lived in villas above the timber coves west of the town. The shipbuilders lived beside their yards, the more successful and affluent residing in stone or brick houses, with room for the family and a couple of apprentices, even an office. Many of the skilled ship craftsmen lived in modest homes along Champlain Street and in the district of St. Roch by the St. Charles River. Along narrow alleys labourers, ship loaders, and their families dwelt in cold, damp quarters, the poorest of them in stone houses "with broken windows pasted over with paper or stuffed with rags."[11]

The anglophone merchant class dominated the business of ship-owning and cargo chartering, but not necessarily the shipbuilding. Both French and English participated. During the years when Henry was in Quebec, 40 percent of the largest yards — that is, shipbuilders known to have built ten or more ships — on average, were French Canadian–owned.[12] Shipbuilding was not some alien manufacturing process directed by emissaries from foreign corporations boasting savvy and technological training unavailable locally. Shipbuilding existed in Quebec long before the British victory on the field above some of the principal yards, and French Canadians were renowned for their superior woodworking skills.

After he arrived in Quebec in early 1854, Henry took up lodging in the hotel Russell House on Palace Street in the lower town. Russell, the hotel's owner, knew everyone of consequence in town. "One Sunday," recalled Henry, "I asked Mr. Russell if there was a Baptist church in the city. Mr. Russell replied that one was being built, but that in the meantime Reverend Mr. Marsh preached in St. Andrew's schoolroom. Thither I went, and was much struck with Mr. Marsh's simple, earnest, loving way of speaking."

The pastor was a thickset man of medium height, with eyes that radiated a kindness to anyone, rich or poor, who met him. Marsh spoke softly, deliberately, and earnestly.[13] "He delighted to dwell on the infinite love of the Father as displayed in the work and death of his Son. From that hour commenced a friendship which, outside my own family, was the warmest and tenderest I ever knew."[14]

If overwork had ever been the cause of Henry's affliction, it surely was not so now. Twenty-eight and soothed by his Baptist faith, he entered a whirlwind of friendships, deals, business, wheeling and dealing, working off longstanding connections with Whitwill of Bristol, where he'd trained. In one of his first business deals, he travelled down to Rimouski, on the south shore of the Gulf of St. Lawrence, and spent six hundred pounds to take possession of a ship, the *J.K.L.*, which had run aground.[15] Later, when two Whitwill-owned ships became trapped in the river ice, Henry organized their rescue. His actions impressed the underwriters and Lloyd's, enabling them to escape paying insurance on the ships had they been destroyed. Lloyd's awarded Henry eight hundred dollars (roughly $20,000 today). Two years later, they would award him a finer prize, appointing him Lloyd's agent for the St. Lawrence River stretching all the way from Sorel, east of Montreal, to the remote Gaspé Peninsula.

5

1854-56
Transatlantic Feud

In 1854, Henry received a demanding letter from his former employer in Bristol. The correspondence would bring him no end of trouble. In it, Mark Whitwill asked Henry to "buy one or two ships and draw upon me for the cost."[1] The request immediately put Henry in a quandary. Because of the Crimean War, the demand for ships to transport troops and war materials had soared, and with it the price of ships. It wasn't a good time to purchase. But Henry felt he had to fulfil Whitwill's request.

Fortunately, he'd run into a lively, enterprising Quebec shipbuilder named Henry Dinning, a man seldom without a boat on his hands to sell. Taking advantage of the market, Dinning set a price of $15,600 (about $400,000 today) for a three-hundred-ton barque named the *Hinda*, built by another yard the previous year. Henry decided to pay the "very high cost," trusting Whitwill to cover him.

The *Hinda* was the first of a dozen or more deals that Henry would cut with Dinning over the next twenty-three years. For *Hinda* he found a cargo of coal at Pictou, Nova Scotia. The ship carried the coal to Boston then sailed north to St. Stephens, New Brunswick, where Henry had arranged a load of lumber for her to carry to England.

Henry had been in North America for almost a year when, in November of 1854, he decided to go back to England to settle his differences with Whitwill. He sailed out of New York aboard Cunard's two-year-old wooden-hulled *Arabia*. The steam packet, with paddlewheels and sail, was 285 feet long with a 40-foot beam. The ship's engines, with a nine-foot stroke, consumed a colossal 120 tons of coal per day.

Arabia was a swift ship, able to steam as fast as fifteen knots. But for passengers, the North Atlantic was a rough ride in November. Henry described a typical voyage:

> In the cabin, the gyration of one's hat and the swinging of garments on the pegs were maddening, especially to those suffering from sea-sickness; no hot water could be

Pen-and-ink illustration by Henry Fry, 1891.

A raw deal: *Henry Fry bought the sailing ship* Hinda *for his former employer, who later denied he'd authorized the purchase. When the ship was loaded with hay destined for Crimea,* Hinda *was barred from leaving port until Henry found the money to pay for her.*

had, nor even your light extinguished, without bawling "Steward!" perhaps a dozen times, when the reply would be heard in the distance, "What number, sir?"

In the early Cunard steamships, a "state room" was only six feet by six feet, with two narrow bunks, two wash basins and jugs. Of ventilation there was practically none, except on very fine days when the stewards were allowed to open the side ports. If you wanted a smoke, you had to go to a wretched little place over the boilers, where the stokers were hoisting the ashes, and where you often got soused with salt water. Books were kept under lock and key, and a special application was necessary to get one to read. At meals you often had to climb over the backs of long benches to get to your seat.[2]

Arabia reached Liverpool in eleven days. Henry went immediately to Bristol, where he happily reunited with his parents, brothers and sisters, and friends. They'd been upset by his breakdown and subsequent absence, and were joyous upon his return, seemingly well again and prosperous.

But in another way, Henry's return was unpleasant and disillusioning: "When I got home to Bristol in December 1854, I went to see Whitwill at his office on Grove Avenue. I told him about the high price that I had been forced to pay for *Hinda*, and how I had found cargoes for her."[3]

An angry confrontation ensued. "I gave you no authority to buy a ship," said Whitwill dryly. "You've done this on your own."

Furious, Henry pulled out Whitwill's original letter and flashed it in front of him. "Here is the authorization you gave me in writing!" Henry declared.

Whitwill read it. He appeared dumbfounded. "I forgot that I wrote it," he said, without apology. Henry, angry, left. Over the next few days, Whitwill, "a very arbitrary and determined old man," continued to nag him about the *Hinda*. Knowing that shipping prices were still high, Henry returned to the office.

He angrily faced Whitwill again. "All right, I will take her off your hands," he said, almost shouting. "Just give me time to pay for her."

"North Britain."

Capt Spong, off Cap. Jone & F.L. 29 April 1859. Machinery temporarily disabled, & 40 Icebergs in sight at 2 P.M. (A. Zottrige onboard.)

Pen-and-ink illustration by Henry Fry, 1891.

Coarse crossing: *During winter the North Atlantic, often traversed by Henry in the 1850s on steamships like* North Britain, *makes for a rough ride. Seasick passengers had a sink, but often no hot water.*

Maritime Museum of the Atlantic, Halifax. Photo by the author.

Henry wasted no time putting *Hinda* to work. "I brought her round to Bristol Channel, and chartered her at a high rate to carry pressed hay from Chepstow to Balaklava for the Crimean army. Cavalry horses in the Crimea were dying of hunger."[4] Yet just as *Hinda* was about to sail, Whitwill confronted him again.

"I will not allow that ship to leave," he demanded, "until you have the money to pay me one half her cost."

"This is a very mean trick, Mr. Whitwill," replied Henry. "I am under contract with the British government to sail without an hour's delay." But he was powerless. He had somehow to find the money to pay Whitwill quickly, so he went to George Cole, a rich pawnbroker, who had a fancy for ships. "I begged him to buy half of the *Hinda*. He agreed to do so, but I had to sacrifice some £300 in the price."[5] At last, *Hinda* was able to leave with its load of hay for the Crimea.

During the winter months of 1855, Henry lived in Bristol near the docks on Coronation Street, drumming up customers for cargoes that could be loaded on the *Hinda* and on ships owned or operated by Whitwill, and now Whitwill's son. He was earning one-third of the profits from concerns they owned. But as his mistrust mounted, he knew that he must separate his future from Whitwill. It was springtime. Across the Atlantic in Canada the port of Quebec would soon be filling with rafts of logs ready to be culled and shipped to Europe. Business was waiting there. More and more, he realized that Quebec would be his home, at least for eight months of the year.

One matter needed his attention before he left Bristol: the uncertain, turbulent restiveness of his soul. After coming to know Reverend Marsh in Quebec, he was now determined formally to join the Baptist Church. In April he met with Nathaniel Haycroft, pastor of Bristol's famous Broadmead Church. Henry was willing to make the open confession that he'd earlier rejected.

"The teachings of Mr. Haycroft convinced me that I was wrong," he stated in the presence of witnesses. He went on to say:

> I had been determined to join, when from mental over-exertion and late hours of business my health suddenly gave way and both body and mind became

almost prostrated. This event led me to a foreign land where, on recovering, my earliest resolution was such that I now seek to fulfil in humble dependence on the grace of Christ and in the hope that he will keep me "faithful unto death." My views of Christianity accord with those of Mr. Haycroft and tho' I do not sympathize in the importance often attached to the mode of baptism, I believe immersion to be the most literal form of obeying the command of Christ. Earnestly imploring in interest in your prayers and sympathies, I am your brother in Christ.[6]

A month after this confession, in May 1855, Henry boarded the steamship *Baltic* in Liverpool, bound for New York. While at sea, the ship was delayed when a crank pin broke. In dense fog, the *Baltic* then narrowly missed colliding with a Boston-bound ship, *Curling*, carrying 570 emigrants.[7]

When he disembarked at New York, he would have had several options for travelling north to Quebec. One was to entrain for Maine, then ride the railway from Portland on Grand Trunk Railway's line through Vermont to Montreal and along the south shore of the St. Lawrence to Levis, across from Quebec. That was the winter route. In May, Henry more likely would have travelled by steam-powered river boat up the Hudson, gone by rail or by boat through the locks of the Champlain Canal to Whitehall, New York, by boat part the way up Lake Champlain, then got on a train to Montreal and down the south shore to Levis.[8]

Once in Quebec, he found rooms at 12 Rue Mont Carmel in a neighbourhood in the upper town favoured by retired shipbuilders, known as The Cape. At the end of the street the land rose steeply to the Plains of Abraham, the scene ninety-six years earlier of the epic battle between troops under Wolfe and Montcalm. Just around the corner from his rooms was the monument to the two generals.

Henry quickly got in touch with Henry Dinning, who'd sold him the *Hinda*. He found Dinning "exceedingly shrewd and smart in business, and good tempered" — a worthy partner. Their first venture in the spring of 1855 was to buy at auction a sailing ship, which, with her cargo of timber, was lying ashore at Matane on the Gaspé Peninsula. The sixteen-year-old *Ant* had been built at Saint John, New Brunswick. She weighed 663 tons and was capable of carrying a large cargo.

"We sent a smart fellow down to Matane," wrote Henry. "He landed all her cargo on the beach, and brought her up to Quebec under sail. Dinning gave her a new keel and sheathed her bottom." Henry transferred the *Ant*'s cargo from the beach to another vessel, and sold the wood to a merchant in Swansea, on the coast of Wales, turning a quick profit.[9]

In the fall of 1855, Henry finally found the excuse he needed to break off with the firm where he'd started to work as a boy fifteen years earlier. Whitwill refused to supply him with enough capital to carry on the firm's ship agency and commission business at Quebec. Henry's anger at the refusal was mixed with relief. On his own he was making more money than the profit furnished by his relationship with Whitwill. It was time again to return to England and settle scores. In November, he travelled by train from Levis to Halifax and boarded Cunard's paddlewheel steamer *Asia* bound for Liverpool. The voyage would take just ten days.

Upon his arrival in Bristol, more acrimonious discussions with Whitwill took place. "I finally severed my connection with his firm," Henry recorded, although he still owed the old man money.

While he was in England, Lloyd's, remembering Henry's work salvaging the two wrecks in the St. Lawrence in 1854, rewarded him further. Recognizing his precocious knowledge of ship construction, of cargo valuation, and of the perils of shoals, rocks, and islets dotting the St. Lawrence, on January 30, 1856, the insurance group in the City of London appointed Henry Fry its agent for the river from the Gulf of St. Lawrence to almost as far upriver as Montreal.

In a history of Lloyd's that he later wrote, Henry recorded his impressions of its London office:

> A lofty, well proportioned room about 100 feet long. On the floor are three rows of small, oblong, mahogany tables and low back seats. Each table is usually occupied by two underwriters [offering insurance] and two clerks, and supplied with two copies of "Lloyd's Register

of Shipping." The spaces between the tables are crowded with brokers [seeking insurance]. The hum of voices almost amounts to a roar. The business proceeds with marvelous rapidity and smoothness. Each broker holds a handful of slips, each with the name of a ship, captain, voyage, risk, amount of risk, and rate of premium. He hands the slip in; almost as quick as a flash of light the underwriter realizes the risk and will either hand it back with a shake of his head but without uttering a word, or will initial it. If he is in doubt, the underwriter refers to his *Lloyd's Register*, and in a few seconds ascertains the age and class of the ship, the names of her owner, builder, and captain, then he decides in a moment.

Lloyd's had originated in a seventeenth-century London coffee house owned by Edward Lloyd. The Committee, as Henry called it, didn't establish insurance premium rates or settle claims, as some people thought. Rather it collected marine news by telegraph and post, published daily in *Lloyd's List*. Much of the information came from Lloyd's agents. At the time of Henry's appointment, more than a thousand agents operated around the world. They worked for little direct compensation, even as "the duties are onerous, and occasionally subject the agent to much opprobrium," Henry remarked. But the information possessed by a Lloyd's agent put opportunity in his way. "Captains are always anxious to secure their advice and assistance when in distress," he wrote. The agent must "forward instantaneous advices of accidents or wrecks by telegraph, and regular advices of arrivals and sailings, superintend surveys and sales of wrecked ships and good, and investigate frauds."[10]

In the first year of Henry's appointment as Lloyd's agent, the Halifax *Nova Scotian* reported that a castaway barque, *Thomas Jones*, wrecked in the course of a voyage from Gloucester to Quebec, was consigned to Mr. H. Fry of Quebec.[11] It was a precursor of the many damaged ships and wrecks that he would encounter through his work with Lloyd's in the years ahead.[12]

Armed now with the prestigious title of Lloyd's agent, and all but free of his earlier dependence on Whitwill, Henry left England, sailing on

Arabia, the same steamship that had carried him to America two years earlier. He disembarked at Boston, and by April of 1856 he was back in Quebec. A new life had begun.

№ 4

"Ant."

663 tons, 1855/59.

Pen-and-ink illustration by Henry Fry, 1891.

A rescued ship: *Henry and Dinning frequently bought ships in distress, including the sixteen-year-old Ant, at auction. They offloaded and sold her cargo of wood, keeled and re-sheathed her bottom, put her back to sea, and eventually sold her, pocketing a nice profit.*

6

1856-59
Crime, Business, and a Wedding

In the year 1856, Quebec briefly became the capital of the Dominion of Canada by vote of the Legislative Assembly.[1] At the same time, Henry Fry & Company came into existence, occupying an office on the most prominent business street in Quebec's Lower Town, St. Peter Street (now Rue St. Pierre). The first horse-drawn streetcars began to rumble through Lower Town.

Henry's financial condition, and that of his company, wasn't especially robust. He had less than £1,000 of capital ... not much when a year could pass between the time you purchased goods and paid for shipping them and when the customer in England finally paid you. But William Yeo, who'd helped Henry after Whitwill put the screws to the young shipbroker, kindly lent him $25,000 to capitalize the business.

"I made such a good year in commissions, lumber contracts, etc., that I cleared $7,000," recorded Henry.[2] With the money he was able to pay off his debt to Whitwill.

In 1856, a total of forty-two sailing ships were launched from Quebec yards, an annual amount typical for the 1850s.[3] Plenty of skilled manpower was available to build the ships. The local population's shipbuilding skills, however, weren't matched by any indigenous seafaring skills. Quebec-born sailors were in short supply. When a ship was launched from Quebec yards, the captain had to recruit the crew elsewhere, perhaps from Boston or New York, or from men running away from other ships. As many as a thousand runaways manned new ships sailing out of Quebec in 1856.[4] The runaways themselves were frequently victims of crimps — thugs who boarded an arriving ship and captured its crew members, or who got them drunk in taverns ashore, seized them, then delivered them to another ship about to sail out of Quebec.

"The shortage of labour in Quebec was so severe that it turned the seaman into a high-priced commodity whose arranged desertion became the staple trade of the Lower Town of Quebec," writes Judith Fingard in *Jack in Port*.[5] "There were 200 to 300 crimps in Quebec at mid-century, composed of the lowest characters in the city.... In their resort to chicanery, force, assault and murder, the crimps of Quebec could hold their own with their counterparts in New Orleans, San Francisco or Shanghai."

The cruelty and corruption angered Henry, and in 1856 he wrote to the *Times of London*, a letter subsequently reprinted in Quebec newspapers:

> The crimping system has now reached such a pitch [that] the force of law is completely set at defiance. Night after night ships in this harbor are boarded by crimps well armed with revolvers, the crews carried off, masters and officers threatened with instant death if they resist or interfere, and the owners' property plundered whole-sale. And for this state of things, the authorities here either cannot or will not find a remedy. I can cite scores of instances to prove the truth of the above. Piracy stalks abroad unchecked in the midst of a British population, and under the very walls of a British fortress.

Not everyone shared his views on crimping. Some resented Henry airing the seamy side of Quebec maritime life in the pages of London's foremost newspaper. "Writing letters of complaint to newspapers is a very common way of evading duties," declared the *Quebec Mercury* in an editorial critical of Henry's letter to the *Times*.[6] The *Mercury* declared that the city's crimping was no worse than in other major ports around the world. The newspaper blamed the stinginess of merchants like Henry for Quebec's insufficient supply of seamen. The ship-owners and masters could easily arrange to bring able-bodied sailors from England to meet the crewing needs of outgoing ships. "Neither seamen nor crimps are responsible for the existing state of affairs," stated the *Mercury*. "The remedy must be applied by the mercantile community."[7] Easier written than done, however.

Crimping wasn't the only trouble on Henry's mind. The international economy was in a swoon. The price of deals (sawn softwood timber, typically a thick plank of pine or spruce) had fallen by half since 1854, and ships and freight by almost as much. "In 1857 came the Indian Mutiny [leading to the collapse of the East India Company] and terrible panic," he wrote.[8] "Five English and Scottish banks failed. The panic in the U.S. was also severe."

Henry had been half owner of the sailing ship *Hinda* since the late winter of 1854. Already burdened by paying interest on the original purchase price, he now faced the fact that the ship's value had plummeted, an early victim of steam's superiority over sail. "The Crimean War was winding down," he wrote, "and the British government was chartering steamships, rather than sailing ships, to bring the troops home."

He decided to sell his half of *Hinda* to the Bristol pawnbroker Cole who owned the other half and was managing her. "Owing to a petty act of attempted fraud on his part, I sold the other half to him at a sacrifice, losing on the whole, some £600."

While the worldwide depression disadvantaged Henry as a seller, he could now buy cheaply. In the spring of 1857, the sailing ship *Lotus* was for sale in Bristol. He saw her as a large ship admirably suited for the Quebec trade, although sixteen years old. "As I had not the means to pay for more than one-quarter of her, I induced Mr. Yeo to take 1/4, and two very dear friends, Captain Joseph Samson and Mr. R.S. May, consented to take 1/4 each. So we bought her for £3,900."[9] As for his own share, he appears to have bought it mostly with other people's money, notably $25,000 from the munificent William Yeo in Devon.

The three-masted, 841-ton *Lotus* had been built in 1841 at Saint John, New Brunswick, primarily of spruce and birch. Soon after the purchase, Henry wrote, "Captain Samson and Mr. May both died, and I bought their shares from their Executors, and ultimately Mr. Yeo also." Henry got her profitable work carrying rails and coal, and over the next nine years *Lotus* cleared him a profit of about $35,000.[10]

In December 1856, he had travelled from Boston to Liverpool on the steamer *Canadian* with his twenty-year-old sister Lucy, who was visiting Canada. It was a violent voyage. In a storm off the northwest coast of Ireland, Henry recounted that he "saw the 1st officer washed off the bridge, five lifeboats smashed, [and] the ship's gun hurled into the engine room." It was hardly a singular accident. During the seven years,

Using other people's money: *Built in Saint John, New Brunswick, in 1841, the sailing ship* Lotus *was in Bristol Harbour when Henry bought her, mostly with borrowed funds. After arranging cargoes of rail and coal, he was able to repay his lenders.*

1854–1860, when Henry crossed the Atlantic a dozen times, as many as two thousand unfortunate men, women, and children tragically lost their lives in Atlantic steamship catastrophes. The year 1854 alone saw the loss of as many as eight hundred lives, more than half the number who would go down on the *Titanic*. For example, the *City of Glasgow* left Liverpool in March for New York, with 480 persons aboard, and was never heard from again. The same year more than three hundred passengers and crew perished after the American Collins Line's steamer *Arctic* collided with another ship in the fog off Cape Race, Newfoundland, and sank. On board the German steamer *Austria* in 1858, an officer trying to fumigate the steerage quarters caused a fire and the loss of all but 67 of the 538 persons on board.

Henry's wintertime transatlantic crossings were often brutal. He was aboard Cunard's steamship *Canada* travelling from Boston to Liverpool in December 1857 when a hurricane from the southwest struck the ship off the coast of Ireland, tossing the pathetic passengers about for twenty-six hours in "awful" seas. When he returned four months later, again on the *Canada*, the ship ran into a violent gale and thick fog and nearly went ashore on Sable Island off Nova Scotia.[11] Transatlantic autumn and winter ocean travel was unpleasant at best. Statistically, you put your life on the line each time you crossed. Henry did it repeatedly.

In England he worked out of Bristol, and likely travelled to London on business. He assuredly spent time with family. His father, George, was seventy-four years old, and would live another eleven years. His youngest brother, Edward, was fifteen. Perhaps Henry went down to Winscombe to see the old family farm. Not far away in Devon he discussed his affairs with William Yeo.

Yeo, in addition to partnering with Henry in ship investment, took a paternal interest in the younger man, and may have asked Henry, now age thirty, if he intended to marry. Similarly, friends and family in Bristol good-humouredly asked if he intended to cling to his bachelorhood. But only five years had passed since his nervous breakdown. Inwardly, he worried that he might be a burden to a bride, a failure as a father.

A keen book purchaser, Henry knew Samuel Edward Dawson, the Montreal book dealer. Henry and Sam also shared an interest in the

St. Lawrence River. The Dawsons, like the Yeos, were originally a Prince Edward Island family. Sam had a younger sister, Mary Jane. Nothing is recorded about how Henry met Mary, but meet her he did. It may have been a socially daunting experience for Henry to visit the Dawson home in Montreal. The Dawsons possessed an impressive lineage. Mary Jane's mother, Elizabeth Cobb Gardner, was a descendant of Richard Warren, who'd arrived in America on the *Mayflower*. The family was descended from Thomas Dawson, who fought under Cornwallis in the American Revolutionary War, then returned to Ireland. In 1801, Thomas took his family to Prince Edward Island where he purchased six hundred acres of farmland. He achieved notoriety on the island as a fiery preacher and fanatical Methodist.

Mary Jane and her eight siblings were well educated at schools in Halifax and Montreal. The most talented was her brother Samuel Edward, who would become a close friend of Henry and executor of his will. Together with his brother, Sam expanded the family business, which embraced book publishing and retailing, stationery, and newspaper and periodical agency operations. He later left the business to write books, including a history of the St. Lawrence River, and he was an expert on copyright law, becoming Queen's Printer of Canada.[12]

The woman Henry proposed to bore herself impeccably. She was relatively tall for a young woman of the mid-nineteenth century, about five feet seven inches. She had a finely sculpted, thin face with childlike eyes. Nothing was juvenile about her actions, though. Mary Dawson in her long life would prove to have a sharp eye for real estate and investment. Her 1858 marriage contract today would be called a pre-nup. The contract may have been engineered by her father. In later years she used it to advantage. Not only was there total separation of property, but she brought no dowry to the marriage. Quite the contrary, a condition of Mary marrying Henry was that he give her $4,000 (about $83,000 today)[13] to be invested in her name.[14]

Henry had found himself a superb partner … a slender beauty, twenty-two, whose parents had roots in the Maritimes and pristine New England, and a family name traceable to eleventh-century Norman nobility. The bridegroom, ten years older, was a fine-cut exemplar of the Anglo Saxon race, outgoing and already a business success.

On December 9, 1858, Henry and Mary were married in old Montreal in the St. James Methodist Church. Where else? The Dawsons were fervent Methodists. Behind the church's high Gothic towers fronting on St. James Street, the ceremony took place. Benjamin Dawson, Mary Jane's father, was present to give away the bride. Best man was Henry Dinning, the Quebec shipbuilder. Mary's wedding dress, which today is preserved in the Nova Scotia Museum in Halifax, was a wide-necked affair of ivory silk taffeta, with boned bodice, pagoda sleeves, and a two-tier skirt gathered all around into a pointed waist.[15]

It remained now for Henry and Mary to settle the matter of their religious affiliation in Quebec. If he had surrendered to the formality of a Methodist marriage, she should surrender to formal registry in the Quebec Baptist Church. Mary agreed, but with a certain lack of grace. Later, after taking up residence in Quebec, she refused to submit to immersion, evoking a protest from a congregant, Mr. McFarlane. Henry was the little church's most generous financial supporter. The protest was ignored.

A few days after the wedding, accompanied by Henry's sister Lucy, who'd come from England on his sailing ship *Ant* to serve as a bridesmaid, the couple travelled by train across snow-covered New England to Portland, where they boarded the steamship *North Briton* for Liverpool. After an eleven-day crossing, they sped down to Bristol, where Mary encountered for the first time Henry's parents and the rest of his siblings.

As a honeymoon — crossing the storm-tossed North Atlantic and wintering in England where Henry carried on business — the four-month trip fell disappointingly short of, say, a sojourn in Bermuda. But the new husband compensated his young wife. They spent time in London, and here Henry commissioned the celebrated artist Edmund Havell, portraitist of Elizabeth Barrett Browning, to do a head-and-shoulders watercolour of Mary, a delicate oval shape placed in an fine square gilt frame.[16] In the portrait Mary wears an exquisite broach of solid gold leaves floating on a twisted coil of gold tubing, with a spectacular oval aquamarine in the centre, plus matching pendant earrings, wedding gifts from her new husband.[17]

In April 1859, Henry and Mary re-crossed the Atlantic on the same steamship that had brought them to England … this time thrilled by seeing forty icebergs off the coast of Newfoundland. Back in Quebec, they moved into a rented cottage on the Plains of Abraham, above the ravine that British troops scaled on the night of September 12–13, 1759. Henry partly furnished the cottage with tables, chairs, carpets, glassware, cutlery, and art that he'd transported on the *Ant* from London. Even as a bachelor, he'd collected marble vases, a marble clock, cigar stand, bagatelle board, port and sherry glasses, statuettes of historical figures, a Brussels carpet, and a black sheepskin rug.

Henry and Mary were now living next to the site where a hundred years earlier men had fought the battle that shaped the future of North America's political boundaries.

Photograph by William Notman; courtesy of Dick Avison.

Newly wedded: *Henry Fry and Mary Jane Dawson, after marrying in December 1858 in Montreal, visited the recently opened studio of pioneering Scottish photographer William Notman. His camera captured their image in a rare early photographic process known as ambrotype. The glass surface has become slightly scratched over 150 years.*

7

1859-60
Lessons of Losses; A Princely Visit

For the owners of square-rigged, tall-masted wooden sailing ships, the 1850s were an ominous decade. Ocean transport was on the threshold of a shocking transition from wood and sail to iron and steam. No one could fail to foresee that the wooden sailing ship's days were numbered. In rapid leapfrogging progression, steam replaced wind propulsion, iron hulls replaced wood, the screw propeller replaced the inefficient paddle wheel, and the compound engine sharply reduced the coal burned in moving a ship across the seas.[1]

Nevertheless, at the beginning of the 1860s, sailing ships still carried the bulk of the world's freight. Of the almost one hundred thousand ships registered by Lloyd's in 1864, 96 percent of them were still wooden. Across the sea lanes of the world, coal smoke from steamers sprouted only occasionally on the horizon, while sails were everywhere. "Steamships could not compete with the mass of sailing vessels which carried the growing trade of the world," wrote the maritime historian Basil Greenhill.[2]

"The years 1850 to 1865," remarks Greenhill,[3] "were the heyday of the wooden, square-rigged merchant sailing ship.... If she was built at comparatively low cost in labour and materials in Canada, she represented by far the cheapest way of carrying goods by sea." Coves all along the St. Lawrence, the Nova Scotia coastline, Saint John, New Brunswick, and Prince Edward Island witnessed the launching of hundreds of sailing ships, barques, brigs, snows, schooners, and countless small sloops. Canada was among the world's half-dozen greatest ship-building nations, and statistically, Henry calculated, it was the world's largest ship-owning country in proportion to population.[4]

Nowhere was the raw efficiency of low-cost sailing ship construction more focused than in Quebec, where it was aided by the inexpensive, seemingly inexhaustible supply of wood and by the skills of carpenters, joiners, plankers, mast and spar makers, riggers, sail and rope makers, blacksmiths, glaziers, caulkers, and painters. In the nineteenth century, most of the large square-rigged sailing ships built on the St. Lawrence were launched at Quebec.[5] At its peak, the port city was home to twenty-seven shipbuilding yards specializing in sailing ships and barques, mostly for sale in England. In 1863, fifty-five large sailing ships were built in Quebec, rivalled by Saint John, New Brunswick, where forty-five were built the same year.

The shipping boom contrived sporadically to enrich Henry Fry, even as he knew that the era of wood would wind down. His frequent

National Archives, Ottawa, Fig. 64, *Charley-Man* (with thanks to Henri Dion).

Quebec shoreline, 1865: *Below the Plains of Abraham, coves on the St. Lawrence teemed with ships under construction, and with moored ships waiting to be loaded with wood. The yard in the immediate foreground was Henry Dinning's Cape Cove.*

partner on his path to prosperity was shipbuilder Henry Dinning. Men are sometimes inclined to choose friends for qualities absent in themselves. Henry judged himself to be a prudent man. Dinning, by contrast, he found to be daring, "often reckless, lacking in judgment."

As for Dinning, he perhaps saw in Henry a man whose nature, certainly his physique, contrasted with his own. Dinning was a tall, taut fellow, active, thin in a way that exaggerated his height. His eyes were narrowly set, bridged by a slender, arched nose. His head would have appeared narrow too, except for the bushy black hair that sprouted wildly above his ears, his chin weak except for a wiry beard that grew on both sides of it. He looked every bit the gambler.

In 1858, Dinning had managed to bring a wreck of a ship, the *Riverdale*, up to his yard in Quebec, where he repaired it. Or thought he had. On that premise, he persuaded Henry to buy *Riverdale*. Henry put his Uncle Holmes, an experienced sea captain, in command of sailing her across the Atlantic. The ship leaked miserably. Fortunately, she made it safely to Liverpool. There she was dry-docked, and water pumped under pressure into the hull revealed a leak in a plank of red oak like a sieve. "I made nothing out of her," wrote Henry. "Such were my early struggles as a ship owner."[6]

Not all of his losses were necessarily disappointing. In the fall of 1859, the sailing ship *Ant*, which he owned with Dinning, sprang a leak in mid-ocean. "As her cargo was salt in bulk, it melted," wrote Henry, "and she had to be abandoned. But as she was insured for $10,000 [about £2,050] she left me, on the whole, a fair profit."[7]

Seven years later, he began to do more self-insuring after learning a lesson with the ship *Columbine*. He'd insured her for £1,500 sterling, only to discover that five of the companies providing the underwriting had failed. Consequently, he recovered only £1,000 when *Columbine*, hopelessly leaking, was condemned. "This so vexed me that I resolved to become my own underwriter, commencing at £1,000, gradually increasing my risk to £2,500 on each ship. It paid me well, although I lost two ships in 1871 and eighty percent on a third in 1873."

Henry didn't hesitate to hire relatives to sail his ships. His Uncle Holmes skippered the *Riverdale*, and he had placed in command of *Ant* his brother Charles, who'd followed Henry into shipping, not as a

Notman Collection, McCord Museum, I-2837.1.

Daring shipbuilder: *"Often reckless, lacking in judgment" was how Henry Fry assessed his Irish-born friend and frequent business partner, Henry Dinning, among the top ten Quebec shipbuilders in the nineteenth century. His yard was one of twenty-seven that built square-riggers to sail the world's oceans.*

merchant, but as a sea captain. Six years younger, Charley was built somewhat like Henry, with a long torso that made him appear somewhat short of leg. He had a round face, clean-shaven except for bushy whiskers that sprouted off the sides, covering his jacket lapels. His eyes were earnest, inquiring, and determined, but not aggressive. He appeared friendly and honest — a man you could trust. Then there was a younger brother, Sam. Henry promoted Sam from first mate to captain of *Lotus*. Some would label these to be acts of nepotism. But in a mercantile world full of the potential for corruption, who wouldn't want to put a trusted brother or uncle in command of a vessel they owned, carrying a cargo whose loss could make or break you financially?

Disputes with customers added to the stress of business. In 1859, after Henry delivered a cargo of coal to Quebec, the Richelieu Company complained about its quality and refused to accept it. Henry dumped the coal on the wharf. The case went to litigation, and Henry won.[8] His fortunes, like the incoming tide, now began to flow: "Change soon came, and success rewarded my perseverance."

One evening in the fall of 1859, Dinning visited Henry and his bride in the cottage they were renting on the Plains of Abraham. "Wood is so cheap now, Henry," said the persuasive Dinning. "Wages, too, will be low this coming winter. Good carpenters will work for fifty to sixty cents a day."

"What do you have in mind?" asked Henry.

"I can build you a good ship of 850 tons at $34 per ton."[9]

Henry reflected. The price was tempting. "I will take half of her," he responded. Six months later, by the spring of 1860, when the ship was ready to launch, prospects looked even brighter. Bright enough that Henry bought Dinning's half of the ship. By that time he'd laid out $31,450. He called the ship *Devonshire*, perhaps to please his friend and financial backer William Yeo back in Devon. She was built of rock elm and tamarack and was 150 feet long and 34 feet abeam. Like all such sailing ships, *Devonshire* had three masts, including the mizzen aft. Square-rigged, her fore and main masts each bore five sails. Over the bow were no fewer than four jibs — fore topmast staysail, inner jib, outer jib, and flying jib.[10]

Henry gave the command to his brother Charles. The maiden voyage took *Devonshire* to Liverpool where an eager buyer was waiting, and Henry promptly sold her for almost $40,000. "She left me a clear profit of $7,000 [roughly equivalent to $147,000 today] in a few months. I was so delighted that I offered Dinning a valuable horse as a present."

Henry could not help but listen when Dinning called on him to invest in another ship. Five years earlier, the impetuous shipbuilder had purchased for two thousand dollars an old Saint John–built barque, *Columbine*, which had gone on the rocks.

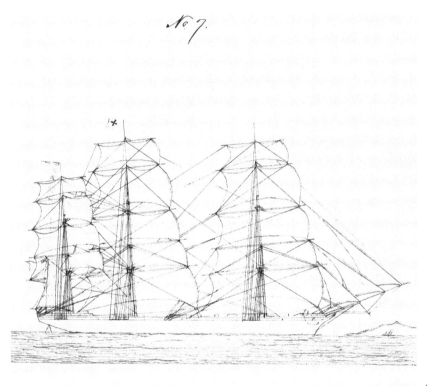

Pen-and-ink illustration by Henry Fry, 1891.

Quick profit: *Dinning built the ship* Devonshire *for Henry Fry in the winter of 1860. When spring came,* Devonshire *made her maiden voyage to Liverpool, where Henry promptly sold her at a profit, equal today to more than a hundred thousand dollars.*

"Burn her!" Henry urged. But Dinning wouldn't listen. He invested heavily that winter in repairing *Columbine*. Then regretted it.

"Take her off my hands," implored Dinning. "I'll take whatever you think she's worth."

Henry consented. "I pitied him … so I bought half of her for $3,750 cash, and lent him $3,750 in my notes on the other half. The new top did not agree with her old bottom, and he never could make her tight."

Henry found a highly profitable charter for *Columbine*, but after the cargo was loaded, the ship broke out again leaking. There followed more repairs, and the detention of the cargo turned profit to loss. Dinning was unable to make payments on the loan Henry had made for him to own half of the ship. From there, things got worse. "I was induced to give command of the *Columbine* to a stranger, John Rofe, who turned out a drunkard, and the only Captain who ever gave me serious trouble. In 1867, when bound from Savannah to Gloucester, *Columbine* finally put in to the Island of St. Thomas, so leaky she was condemned and sold for a trifle — the brute. She made me a little money, but she cured me forever of buying wrecks and gave me more trouble than any ship I ever had to do with."[11]

Henry spent the winter of 1860 in England, returning with his brother Charley in the springtime. They landed in Portland, Maine, and rode the train up to Levis. Across the river toward Quebec they looked upon an aqua-panorama teeming with rafts and tugs and masts and hulls — ships sailing up, ships sailing down, ships swinging at anchor. Upstream, squared timbers floated all over the river. Historian William Wood described the scene: "The distinctive feature was the rafts, some so enormous and so populous that they form little floating settlements of shacks and tents and wigwams, with captain's house and store-room, sometimes a farmyard full of chickens, and often milch cows…. Half the townspeople are in the ship and timber business, while most of the other half depend on it too. Quebec is nautical all over."[12]

The town was in glorious turmoil, excited as it prepared for the official visit in the summer of 1860 by Queen Victoria's eldest son, the nineteen-year-old HRH Albert Edward Prince of Wales, heir to the throne. In the 1790s, the prince's grandfather, Victoria's father, the Duke of Kent, had been stationed in Quebec in command of the 7th Fusiliers.

He lived with his mistress, Mme. St. Laurent, in a house on St. Louis Road, where Henry and his bride Mary were at that time ensconced in a cottage.

The future King Edward reached Quebec on August 16 on the sailing ship HMS *Hero*, which was equipped with an auxiliary steam engine. Accompanying the prince was a whole flotilla of ships — both steam and

... and a loss: After running onto rocks, the ship Columbine *was repaired by Dinning, who persuaded Henry Fry to buy her.* Columbine *leaked badly and was eventually condemned. "She cured me forever of buying wrecks," remarked Henry.*

sail. The British naval vessels erupted with a deafening roar as they delivered a ceremonial gun salute. Tens of thousands of residents thronged the shore, and more looked down from the upper town at the royal teenager's arrival. Thousands more visitors arrived in the port from up and down the St. Lawrence, and from the United States. Government and commerce were at a standstill.[13]

The *New York Times* correspondent gushed at what he saw: "All the banks, public halls, hotels, markets and saloons are gaily decorated. Triumphal arches, equal to any we have ever seen, are encountered in every principal street."[14]

Twenty-four riding horses and twelve elegant carriages were placed at the disposal of the prince's party. No fewer than 1,500 people attended a lavish ball, illuminated by an immense number of gas-burners. The *Times* correspondent enthused about the inspiring music of the two bands and the decor — "wreathes of green, alabaster vases of beautiful flowers, elegant carpets, showy uniforms, bright buttons, fair damsels, bewitching eyes." The heart of every unmarried Canadian girl was aflutter at the prospect of glimpsing the prince, hoping to receive a return glance, to say nothing of the miracle of being chosen to dance in the arms of the world's most eligible bachelor.

The royal visit may not have excited Henry as much as it did other Quebecers. While he worshipped the Empire and its surpassing industriousness and trading successes, drowning it in a tidal wave of verbal praise, he was mute about the queen, and even dismissive of her son, the prince. He described London's Rotten Row, along Hyde Park, as a place "where the fashionable may be seen living, or driving every afternoon, including the Prince and Princess of Wales."[15]

For Henry it was important to cherish and defend, not the Crown, but rather "the sacred cause of civil and religious freedom for which his forefathers fought and died." Of English governance, he commented, "In reality it is a republic with a nominal monarchical head." He described the annual Lord Mayor's London procession to the Courts of Justice in November in order to receive the queen's approval as "almost ridiculous, an allegorical show."[16] He may have thought the same of the young prince's Canadian visit. The fawning, scraping, and bowing were over the top.

In any event, Mary, overdue with child, was in no condition to attend balls, and Henry was happy to spend an evening at home in the cottage, chatting with his friend, the Baptist minister David Marsh. And some intense, robust discourse it was. "Marsh was not only a good Greek scholar and theologian," wrote Henry, "but he made considerable attainments in chemistry and astronomy, on which he sometimes lectured. In intimate conversation, he was remarkable for his great tenderness and suavity of manner, his sweetness of temper … and his love of children." An evening at Henry's included hymn-singing. Marsh "was a good musician, both a singer and composer, and delighted in the sacred compositions of Bach, Handel, Weber and Mozart."[17]

Henry readily matched Marsh in conversation. He was an inveterate reader, and had brought to Quebec his growing library of books. Among them were Macaulay's *History of England* and his *Essays*; Francis Bacon's *Essays*; Schwegler's *History of Philosophy*; Montaigne's *Essays*; Paley's *Natural Theology*; Chalmers's *Natural Theology*; John Stuart Mill's *Principles of Political Economy*; Pepy's *Diary*; a book of Henry Wadsworth Longfellow's poems; Dickens's *Nicholas Nickleby*; to say nothing of 21 volumes of the *Encyclopaedia Britannica*.

October 14, 1860, marked the birth of the Frys' first child and, as it would happen, their only daughter — little Mary would come to be called Mame within the family. The delivery was made by Dr. James Arthur Sewell, who would go on to attend the births of all of Mary and Henry's sons.

Henry, meanwhile, continued to work long hours in his office at 21 St. Peter Street in the Lower Town. In November of that year, Abraham Lincoln was elected president of the United States, and within weeks the American Civil War broke out. That awful conflagration would bring death to more than half a million men. But it brought unexpected commercial prosperity to Canada.

The *Mary Fry*: In 1861, Henry commissioned Dinning to build this ship, which he named for his wife, who'd just given birth to their first child. Mary joked that she hoped "not to read in the paper that I have been hauled into dry dock to have my bottom scraped."

Pen-and-ink illustration by Henry Fry, 1891.

8

1861
The Mary Fry

Business booms are often linked to morbidity. During the devastating U.S. Civil War the Union Army's demands for the replacement of slain horses and for wood to replace destroyed ships brought unexpected prosperity to Canada. Canadian agriculture experienced soaring demand.[1] Not only farmers, but shipbuilders and livestock breeders benefited, as did Canadian manufacturers of clothing and shoes, who saw an upsurge in orders when their American competitors were forced to neglect exports in order to focus on the needs of the Union Army and home demand.

Henry, in his later *Essays*, saw the era as once again vindicating his belief in the benefits of free trade: "The Civil War developed such a demand for our exports from 1862 to 1866 [that] duty or no duty, the Americans will buy what they want and must have, and the duty makes little or no difference in the prices they pay us or the quantity they buy."[2]

Above all, it was an era that spurred shipping and shipbuilding.

"Dinning offered to build me a tip-top ship of 1,000 tons at $42," Henry recorded. "I had such implicit confidence in him that the contract was written on a half-sheet of notepaper and merely initialled."

Dinning agreed to buy one-third of the ship for himself — money, however, that he had to borrow from Henry.[3] In his Cape Cove yard, under the cliffs topped by the Plains of Abraham, men laboured through the winter of 1861 constructing the 986-ton ship of rock elm and tamarack. While they worked, Henry was in England seeking cargoes that the new ship might carry. He returned in early April after two and a half months abroad, taking passage on the luxury steamship *Persia* and crossing the North Atlantic in record time — under nine days; the stretch from Ireland to New York took only three.

Not long after he returned to Quebec, two memorable events occurred in the harbour, one rather calamitous and the other happy. In May of 1861 the shipping of timber to Europe was fully underway and the river was crowded with ships waiting to be loaded. A pilot anchored Henry's sailing ship *Lotus* in such a way that when a fresh breeze came up and the tide turned to ebb, adding force to the river's natural flow, the ship broke her sheer, swung around, and collided with another ship, *Washington*. The latter's jib-boom passed between the main and mizzen masts of *Lotus*, and the two ships became hopelessly entangled. Their anchors dragging, they drifted downstream, becoming entangled with three other ships. The five ships' anchors eventually held them off the west shore of Île d'Orléans. What a mess it was! The *Washington*'s owner sued Henry and his partners who owned *Lotus*. The court rejected the suit, judging that *Lotus* had been under the control, not of her master, but of the pilot.[4]

The good news was that Henry had arrived back in Quebec in time for the launching of the sailing ship that Dinning's men had built during the winter, equipped with Cunningham's patent self-reefing topsails. "She was a handsome ship," Henry remarked with pleasure. His brother Charley, twenty-eight, had recently married Sarah Bryant in Bristol. Henry offered him command of the new ship, and allowed him to work with Dinning in designing the poop cabins to his own taste so that Charley and his bride could sail the world together.

"I was in the full tide of domestic bliss," Henry later wrote to his oldest son, his namesake Henry. "Our baby girl was just six months old. So I had your mother's portrait roughly carved in wood for a figurehead, and named the ship *Mary Fry*."[5]

Mary Dawson Fry found the honour amusing. "I hope not to read in the paper that I have been hauled into dry dock to have my bottom scraped," she joked.[6]

The *Mary Fry* came to generate a robust return on Henry's investment. On a single 1862 voyage she made a profit of $12,500 carrying sugar and hemp to Australia, bringing back twenty-six Spanish officers

Notman Collection. McCord Museum, 1-716.1.

Mrs. Henry Fry: *In the year of the ship* Mary Fry's *launching, the honoree, twenty-five years old, found her way to William Notman's studio to be photographed.*

and their wives from Manila, along with valuable cigars. She carried rails to New York and teak to Naples. "From Naples she went to Calcutta," wrote Henry. He continued:

> On her way back to Hull in 1865, she lost all three topmasts in a sudden squall near the Equator. It cost $15,000 to put her in good order, two-thirds of which I recovered from the underwriters. On her next voyage she got a good freight from Shields to Bombay, then went to Calcutta for rice, and on her return to Bombay carried stores for the army in Abyssinia. In the fall of 1869 she loaded at Trois Rivieres for Callao, Peru, was detained too late, and had to winter at Indian Cove. In 1871 she carried guano* from Peru to Hamburg.

In late 1873, the *Mary Fry* brought a cargo of teak from Rangoon to Greenock. "We were all in England when she arrived," Henry recorded. "As the price of ships was then very high, I sold her for £7,000, or about 75 percent of what she had cost 13 years before. On the whole, from first to last, she cleared about $30,000 net. Charley, who joined her without a penny, left her worth $15,000. As he had no children, Charley's wife Sarah went everywhere with him. He made one more voyage to India and then retired from sea life, becoming ships' husband to a line of steamships, and owning parts of several ships and steamboats."

Back in Bristol, Henry's Uncle William designed a house flag for the *Mary Fry* and for the other Fry-owned ships — a red Maltese cross on a white ground — to be flown whenever in port. And from across the Atlantic came Henry's youngest brother, Edward, nineteen, who'd attended Bristol Grammar School and had apprenticed as a sailor and navigator on Henry's *Lotus*. Edward joined Henry Fry & Co. as a junior merchant and office "gofer" in the Quebec office.

Henry extended the lease on his office on St. Peter Street at an annual rental fee of £50.[7] His life now was at a crescendo of deal-making. Along with two Quebec lumber merchants, in 1861 he had purchased the use of

---

* Guano is the excrement of seabirds and cave-dwelling bats, highly desirable as a fertilizer due to its high levels of phosphorous and nitrogen and odourless compared to livestock manure. Guano was also an important source of nitrates for gunpowder.

Sillery Cove for £11,571, payable in annual installments of £1,000 a year.[8] They could use the cove, located midway between today's lower town and the Pierre Laporte Bridge, to hold wood in readiness for sawing and shipbuilding or wood they'd sold for shipment abroad, or earn a return from other merchants who used the cove. The investment would one day enrich his wife, Mary.

A sudden squall: *The Mary Fry transported cargoes to Australia, teak to Naples, rails to New York, and guano from Peru. Sailing from Calcutta in 1865, she lost all three topmasts in a sudden squall near the equator. Henry imagined how she would have appeared.*

9

1861-62
Family Time

On what is today Dufferin Terrace, Mary Dawson Fry took title in 1861 to a two-storey row house, 3 Rue des Carrières, at a cost of £1,500. What a location! The building's front windows afforded one of the most prized urban views in the world — in the foreground a grassy lawn and garden, then, below the mighty St. Lawrence, the south shore, and beyond the hills of the Beauce country all the way to the Maine border. In winter they could see the river shining brilliantly, white with snow and ice. In summer the water's surface bristled with the breezes and the agitation of tidal currents battling or coalescing with the river's flow, never limpid or calm, teeming with masts and sails and little tugboats.

Henry, Mary, and their infant daughter moved out of the cottage that they'd been renting on St. Louis Street and into the house on des Carrières. Henry promptly left for England, returning in April on the steamship *Persia* in an unusually fast North Atlantic crossing of only eight days (refuelling in Queenstown, Ireland) to New York.[1]

Arriving in New York, he read newspapers headlining the beginning of the Civil War. On April 15, President Lincoln declared an insurrection of the southern states. New York's most influential citizens organized a gigantic mass meeting that drew more than a hundred thousand people to Union Square. The excitement in the streets was palpable. Men rushed to enlist. The war, Henry suspected, would bring a boom to the shipping industry and to Canadian exports. Nor could it escape his attention either that a new industry had come to New York Harbor — the refining of oil from Pennsylvania to produce and export kerosene, the cheapest illuminant known at the time.[2]

Back in Quebec, on a June night, asleep in the family's new home, Henry was awakened by a furious knocking on his bedroom door. It was his brother Edward. "The *Mary Fry* has gone ashore on a bed of rocks!" he cried. The new ship, launched only a few weeks before, had been coming downriver from Montreal, heavily laden with a cargo of wheat and flour. If she remained stranded on the rocks at low tide, she could easily break in two. Henry leaped out of bed, threw on his clothes, and rushed down to his office. He quickly dispatched a tug with men and cables to pull the ship off. But the aid wasn't needed. "In the afternoon, to my delight, she made her appearance with flags flying," he later wrote. Although her sternpost had been on the rocks, her bow had apparently kept afloat and she came off all right at high tide.[3]

In autumn 1861, the *Mary Fry* was scheduled to sail to London. Mary's brother, Sam Dawson, twenty-eight, was sick and weak at the time. Henry offered him free passage so that he could see doctors in

Archives Nationales, Quebec.

Quebec's famed terrace: *This was the condition in 1850 of what would become Durham, later Dufferin Terrace, and the future site of the Château Frontenac hotel. Visible in the back centre of the gravure are row-houses, the middle one of which Mary Fry would purchase eleven years later.*

Notman Collection, McCord Museum, I-534.1.

Lost and found: *Samuel Dawson, historian and future Queen's Printer of Canada, was Henry Fry's brother-in-law and close friend. His 1861 voyage aboard the* Mary Fry *to seek medical help in England took more than two months.*

London. The ailing Dawson might have done better to find the cure for his illness in his native land, or bought himself a steamship ticket. The wind from the east blew so hard that the *Mary Fry* beat about the Gulf of St. Lawrence for a whole month. After eight weeks the family had heard nothing from England about the fate of the ship. "We all waited and waited to hear of her arrival in vain," Henry wrote. "I got dreadfully anxious and feared the worst." Finally, in January, just after New Year's 1862, a telegram arrived from Charley, the skipper: "Arrived, all well."

"I almost shed tears of joy," wrote Henry.[4]

As with the *Mary Fry*, Henry later used his sailing ship *Sunbeam* to offer no-expense transatlantic passage to relatives and friends. "I gave so many invalids a free passage to London in *The Sunbeam*," Henry wrote, "that I called her my 'hospital ship.'"

Canadians like Sam Dawson and his sister were propelled to cross the dangerous North Atlantic at the stormiest time of year to seek medical help in England for the same reason that medical students went abroad to study. The most prestigious universities and hospitals were in Great Britain, France, and Germany.[5] More than likely, too, anglophiles like Henry, imagining all things British to be superior, travelled three thousand miles to Harley Street seeking medical skill more advanced than what they thought was available in Quebec or Montreal.

At the time Henry received the telegraph advising him that the *Mary Fry* had successfully reached Europe, he was aboard the steamship *Hibernian* in the harbour at Portland, Maine, ready to cross the Atlantic. Mary Dawson Fry was also ill, and Henry had decided that she, like her brother, must go to England for medical care.

Henry, Mary, baby, and nurse, along with Sam Dawson, spent more than four months in England. In May 1862 they all returned together on the steamship *Nova Scotian*. Not only was Mary's health restored, but she was pregnant with her second child. The return voyage included a narrow escape from a collision with heavy ice off Bird Rocks, east of the Magdalen Islands, when the ship was buffeted by a gale. After a sixteen-day crossing, the ship steamed into the port of Quebec, where horse and carriage greeted the weary travellers at dockside and bore them up the steep incline that took them home.

* * *

The walls of the house on des Carrières, bordering the terrace, were filling up with paintings, drawings, and engravings. Henry had "discovered" the now celebrated Cornelius Krieghoff, the *bon vivant* Quebec artist chronically short of money. Between 1863 and 1871, three auctions of Krieghoff paintings took place in Quebec. Henry acquired two more of the artist's paintings, today worth as much as fifty thousand dollars.[6] On his house and office walls hung paintings of ships that he'd commissioned. The subject matter — the sea, and his native Somerset — attracted Henry's eye. Here was a brig beating up the English Channel by Poole, and there was a watercolour by the Bristol painter John Syer showing sailors pulling a trawler up on the shore. A large Syer oil-on-canvas of Wells Cathedral Henry purchased for two hundred dollars. "You could get a thousand dollars for it," he was told by young Edward Fry. "Well, it is not for sale," snapped Henry.[7] He gave to his pal Dinning a picture by the well- known British artist Edwin Weedon of the *Ocean Monarch*, drawn before that ship had tragically burned with the loss of four hundred lives in 1848.

On November 30, 1862, Mary gave birth to a boy. The first son, he received his father's name, Henry. Two years later, William Marsh Fry was born, taking his middle name from the good Reverend Marsh. A model of Victorian motherhood and child-bearing, Mary bore six sons over twelve years — biennially, like clockwork.

Row house on Dufferin Terrace, Quebec: *The middle building — today the Hotel Terrasse Dufferin — was the Fry family home for over twenty years, starting in 1861. The brick and green-mansard-roofed building on the right is the U.S. consulate.*

Photo by the author.

Notman Collection, McCord Museum, I-7059.1.

Mother and first child: *Mrs. Henry Fry and her firstborn, only daughter Mary Dawson Fry, known as "Mame," in 1863. Mame was destined to have six brothers.*

Notman Collection, McCord Museum, I-17498.

Photo by the author.

Views 145 years apart: *Looking down on Quebec's lower town and harbour in 1865 (top), and in 2010 through a window of the Hotel Terrasse Dufferin.*

With the burgeoning brood of children, nannies, and cooks, the house on des Carrières was bursting, necessitating the addition of a third floor. After the renovations, the house boasted eight rooms upstairs for sleeping, two bathrooms, and a sitting room. On the ground floor, the spacious, heavily curtained drawing room was filled with a half-dozen easy chairs, a couple of footstools, a piano, fireplace tools, a cribbage board, busts of Queen Victoria and her husband the Prince Consort Albert, and on the walls oil paintings and engravings.[8] Also in the drawing room was an ornate, exquisitely carved wooden Bombay Chair, Henry's favourite.

From the street, visitors to the Fry home entered a lobby with a cloakroom. At the rear of the house was a door leading to the horse stable. The kitchen and pantries were filled with the necessities of Victorian life — an icebox, a large stove and wood box, a water barrel, fish kettle, roasting pans, soup tureens, a gravy strainer, bread box, marmalade pots, pudding bowls, jelly moulds, a bread box, cake and biscuit tins, a milk skimmer, and weighing scales.[9]

In December 1862, Henry once again left his family at home in Quebec, travelling to England to find cargoes and to cut deals for the next year. But first he stopped in New York to look at a ship he'd long yearned to own.

10

1861
A Very Public Controversy

It had been love at first sight in 1859 when Henry first eyed the sailing ship *Sunbeam* in Boston Harbor as she was loading a cargo for London: "I saw at once that she was a splendid ship with a heavy white oak frame, planked & ceiled [*sic*] with pitch pine, and the workmanship superb."

Capable of carrying large cargoes, *Sunbeam* measured 168 feet long with a 34-foot beam. She'd been built in the Medford, Massachusetts yard of Paul Curtis in 1845 for Augustus Hemenway of Boston at a cost 50 percent more than what normally would be paid for such a ship. But Hemenway could easily afford it. Rising from lowly clerk, he'd become a millionaire from copper mining investments in Chile, as well as owning a fleet of ships. Henry never forgot *Sunbeam*. After Hemenway suffered heavy financial losses, forcing him to sell off most of his ships, Henry seized the opportunity to buy *Sunbeam* in December 1862.

"The Civil War was raging," Henry later recalled, "and gold was at 33 percent premium. Silver even had all disappeared, and shinplasters[1] down to five cents were the only currency. *Sunbeam*'s price was $24,000 in greenbacks, and I closed at once. The broker thought I had paid a long price as she was 17 years old." But the Yankees could not see that their paper dollar, or "greenback," didn't have the nominal value printed on it. "In truth, she only cost me $18,000 Canadian money. The *Sunbeam* was by far the cheapest and best ship I ever owned. At Quebec and Montreal, I usually loaded her with grain and flour. She soon cleared her initial cost."[2]

Times were good. The prosperity was attributable, in Henry's mind, to the free play of the markets and open trade. The cost of labour was akin to the cost of a commodity — subject to the vagaries of the marketplace. Henry bore an unconcealed hostility toward the idea that workers should control the price of their labour. Trade unions, he believed, were "obnoxious, leading to strikes ruinous alike to the working man and his employer."[3]

Sunbeam: "By far the cheapest and best ship I ever owned," wrote Henry Fry of the splendid sailing ship Sunbeam. *He bought her in 1862 at auction from Bostonian Augustus Hemenway, the American copper mining millionaire who'd fallen on hard times.*

Pen-and-ink illustration by Henry Fry, 1891.

The issue became personal for him early in 1861 when Quebec's stevedores attempted to persuade the government to allow them to form an association regulating the loading of ships in the port. The struggle ignited an explosion of angry letters to the editor of the *Quebec Morning Chronicle*, in which Henry publicly threw himself into the fray.

The loading of ships was hot and dangerous work. It was typically done hurriedly, in a small space through a square port in the stern. After the ship was fully loaded the port was plugged and caulked for the ocean voyage. The direction of the work required skill and knowledge. A cargo improperly stowed could shift about, causing the ship to capsize in heavy seas, or, if wrongly distributed, cause the hull to break if the ship was loaded fore and aft with nothing amidships. Of critical importance was the correct distribution of cargo over the length and breadth of the ship in order to minimize the danger of excessive weight bearing on the ship's inner lining. If there was deck cargo, ballasting knowledge was essential. There should be clear standards, insisted stevedores, for teaching, apprenticing, and licensing stevedores.[4]

A further reason to regulate ship loading was the need to discourage corruption. To obtain jobs stowing wood on ships, hustling stevedores often resorted to kicking back a portion of their pay. Bribery, not necessarily competence, won the job.

"After landing on the wharf," reported a writer to the *Quebec Morning Chronicle*, who signed his letter "Experienced Stevedore," "the ship's master is surrounded by grocers, butchers and their runners, wanting to supply the ship with beef, others with groceries, and all eagerly trying to recommend some stevedore. The class of stevedores these people generally recommend are not those capable of loading a ship properly."

What was required, insisted the stevedores, was governance — organization. Henry disagreed, and wasn't shy about expressing his opinion. A stevedore organization, approved by Parliament, he said, was unnecessary, even "injurious." Supposing some stevedores were incompetent, the ship captains, he wrote, "are not bound to employ them. They have an ample choice of good men. The stevedores are well paid, and if any of them fail to make a good living, it is only because of natural law." *Tant pis*. It was implicit in Henry's mind that the invisible hand of laissez-faire would design the path to what worked best. "Leave every man to get his own living as best he can, without let or hindrance," Henry explained to the editor of the *Morning Chronicle*. "Supposing a spring fleet of 300 ships hove, and say there are only 100 licensed stevedores. During the height of the busy season, it is usual for a stevedore to superintend the stowage of more than one ship at a time. With a competent assistant at each, he can do so easily," especially when the ships were at one log boom. Under the bill proposed by the stevedores, however, only one ship could be stowed at a time. It would require far greater numbers of stevedores, wrote Henry, inevitably forcing skippers to hire less competent ones. Nothing was wrong with the present system, he insisted.

Notman Collection, courtesy McCord Museum and Eileen Marcil, I-76319.

Stevedoring fight: *Loading deals and squared timbers onto ships in Quebec Harbour was hot, dangerous, tricky work. When the stevedores wanted to unionize, Henry vocally led the Quebec Board of Trade in opposition.*

"I cannot believe that the great majority of the stevedores themselves are in favor of change. If they are, I warn them that they are preparing a rod for their own backs."[5]

Henry's dismissal of the stevedores as a bunch of unjustified whiners infuriated their leaders. "There are men engaged in this affair," wrote one of them in a sarcastic letter to the *Chronicle*, "who are as capable of thinking and acting for themselves as Mr. Fry is of doing so for them. Mr. Fry says he speaks from practical knowledge. I never knew that he ever was, or is, a stevedore. If he is, we will offer him the hand of welcome, hoping that on some future day one of us may attain the position of Lloyd's agent.

"Mr. Fry," the letter writer continued, "says it would be injurious to the trade if the stevedores were to have a board of examiners. Mr. Fry should take a wider field for his letter writing, and tell people that ship masters should have a board of examiners for granting certificates to mates and master." For sure, a stevedore should not be directing the loading of more than one ship at a time, and "Mr. Fry cannot point to a time when a ship was detained for want of a man to stow her."[6]

Henry lashed back, accusing the letter writer of "failing to answer one of my arguments. If he has the manliness to state his charges explicitly over his real signature, giving names, I, for one, will meet them fearlessly." Meanwhile, he advised the *Chronicle*'s editor that the Quebec Board of Trade (Henry would become its president) opposed the stevedore bill, and that the town's merchants "are, I believe, without exception, opposed to it."

Well, not quite. A week and a half later, one of Quebec's merchants furnished the newspaper with reasons why stevedoring should be reformed. A proper stevedoring association would destroy the influence of merchants, chandlers, butchers, and pilots who meddled in recommending stevedores to captains. It would take responsibility off the captains, who were blamed for employing bad stevedores. It would be a boon to captains unfamiliar with the port's practices. It would eliminate a great deal of litigation, which generally ended in the defeat of the captains and loss to the owners. And there would be fewer ships getting waterlogged as a result of bad stowing.[7]

The Quebec Board of Trade prevailed, nonetheless, and the stevedoring bill never passed. The stevedores did not totally lose, though.

In June 1862, legislators passed an Act to Incorporate the Quebec Ships Labourers Benevolent Society. The society's ostensible aim was to assist the families of members reduced to distress by illness or death caused by the hardships and accidents incurred in ship loading.

Under the guise of operating as a charity, the society's goal was to gain for its members — Irish, and Irish descendants mostly — an exclusive grip on port work, demanding ship stowage wages as much as 40 percent higher. Hundreds of French-Canadian port workers were excluded. They did not react passively.

"French-Canadian laborers, who preferred low pay to none at all, were prepared to undercut them, and they formed a rival society in 1865," records Quebec maritime historian Eileen Marcil.[8] Fights between the French and Irish became a frequent occurrence in the lower town and around the docks.

Quebec's religious, ethnic, and economic interests were a muddle of confusion. By religion, both the French-speaking workers and the English-speaking Irish were Roman Catholic, even as they fought one another. The French-Canadian shipbuilders, also Roman Catholic, had economic interests in common not with their French-speaking Catholic workers, but with the English merchants and owners of other yards, virtually all Protestants.

Ownership of the yards was by no means English-dominated. For a while in the 1860s French-Canadian shipbuilders — father and son Charland, F.X. Marquis, the brothers Samson, Pierre Brunelle, Narcisse Rosa, the Valins, Toussaint Valin, Edouard Trahan, and more — actually outnumbered the English builders. Lloyd's surveyor considered the quality of Pierre Brunelle's Quebec-made, fully rigged sailing ships equal to work done in the Royal Dockyards.[9] His eponymously named *Brunelle* was one of the fastest wooden sailing ships in the world. Among the last of the great sailing ships, Guillaume Charland's *Lauderdale*, built in 1880 across the river at Lauzon, earned the highest Lloyd's rating of any ship ever built in Quebec. The intrepid Captain J. Elzear Bernier, before setting out on his historic Arctic exploration, was acting superintendent in a shipyard.[10]

Quebec's social fabric differed from the later French-English two solitudes, characterized by separation of language, religion, and wealth.

The situation in 1860s Quebec City was more nuanced. It was not unilingual as it is today, but rather cosmopolitan, not unlike Montreal today, where amid the majority of French and English Canadians is relatively small numbers of Italians, Greeks, and others. The term *anglophone* had not been invented. English-speakers saw their identity as Scottish, Irish, English, or Jewish. If you were not a Roman Catholic, you were Anglican, Methodist, Presbyterian, or Baptist.

Five years after Henry took up residence in Quebec, the city covered two square miles. Of its 51,000 inhabitants, 44 percent were English and Scottish, Irish working class, and a heterogeneous collection made up of about seven hundred Germans, Italians, and other assorted nationalities.[11] Three thousand British troops were still in garrison, remaining in Quebec as part of the fledgling nation's military defence against incursions from the United States, most recently from vengeful Irish Fenian raiders. The garrison was a legacy of Wolfe's victory on the Plains of Abraham a hundred years earlier. The resident troops had initially been necessary to ensure order in a town predominantly made up of conquered French inhabitants, and to defend against invasion from the south. In any event, during the middle years of the nineteenth century, the historic francophone dominance of Quebec was not plain to see. The port city's population was only 55 to 60 percent francophone, compared to 97 percent today.

The stevedoring controversy publicly revealed, through published letters, an aggressive, righteous strain in Henry's character.

He could number himself among the Anglo-Canadians who well into the twentieth century saw society as a kind of layer cake, made up of the low or working class, the middle class, and the wealthy and people of noble family. If a man were poor, it was his own fault. "Ability and intelligence meet their due reward," wrote Henry, "whilst incompetency falls to the poor."[12] Twentieth-century libertarians like Sam Walton and Ayn Rand would easily have endorsed Henry Fry's view. Not that he was insensitive to the plight of the deprived and exploited. There were charities to care for the most indigent, and few wealthy men in Lower Canada equalled Henry in their philanthropy.

11

1863-65
Cargoes, Conflagrations, Confederation, Committees, and Church

A cheap U.S. dollar lured Henry in late 1863 to go shopping for a ship south of the border. The *Sunbeam*, which he'd bought in Boston in 1859, had proved to be a hugely profitable vessel. During the eight years Henry would own her, *Sunbeam* would clear $30,000 net for him, the equivalent today of as much as $800,000.[1] He was so pleased with the bargain-basement price he'd paid for her that he went to New York to see about buying another ship.

When Henry arrived in Manhattan in December 1863 at the height of the Civil War, the city's economy was booming. Hotels were full, and railroads and manufacturing prospered. In the streets he would have witnessed uniformed soldiers, among them stump-legged amputees, back from the front. Clip-clopping past them, prize horses drew magnificent carriages bearing the city's wealthy denizens to festivities. Millionaires dined on partridge at Delmonico's. The nouveaux riches shopped for pearls and diamonds at Tiffany's. The upper 1 percent of the city's income earners accounted for 60 percent of its wealth.[2]

While in New York, Henry later recalled that he "did what I never did before or since." He bought, sight unseen, the sailing ship *Richard Alsop*, which had left port and was on her way across the Atlantic to Liverpool. "I had loaded her at Quebec in 1855, so I knew something about her. She was built at Bath, Maine, in 1847 for Grinnel & Co of NY — 861 tons, 157' x 35' x 21', fast, but a very different style of ship to the *Sunbeam*, being somewhat slightly built and planked with oak."

Her price was $23,500 inflated greenbacks, actually only about $10,000 in gold-backed currency.[3] "I took possession of her, and renamed her *Miranda*. She proved a troublesome ship. She had a bad leak which we never could find. On one outward passage from Swansea, laden with coal and iron, *Miranda* was struck by a sea which broke five of her lower deck beams, tearing out knees and stringers and throwing 300 tons of iron from tween decks into the lower hold."

Pen-and-ink illustration by Henry Fry, 1891.

A bargain: *Built originally at Bath, Maine, the ship* Miranda *was bought sight unseen by Henry with cheap U.S. greenbacks when he was in New York.*

Nevertheless *Miranda* earned more than she cost, and after seven years Henry sold her.

In the early 1860s, about forty large sailing ships were being launched annually from Quebec yards. "One of the cleverest builders in the province," wrote Henry, "was Edouard Trahan, a conscientious and unassuming man. He could never make more than a bare living. Dinning proposed to me to help Mr. Trahan by giving him an order to build a ship for Mr. D. and myself." So commissioned, Trahan set about building an 848-ton sailing ship, which Henry named *Sea Queen*. After crossing the North Atlantic, she sold in Liverpool for a nice profit, encouraging Henry to order Trahan to build three more sailing ships — *Ontario* (1,068 tons), *Rock Light* (770 tons), and *Shannon* (1,150 tons). The ships were among twenty-two owned by Henry, which he would come to illustrate in extraordinary detail, with pen and ink, in his handwritten book *Reminiscences of a Quebec Shipowner*.[4]

A Daring Rescue from Fire

Over the years, fires periodically devastated parts of Quebec. The human suffering was often terrible. In 1845, two successive conflagrations destroyed most of the wood-built homes of workers in the faubourgs of St. Roch and St. John.

On September 10, 1864, fire struck again — not wooden homes, but the grand Custom House, one of the finest public buildings in Canada. Praised as an architectural triumph, it had been built in the lower town only four years earlier. Located next to the wharves and bounded on the north by Prince of Wales Street, the two-storey building was constructed of finely cut stone, with a portico and colonnade facing the river. It was seemingly built for the ages. But late that Saturday afternoon a plume of black smoke rose from the Custom House's imposing dome. Henry's wife Mary would have been able to see it from the Fry house on Dufferin Terrace, looking out the window as she cradled her second son, six-week-old William in her arms.

The fire spread slowly. Aroused by the cries of onlookers, Henry emerged from his office on St. Peter Street. As soon as he realized it was the

Custom House that was on fire, he raced to where he knew the precious shipping register was located: the record of ships entering and departing Quebec and the St. Lawrence, gateway to British North America, was critical not only to Henry's work as merchant and Lloyd's agent, but to the city's entire shipping industry. He scurried in and out of the building, his arms loaded with papers, as the fire made its way down from the roof.

"The volumes containing the register of shipping were saved by Mr. Henry Fry, Lloyd's agent of this port," reported the *Morning Chronicle and Shipping Gazette* two days later.[5] In the same account, the newspaper fiercely criticized the city's inadequate firefighting. The Custom House could have been saved, declared the paper, if there had been proper hose and decent equipment and if the firefighting companies had not fought among themselves.

Despite the terrible fires, the year 1864 marked a pinnacle, both economically and politically, for Quebec. Shipbuilding reached a peak with the launching of fifty-five new one-hundred-ton-plus wooden-hulled vessels.[6] The great majority would sail under the British flag. Britain and Canada (British North America) now owned a greater tonnage of ships than Germany, France, Holland, Italy, and Norway combined.

Custom House fonds, Michael Ayre.

Saved from the flames: *Quebec was regularly savaged by devastating fires in the nineteenth century. While the grand Custom House burned in 1865, Henry Fry courageously ran inside to rescue the shipping register, containing records vital to the port city's economy.*

Hosting the Fathers of Confederation

Less than a month after the Custom House fire, in October 1864, Quebec greeted the leaders and officials who in three years time would unite the two Canadas with Nova Scotia and New Brunswick. To honour the future fathers of Confederation, the city's merchants, including Henry Fry and James Stevenson (his banker and a future in-law), hosted a dinner in Russell's Concert Hall.

The correspondent of New Brunswick's *Saint John Morning Telegraph* gushed over the affair:[7]

> Flags were suspended from the balcony at the upper end of the room, which was occupied by the band; and the walls were covered with a profusion of bright bunting relieved by wreaths of evergreens placed at intervals. Along the wall on one side were the names *Nova Scotia*, *Prince Edward's Island* [sic], and on the other *Canada*, *Newfoundland*, and *New Brunswick* — all beautifully wreathed. These, with *Union is Strength*, and *Ships, Colonies and Commerce*, made up the decorations of the room.

At the various tables sat the joint premiers of the Canadas, John A. Macdonald and Sir Étienne Paschal Taché, and all the leaders of the Maritime provinces. Guests included the press, lawyers, bankers, and traders. A prominent Quebec merchant sat at each table, as a reminder of who was picking up the tab. The Quebec banker James Stevenson, whose daughter would come to marry Henry's eldest son, presided at the end of one table.

Henry's table may have included Canada's agriculture minister, and certainly one or two delegates from Prince Edward Island, who were happy to know that Henry was married to a girl descended from the distinguished P.E.I. Dawsons. But neither the family connection nor the food and drink was going to persuade the recalcitrant islanders to enter Confederation.[8]

Abraham Joseph, the president of the Quebec Board of Trade — ship-owner, banker, and importer — welcomed the distinguished guests. Like Henry, Joseph favoured Confederation, although not so strenuously, it can be guessed, that he would offend customers and legislators who opposed it. In his toast, Joseph said that, while the merchants of Quebec were not called upon to express an opinion on Confederation itself, they at least desired a commercial union eliminating tariffs between the provinces. Loud cheers erupted when Joseph declared that the merchants above all wanted a union under one flag … of England. Applause arose again when he mentioned the urgent need for an east–west Intercolonial railway in order to bind the new country together. Henry joined further loud cheering when Joseph cited the need for free trade in shipbuilding.[9]

The dinner was one of many given for the delegates during the nineteen days they were in Quebec. Another two and a half years would elapse before Confederation was actually consummated with passage of the British North America Act.

With dinners, conflagration, the stevedoring controversy, ship launchings, the birth of a son, and more, 1864 had been a hectic year for Henry. After celebrating Christmas and New Year's in Quebec, in January he travelled by train down to Portland, Maine, and once again crossed the North Atlantic, this time to Liverpool, aboard the steamship *Peruvian*. He spent two months doing business in England. Lewis Carroll's *Alice's Adventures in Wonderland* had just been published, and he purchased a copy for his children.

In April 1865 he re-crossed the Atlantic on Cunard's *Persia*, the vessel restricted to two hundred first- and second-class passengers bound for New York. The sail-equipped paddlewheel steamer suffered a brief engine breakdown off the south shore of Long Island. When the pilot boarded the ship, Henry and the passengers learned that Union forces had captured Richmond, ending America's bloody Civil War. By the time the ship reached Sandy Hook and the entrance to New York Harbor, they learned of President Lincoln's assassination.[10] Already ships in the harbour were draped in black muslin.

Meetings, Boards, and Committees

In 1865, Henry, now nearing his fortieth birthday, travelled to Detroit to attend a joint convention of the Boards of Trade of the United States and Canada. Central to the discussion was the future of tariff reciprocity between the two countries.[11] Henry advised the Americans to repeal an antiquated law forbidding the registry in the United States of ships built abroad. Other nations had rid themselves of the rule, which failed to achieve the protection it was supposed to provide. The registry prohibition was stunting U.S. shipbuilding and forcing American merchants to purchase or charter ships under foreign flags. End it, urged Henry.

Back in Quebec City later in 1865, he took over as treasurer of the prestigious Literary and Historical Society, known to locals as the "Lit and Hiss." Located today in the Morrin Centre, its library contains the finest collection of English-language books in the city. As treasurer in 1866, Henry oversaw a transfer that further enriched the Society. The Quebec Library Association had fallen on hard times and was in debt five hundred dollars. In return for paying off the Association's debt, the "Lit and Hiss" received the Library Association's entire collection.

Notman Collection, McCord Museum, I-70327.1.

Man in full: *(Above) Henry Fry in 1872, at the apex of his career. He was at the time president of the Dominion Board of Trade and served on the boards of multiple organizations. (Left) A page from Henry Fry's* Reminiscences of a Retired Ship Owner.

Henry joined the Protestant Home Advisory Board in 1865, and also became a member of the Ladies' Protestant Home Advisory Committee.[12] A year later, perhaps anticipating his children's future education, he joined the board of the High School of Quebec on Rue St. Denis. Today Quebec's schools are mostly segregated by language, but prior to 1977 they were organized by religion, Protestant and Catholic. The well-off English Protestants sent their children to be educated at the high school. The children could start at the equivalent of grade one and proceed to graduation, so a boy could go to HSQ[13] for his entire schooling. While on the board, Henry offered a prize to the boy who showed the greatest proficiency in English composition and the most knowledge of language and literature.

The Fervent Baptist

Henry was dedicated to religious reading. Eight years earlier he'd joined the Quebec Bible Society. He belonged as well to the Religious Tract Society. Based in England, the Tract Society published books, especially in the wake of Darwin's *On the Origin of Species*, designed to ensure that tens of thousands of readers understood the new sciences in a way that would not cause them to abandon religion. Nothing about science, they believed, should contradict Christ's teaching.[14] The books arrived in a steady stream from England, and were avidly consumed by Henry.

His religious observance was strict. It even carried over to Sundays when he was crisscrossing the North Atlantic aboard steamships. On the Inman Line ships, Henry praised the "provision made for divine service on the Sabbath Day.[15] He avoided travel on French liners. "Though they are beautifully decorated and fitted with every luxury, they do not suit the British taste inasmuch as no notice is taken of the Sabbath day, while on British ships Divine service is always held at 10:30 a.m. and it is often very impressive."

Henry's strict observance was emulated by his wife, Mary. A half-century later, when she found her great-granddaughter, eleven-year-old Mary Dawson Fry, playing cards on the Sabbath, she admonished the child. "You must not, on Sunday."

The Religious Tract Society and the Bible Society appealed to an evangelical fervour in Henry. He intensified his involvement with the Baptist church on McMahon Street, keeping it afloat financially. He paid for the addition of an end-gallery, and he brought over from Yorkshire on one of his ships a small organ to improve the music in the small building.[16]

The little church's pastor, Reverend Marsh, beckoned all who adored Christ to come to his services. "Quebec citizens of all Protestant denominations," Henry wrote, "came to listen to Reverend Marsh, attracted by his simple, fervent piety and catholicity of spirit. He welcomed evangelical Christians of all denominations to membership."

The open welcome made Marsh a *persona non grata* in the exclusionary ecclesiastical circles of his time. "All of the churches in Montreal and Ontario looked on him [Marsh] as outside the pale," wrote Henry. "They were addicted to close communion. They refused to admit those who were not immersed."

Marsh suffered in the battle. The formally listed members of his congregation failed to grow in number. "Quebec is not a fertile field for the growth of denominations lacking elaborate organization and central authority," once commented historian Edward P. Conklin.[17] Marsh's congregation oscillated. In 1862, thirty-eight persons were baptized, but during a short time afterward an abnormal number were disciplined. In 1864, a dozen exited Marsh's congregation, but two years later were replaced by fifteen new members.[18]

Having no fixed salary, Reverend Marsh rarely received more than five hundred dollars a year ... that is, until Henry, who served as the church's treasurer, put up the money to ensure that he received not less than $750.[19]

Henry's personal devotion fit with the charitable side of his nature. He wanted to help poor pastors, shipwrights out of work, feed the needy widows of sailors lost at sea. It did not occur to him that their misfortune may have been a consequence of societal failures correctable by better laws and a more equitable distribution of wealth. Henry dwelt in a paradox: As a capitalist he believed in minimizing the cost of labour in the name of efficiency, while as a devout Christian he bore the responsibility of aiding the very same class of people when they were impoverished.

12

1866-69
Good Deeds Rewarded

Henry's business fortunes rose and fell, yo-yoing almost as wildly as shipping and timber prices. The reason was timing. Investment in labour represented the main cost of getting the timber and raw goods from Canada's interior to the shipping ports, principally Quebec. Merchants advanced the money to cover the costs. A year or more could pass before they got it back, and who knows what would happen during that time. It was a credit structure unintentionally designed to exaggerate fluctuations in prices and profits. "Little wonder that the psychological traits of mania and despair were so identified with the timber trade," reflected a twentieth-century historian. "A breath had made it, and a breath might take it away."[1]

Widespread financial panic occurred on May 11, 1866, when the greatest private banks in England unexpectedly failed. "Black Friday was the darkest day London has seen since the South Sea Bubble burst of 1720," observed Henry.[2] Later that year the pace of business became more hectic with the completion, finally, of a fully functional telegraph cable from Newfoundland to Ireland. Newfoundland was linked to New York.[3] Transatlantic trade was revolutionized. Instead of a message crossing the ocean by ship in ten days, it now took minutes.

After the banking crisis, mercifully, three years of prosperity ensued. Henry had become the sole owner of *Lotus*, one of his favourite ships (see chapter 6). He put her in Dinning's dock, where he spent $9,000 on repairs, among them the replacement of deck, topsides, and top timbers. Much as he loved *Lotus*, though, the ship had given him trouble — human, not maritime. The trouble arose when two of Henry's strongest character traits had come into conflict — ship management versus family obligation.

"As eldest son," he said, "I deemed it my duty to do all I could to help my brothers." In 1863 he'd put twenty-five-year-old Samuel Holmes Fry, formerly first mate, in command of *Lotus*. The trouble was that Sam, in Henry's words, "had a queer temper, and in 1865, in a very surly manner, declined to sail the *Lotus* any longer, as he said he wanted a better ship. I was vexed, as prices were high, but … I went up to London and bought for 4,300 pounds a very fine New Brunswick–built ship specially for him, *Constance*, built by Wright of St. John for the Australian passenger trade. She was a sharp model (178 feet long with a 36-foot beam) and very fast (sailing at a speed of thirteen knots when deeply laden) and in every respect a superior ship."[4]

No good deed goes unpunished. Notwithstanding Henry's generosity, in 1867 his incorrigibly resentful brother grossly insulted him again, in his home. This time, an angry Henry was unforgiving: "I requested Sam to resign. He had saved some £600 while in my employ, and on this he afterwards lived in idleness until it was spent."

As for *Lotus*, she continued to sail the high seas, although not lucratively. "I held on to her too long," wrote Henry later in life. Worst was the tragedy it brought. "In the winter of 1874," he recorded, "*Lotus* shipped a sea over the poop which carried overboard and drowned Captain John Harris, a most worthy man, plus the man at the wheel. Captain Harris' widow died soon after of grief. It was the worst accident that ever befell a ship of mine," Henry wrote.

Canada's Newport

The summer of 1866 had been hot, as often happens in Quebec. In Lower Town, where Henry worked, the high south-facing cliff above partly blocks northern breezes that might cool homes and offices. The previous year Henry had the idea that his growing family would enjoy relief if he were to own a cottage on the fashionable south shore of the St. Lawrence where the river widens into the beginning of the Gulf of the St. Lawrence, and where refreshing air from Hudson Bay and Ungava streams for miles shoreward across the cold water.

Actually, it would be more accurate to say that Henry's summer home idea may have been implanted in his head by the entrepreneurial Quebec lumber merchant and banker Andrew Thomson, who had the idea for a second-home real estate deal — four side-by-side cottages on a cliff overlooking the broad St. Lawrence River. The location was Cacouna, a resort village about 120 miles downriver from Quebec. One cottage would be for Thomson; one for his father-in-law, the Reverend John Cook, minister of St. Andrew's Church in Quebec, who in 1875 would become moderator of the General Assembly of the Presbyterian Church in Canada; and one for Cook's brother-in-law, the wealthy Reverend Charles Hamilton, rector of St. Peter's Anglican church in Quebec City, who later would become the first bishop of Ottawa.

Henry, a sucker for ecclesiastics, was easily talked into purchasing the fourth lot for $175. Less certain is whether the ranking clerics appreciated the close proximity of a fervent Baptist. But it was a delight for Henry. Laymen like Henry with an appetite for knowledge gravitated in their friendships toward clerics who were typically nineteenth-century society's better educated people ... and the higher up the ecclesiastical scale, the better.

The four identical 2,800-square-foot Cliff Cottages, designed by Quebec architect Edward Stavely, with walls built of squared timbers and floors of thick finished deals, were up and finished by November 1866.[5] From the lawn in front of his new second home, with a telescope, Henry could glimpse his own square-riggers plying the river. Tennis and croquet were also played on the lawn, a former potato field, with the Gulf and the Laurentian Mountains on the opposite shore as a backdrop. The ruby-red sunsets have always been spectacular. In the month of May, tens of thousands of snow geese congregated in the vast marshland east of Cacouna before flying north to James Bay. (They still do.) In August, untilled fields and carriage roads were lined with blazing red fireweed, purple loosestrife, and white Queen Anne's lace. Henry fell in love with the place.

Notman Collection, McCord Museum, MP-1984.107.38.

Photo by the author.

Photo by the author.

Bliss on the south shore: *Cliff Cottages at Cacouna on the lower St. Lawrence River, where Henry and two of Canada's leading clergymen made their summer homes in 1867. The Fry cottage, at the far end, as it is now. The cottages face across the river toward the mouth of the Saguenay River, with a view of spectacular sunsets.*

Cacouna was known in the late nineteenth century as "the Newport of Canada," suggesting that it ranked with the Rhode Island summer home of America's upper class. Henry's brother-in-law Sam Dawson, Mary's brother, described it as "famous for the dancing and flirting, and a dangerous place for an unengaged bachelor, or even for an engaged one, if his fiancée be not there to monopolise him."[6]

Cacouna was, as well, a summer retreat for the elite — among them a founder of the mighty Allan Steamship Company, and the banking and brewing Molson family. In nearby St. Patrick, Canada's first prime minister, Sir John A. Macdonald, enjoyed the ownership of a summer home.

Sirs John and Narcisse

During the winter of 1867, Henry was in Bristol, occupied with business; at the same time, in London, the widowed John A. Macdonald was occupied in marrying himself to his second wife, Agnes, while shepherding the British North America Act through Parliament and the House of Lords. With that historic accomplishment, Macdonald and his new bride in April boarded the sail and paddlewheel steamship *Persia* in Liverpool to return to the new Dominion of Canada. As it happened, Henry was one of the 250 passengers on that voyage to New York.[7]

Image from Heritage Web.

Steamship *Persia*: *John A. Macdonald and his new bride, Agnes, travelled home on the passenger ship* Persia *in April 1867 after British government go-ahead for Canada's Confederation. On board as well was Henry Fry. When built in 1856,* Persia *was the world's largest steamship.*

Cunard's *Persia* was "a great favorite with passengers," Henry wrote, "making the Atlantic crossing typically in less than ten days, moving through the water above thirteen knots average."[8] When built in 1856, the 376-foot-long, 3,300-ton *Persia* was the world's largest steamship. The Macdonalds and Henry could stroll on a roofed promenade from stem to stern and take their meals in the main dining salon — sixty feet long and twenty feet wide.

Back in Canada on July 1, 1867, Henry joined the throngs celebrating the first Dominion Day. Bands paraded and fireworks lit the sky. Quebec City was now the capital of the province of Quebec. To celebrate the occasion, the first lieutenant governor, Sir Narcisse-Fortunat Belleau — *avocat*, politician, and former Quebec mayor — sailed down from Montreal. Henry recalled that he was "among a great crowd on the wharf," waiting to greet the new lieutenant governor. Sir Narcisse selected Henry, soon to head the Quebec Board of Trade, to accompany him to the hotel reception.

"It happened that Sir Narcisse looked upon me as a representative English merchant," Henry recalled. "He bestowed on me repeated acts of kindness, which I can never forget. I often dined with him at the Stadacona Club, and on one occasion at Spencer Wood [the lieutenant governor's residence] where I met Prince Arthur [Queen Victoria's son]." Henry additionally admired Belleau for always "looking on the bright side of human nature."[9]

On the occasion of Sir Narcisse's death in 1894, Henry wrote a tribute to the farm-born lieutenant governor in the snobbish, condescending manner that would be infuriating to francophones for another century. "He [Belleau] will long be remembered as a kind-hearted, genial specimen of the old French Canadian regime, which, while not displaying the energy or force of the Anglo-Canadian, had many fine qualities which will be looked for in vain amongst the great majority of the modern 'go-ahead' trading class."

Bibliothèque et Archives Nationales du Québec.

Sir Narcisse-Fortunat Belleau: *The first lieutenant-governor of the Province of Quebec, 1867, regarded Henry Fry as a representative of the British merchant class. Fry, in turn, regarded Belleau as "a kind-hearted, genial specimen of the old French-Canadian regime."*

A Good Deed Rewarded

In November of 1866, Mary gave birth to the couple's fourth child, Arthur Dawson. With the infant, six-year-old Mame, four-year-old Henry, and two-year-old William Marsh, the family spent the winter of 1867–68 in Quebec. The town was still recovering from the devastating October fire of 1866.

"Times were bad," Henry wrote later. "There was much distress among the ship carpenters of St. Roch … so much so that a meeting was called to promote soup kitchens. I attended the meeting and denounced the proposition on the ground that it would tend to make the men paupers. 'What they want,' I said, 'is not soup, but work, and there are wealthy men in this room who can provide it without loss.'" As president of the Board of Trade, Henry believed that the assembled businessmen — merchants, ship-owners, bankers — should fund the construction of a half-dozen ships, immediately providing the money for wages. For his part, Henry would undertake to sell the ships, charging no commission.

"In this way," he told the group, "you will run no risk, get all your money back, and provide for the 5,000 souls. I will undertake myself to build one [ship]." The businessmen enthusiastically approved Henry's initiative. "I supposed them to be sincere, so I went at once to McKay & Warner [shipbuilders] where I signed a contract for a ship of 800 tons costing $38 per ton."[10]

When he looked back, however, Henry found no one following him. A few people donated token money to help the destitute, but none pursued his example of building ships to create jobs.

During the winter he watched and superintended as carpenters and yard craftsman built the ship *Rock City*. In the end, Henry's charity was rewarded:

> *Rock City* proved the most fortunate and profitable
> ship I ever owned. She was a good model, a very handy
> ship, nicely sparred, with double diagonal ceiling,
> extra fastenings. She was launched in May 1868. I ran
> her for five years between London and Montreal, and

she cleared $32,000. Then she ran another five years in the Buenos Aires and Peruvian trade, clearing $25,000 more, in all about $57,000 in ten years. But new wooden ships depreciate fast, reducing her net profits to somewhere about $32,000.[11]

A wooden ship, it's true, did not have the service life of an iron ship, and while wooden shipbuilding's demise was not immediate, its inevitability was. The low cost of iron was causing builders to steer away from wood. And the prospect of the Suez Canal opening in November 1869 would further darken sail's future.

Pen-and-ink illustration by Henry Fry, 1891.

Rock City: A profitable ship built originally in 1868 by Henry to provide winter work, rather than soup kitchens for unemployed yard workers and their otherwise destitute families.

Quebec, however, proved incapable of switching to the mass building of iron ships. It needn't have been so, believed Henry and other shipbuilders. There was an alternative. Quebec could forestall the inevitable by switching to the construction of composite ships, having frames, beams, and stringers of iron, and outside planking and ceiling of wood. On March 9, 1868, Henry led a deputation of the Quebec Board of Trade in appealing to the government.[12] He explained that iron freighters cost not much more than wooden ships to build, and that after twenty years they were still in excellent service, whereas the wooden vessels were near the end of their useful life.

"Are they as safe?" asked then prime minister of Quebec, P.J.O. Chauveau.

"They are stronger afloat," replied Henry, "but break up quickly if they run aground. There are other objections, too, such as bottom fouling and drainage from sugar eating away the heads of rivets." The solution, he said, was a composite ship: "It combines the strength of an iron ship with the safety of a wooden ship. I believe these will be the ships of the future, and they can be profitably built in Quebec. In order to commence building them, however, it will be necessary to import costly machinery, and instruct the workmen in the new mode of construction. Our shipbuilders are men of small means, and cannot at present afford such an outlay."[13]

In effect, a government subsidy was needed to kick-start composite ship construction. The subsidy never came. Two years later, it's true, William Baldwin did lay the keels of two composite ships, with iron keelson, frames, knees, and deck beams.[14] But a few weeks before the ships were ready to be launched, another devastating fire struck St. Roch. The area around Baldwin's yard, and the two ships in it, were destroyed. They were the only composites ever built at Quebec. With the notable exception of the Davie yard on the Levis side of the river, Quebec's shipbuilders stuck with wooden construction.

"The days of wooden ships were fast coming to an end," Henry wrote. "I did not have the capital to build iron ships alone." Perhaps not, but in 1867 he failed to join other Quebec investors in a new venture, the Quebec & Gulf Ports Steamship Company, precursor of the Canada Steamship Lines.[15]

He did make one iron-ship investment, however. Early in 1869, when he was in England with his wife, two small boys, and nurse-maid, he ran into Alex Ramage, a Liverpool merchant and ship-owner. Ramage had the idea of building fast iron sailing ships to run to Montreal. "If you will finance a quarter of one ship," he told Henry, "you can have the Canadian agency." Henry took him up on it, and wound up owning a piece of the 190-foot, 895-ton *Oceola*. "She was almost like a yacht," Henry recorded, "very fast, paying pretty well." The *Oceola*'s life was short, however. In October 1871, the iron barque *Marmion* ran into her off the Welsh coast. *Oceola* sank within five minutes. The captain and most of the crew were saved, but five men who jumped into one of the boats lost their lives. The tragic collision was the fault of *Marmion*, and Henry recovered most of his investment.

George Fry, eighty-five, beloved father of Henry, died in Bedminster, Bristol, in June of 1868. Henry and family did not reach England until November. In the spring of 1869, after four months, they returned to Canada, accompanied by Mary's father, Benjamin Dawson, retired Montreal bookstore owner and magazine and newspaper distributor. Their North Atlantic crossing from Liverpool to Quebec was made in a new record fast time of just under nine days on the steamer *Austrian*. On the final day, the family stood on the port deck and glimpsed the cliffs of Cacouna, where their new cottage stood.

Back in Quebec, they resumed living in the house on des Carrières, behind which a stable housed the family's horse and carriage. On Saturday night, July 14, Henry and Mary took out the carriage and drove to a party. On their way home, a bicyclist dressed in dazzling white appeared out of the darkness on St. Foy Road, pedalling furiously in swooping curves. Henry shouted at him, warning that he could frighten the Frys' horse. The cyclist paid no attention. Terrified, the horse reared up, overturning the carriage and throwing the occupants to the ground. "Mrs. Fry received some quite serious bruises," reported the French-language weekly *Le Courrier du Canada*. "Mr. Fry escaped with a few scratches." The newspaper went on to warn, "If velocipede riders are not more careful, they will end up with a very bad reputation. If they carry on in such a manner, we see no reason why the authorities should not intervene."

Back at home, Henry and Mary's row house on des Carrières was filled with the cries of five children ranging in age from one-year-old Alfred to eight-year-old Mame. The children could play on the terrace. Or they perhaps could walk a hundred yards to the Governor's Garden and gaze at the now famous monument dedicated to Generals Wolfe and Montcalm.

13

1868-69
A Monumental Gift[1]

A couple of hundred yards from the Fry house on des Carrières in the Governor's Garden stood the monument to Wolfe and Montcalm, the heads of opposing armies who died tragically on the Plains of Abraham in what has become a metaphor for Canada's birth pain. Today, a million or more tourists view the limestone monument each year. It was originally erected in 1828, but even before Henry first arrived in Quebec in 1854 it was in need of repair. A crack in the obelisk kept widening. Frustrated attempts to raise money to fix it were reminiscent of the parsimony encountered by the Earl of Dalhousie when he initiated the memorial.

The first monument of its kind in the city, its construction had required a strenuous fundraising effort led by the governor general, Dalhousie. Top-tier Quebec merchants, the Roman Catholic Church, and even a donor from as far away as New York coughed up enough money to get the construction underway. Like a good part of historic Quebec built before the middle of the nineteenth century, the monument was made of limestone. In this case the bluish-grey stone came from a quarry near Montreal.[2] On the thirteen-foot-high stone sub-base was placed a seven-foot-high sarcophagus, from which rose a column or obelisk forty-two and a half feet in height, capped with a stone piece. It is the design we see today.

It was simple in concept, but by the spring of 1828 the funds — seven hundred pounds sterling — for its construction were exhausted.

Dalhousie had to dig into his own pocket to finance its completion. Then he promptly left for India. By summertime the monument was finished, although not exactly open to view. The Governor's Garden was still private, as it had been for a century or more. In 1838, however, the reform-minded Governor General Durham opened it to the public. It was about this time that an ominous vertical crack in the limestone obelisk began to appear. Clearly, restoration work was needed. Yet nothing happened.

"Surely it is not creditable to abandon so popular an undertaking," wrote a reader to the editor of the *Quebec Morning Chronicle* on September 12, 1864. "A few individuals must undertake to save this monument to Quebec."[3] But no one stepped forward.

The daily sight of the deteriorating monument as he walked or was driven to work in Lower Town offended Henry, who became frustrated by the lack of action to repair it. As the head of the port city's most important association of businessmen, he might have led a fundraising drive as Dalhousie had done. But the experience two years earlier, when no one had followed his example in aiding the unemployed ship carpenters, determined him not to solicit the help of others. He decided to rebuild the Wolfe-Montcalm monument himself.

Henry drew up a contract with Quebec master builders Thomas and Henry Hatch to dismantle, repair, and re-erect what Dalhousie and others created forty years earlier. The agreement, drawn up in stages between July and September 1869 by the notary Henri-Charles Austin, called for the Hatches "to take down and rebuild the Wolfe and Montcalm Monument. The contractor is to provide all the necessary scaffolding, tackling, tools, labour, materials, etc., etc. etc. necessary." Henry was obliged to pay, in installments, "one thousand dollars of current money of this Province to the said T. and H. Hatch. The monument is to be carefully taken down and stones cleaned; all the face stones assembled and laid aside after cleaning so that they may be placed in the same position they now occupy in the re-erection."[4] Inferior mortar may have been a source of problems with the original monument, because more than a third of the Specifications Contract between Fry and Hatch concerned the quality of the cementing to be done. The initiation of the complex work was celebrated in a modest cornerstone-laying ceremony on September 8, 1869, reported in the daily *Quebec Chronicle*.[5] "The monument is being rebuilt by private subscription," reported the newspaper, "principally through the energy of Mr. Henry Fry who, anticipating that it would soon fall to the ground a heap of ruin and debris, brought the matter before the public through the columns of the press, and his exertions were soon after crowned with success."

The newspaper expressed disappointment at the absence of the Mystic Order of Masons at the rededication ceremony, since the Order had participated in the original cornerstone-laying. But the ceremony was otherwise impeccable. At the gate to the upper garden, Henry greeted the celebrants, including Lieutenant Governor Belleau. Into a small cavity in the stone Sir Narcisse placed a variety of coins from the reign of George IV, which had been in the original monument. The *Chronicle* went on to report that "a jar was also deposited at the back of the foundation stone containing a tracing of the plan of the Monument, with the following inscription: Wolfe and Montcalm Monument, restored at a cost of $1,000, raised by public subscription in 1869, in the 34th year of the Reign of Her Majesty Queen Victoria."

In the final act, Sir Narcisse passed a trowel over the cement, and the large stone was lowered into place. "His Excellency again took the implements of the art into his hand," reported the *Chronicle*, "and gave the stone the customary three taps, declaring it laid. Mr. Fry and other gentlemen then took up the mallet and went through a similar ceremony." Among those present were Quebec premier Pierre-Joseph-Olivier Chauveau, the historian James MacPherson, and Masonic lodge bigwig James Dunbar.

Before the year was out, the monument rose skyward again. "The workmen, who are skilled in such matters, say the obelisk will remain firm for two hundred years," reported the *Chronicle* in its September 9, 1869 issue. (Their prediction was wrong by about fifty years. In 2010, Parks Canada took down the monument and used all-new limestone in its reconstruction.)

The original monument had been designed by a captain on Dalhousie's personal staff, described in *Hawkins's Picture of Quebec* as "an officer whose taste had been greatly cultivated by foreign travel." Hawkins admired the monument's chaste design, "a combination of beautiful proportions to be found in some of the celebrated models of antiquity."[6] It was simple,

Notman Collection, McCord Museum, I-20740.1.

Notman Collection, McCord Museum, MP-0000.1452.102.

Before and after: *(Above) The Wolfe-Montcalm monument, leaning and cracked, as it appeared in 1866, threatening collapse. (Below) Four years later, the monument, freshly mortared and perfectly erect, after it was repaired by initiative of its neighbour Henry Fry.*

austere — not a physical depiction of dying men or bodies lying on a gory battlefield, but an abstract invitation to contemplate death, heroism, and sacrifice. And so it does.

Montcalm's name appears on the north side of the monument; Wolfe's on the south side facing the river whose rugged escarpment his troops had scaled. Henry and the contractor, Hatch, saw to it that the lettering of the original inscription was properly cleaned and restored. When the original monument was built, a medal had been offered to the person who furnished the most appropriate inscription to go on the cenotaph. The winner was Doctor of Literature J. Charleton Fisher, who wrote: *Mortem virtus communem. Faman historia. Monumentum posteritas dedit.* ("Valour gave them a common death, history a common fame, posterity a common monument.")

The inscription mirrored Dalhousie's sentiment. Sixty-five years after the deaths of the two generals, he had wanted to avoid feelings of conflict and resentment, but rather inspire reconciliation — a model for our own times. The oldest monument in Quebec is perhaps the most meaningful ever constructed in Canada. It is that lapidary tribute to the settling of old scores, the monument to both generals and arguably to both Canadian cultures, which stands in the little park next to the Château Frontenac. One man's effort in 1869 saved it from collapse.

14

1869-72
So Much for Disobeying Orders

In the middle of the nineteenth century, the boardwalk west of today's Château Frontenac hotel, overlooking the river and below the garden containing the Wolfe-Montcalm monument, was less than half its present length. Before it expanded into Dufferin Terrace, the shorter Durham Terrace (named for a previous governor general) didn't extend all the way to the Fry house on tiny Rue des Carrières. Rather, the western terminus was a garden and a sloping snow-covered lawn, and farther on was the steep hill that descends from the Plains of Abraham. In winter it was ideal sledding terrain for children, bundled in their heavy blanket coats with sashes, fur caps, thick woolen stockings, and overboots. Henry spent the winter of 1869–70 in Quebec, one of only four winters between 1854 and 1877 when he didn't travel to England. It gave him time to be with his growing family, and to take on more charitable work.

On January 18, 1870, he attended the first meeting of Quebec's Young Men's Christian Association in Jeffery Hale's Sunday school. Henry's bosom friend, Reverend David Marsh, chaired the meeting. After prayers, bylaws were adopted and the group elected Henry to be the Quebec YMCA's first president. Over the next eight years under his leadership the YMCA hosted readings and lectures by the city's clergy during the winter months. At noon each weekday Henry led prayers. His influence was conservative, to say the least. He opposed readings, for example, from Shakespeare. He insisted that the YMCA meetings have a religious focus, consistent with its name. He also opposed the presence of women at meetings; after all, it was the Young *Men's* Christian Association, and — to make his point — in 1875 he served on the advisory committee that launched the separate Quebec's Young Women's Christian Association.[1]

In 1870, the fledgling Dominion of Canada took over all the territories once owned by the Hudson's Bay Company, spawning the province of Manitoba and the Northwest Territories. In May, Fenian raids intensified along the upper St. Lawrence River and on the Vermont border. The U.S. government did nothing to bar the savage incursions, angering Henry. "Who allows a horde of armed ruffians to cross the new frontier and shoot down citizens of a friendly country, then refuse compensation?" he asked.[2]

Henry's sensitivity to injustice was always at a nervous pitch. It irked him that the towing of sailing ships on the river was pretty much controlled by a combine. The St. Lawrence Towboat Company, in Henry's mind, should not be able to set towage fees and conditions for the river up and down from Montreal, or for pulling ships off when they went ashore. What was needed was competition. In 1870, partnering with the powerful financier James Gibb Ross, he bought for six thousand dollars

Monopoly opponent defector: *Financier James Gibb Ross joined Henry to fight the combine that controlled ship-towing on the St. Lawrence. Ross later reneged on the deal.*

Photo from Eileen Marcil's *Charley-Man*, courtesy of the late Harry Ross.

a quarter-interest in a Scottish-built tug, *Conqueror*. Leasing out the tug would be a chance to fight back against the combine.

The St. Lawrence Co. did not take long to retaliate. In a cunning move, the company chartered the *Conqueror*, offering Ross, the majority owner, a temptingly high price that he could not refuse. Ross had conveniently forgotten the goal of destroying the monopoly and took the money without consulting Henry, the minority owner. Henry wrote of his "disgust" with Ross's short-sighted greed.[3] (In later years when steamships replaced sailing ships, the need for tugs disappeared except around Montreal and the rapid St. Mary's current just below the city.)

In January 1871, Henry left his family in Quebec and went to England on business, returning in April. In May, Britain and the United States signed the Treaty of Washington, leading to the demilitarization of the U.S.-Canadian border, and the evacuation from Quebec of the British troops garrisoned there since Wolfe's victory more than a century earlier.[4] Using his beloved *Sunbeam*, Henry won a charter to transport some of the garrison's supplies to Woolwich, England, home of the Royal Military Academy.[5] So it was that Henry's American-built *Sunbeam* participated in the dismantling of a military outpost which had outrun its usefulness in protecting Canada from American invasion or French insurrection.

In the late spring of 1870, Mary had given birth to a fifth son, Frederick, who would grow up to become a paediatrician. There wasn't yet such a specialist in Quebec, but she surely could have used one. She had borne six children in less than eleven years.

The following summer the whole family departed for the Cliff Cottages at Cacouna, where nannies shepherded the kids down to the gravel beach and the chilling water of the Gulf. Cacouna was teeming with nearly three thousand summer vacationers. Some of the tourists came by rail, but most by ship, debarking in nearby Rivière-du-Loup. If they didn't rent cottages from locals, they stayed in one of four hotels for less than $2.50 a night. The largest of these was the massive wooden St. Lawrence Hall down the road from the Cliff Cottages. Perched a hundred feet above the river, the St. Lawrence offered its guests views across twenty-five miles of water toward Tadoussac and the north shore of the river. Inside the hotel were bowling alleys and a sprawling dining room. Just added was a wing that raised the hotel's capacity to six hundred beds. On the inland side was a new race track. Guests could entertain themselves watching the horses run before dressing for dinner and dancing.[6]

Cliff Cottages was an odd little community of distinctive personalities, whose non-vacation vocational hours were dedicated to commerce and religion. One cottage was owned by Oxford-educated Charles Hamilton, the rector of St. Matthews Church in Quebec — a high-church Anglican who would go on to become bishop of Niagara and then of Ottawa. Hamilton's immediate neighbour was John Cook, a clergyman who was working at the time to unite Canada's Presbyterian churches, and who liked so little of Hamilton's kind of high Anglicanism that he regarded it as papal at heart, a kind of "mongrel medievalism." What a disparate lot they were! Cook and Henry, the ardent Baptist, belonged to the Bible Society, which encouraged its members to use scientific knowledge to gain insight into the Bible's teachings. Both men also served on the board of the High School of Quebec.

Though a cleric, Cook had a reputation for business acumen, so he would have enjoyed conversing with two of Canada's smartest

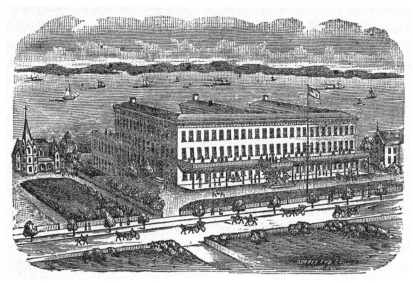

Bibliothèque Nationale.

"The Newport of Canada": *Cacouna in the last half of the nineteenth century was Canada's fashionable summer resort. Its centrepiece was the massive four-hundred-bed St. Lawrence Hall, with dinner-dances, a bowling alley, and a racetrack.*

operators — the risk-taking, deal-making Fry, and the brilliant finan-cier and lumber merchant Andrew Thomson, who had put together the Cliff Cottages real estate deal. Thomson was married to Cook's eldest daughter, Margaret. His deceased first wife had been a Hamilton. These intimate family and social connections, counterpointing acute differ-ences of religious outlook, must have generated lively conversation on the lawn fronting the cottages.

One July day at Cacouna, Henry received a cable advising him that his brother Alfred, forty-one, had returned to Bristol from Africa, where he'd worked for eighteen years as a trader and shipmaster, bartering goods for palm oil, ivory, and gold. Alfred, he learned, had almost died of fever. Henry was alarmed. At once he departed Cacouna, went upriver to Quebec, and boarded the steamship *Scandinavian*, reaching Liverpool in just nine and a half days.

In Bristol he observed that Alfred was "greatly emaciated, and I felt sure he would die if he returned to Africa. But he told me that he must go back to trading in Africa as it was his only means of supporting his family financially."[7] Henry was appalled at the idea. Alfred's savings amounted to about £2,000, yielding only 3 percent. Henry offered him £200 a year for the next three years, and invited him to come to Canada where he could help him with business, staying "as long as he liked at my expense, and I would also pay him his passage home." Alfred accepted, and the two left England in September on the steamship *Sarmatian*. Their arrival in Quebec was delayed after the ship met with foul weather off the New Brunswick coast, almost running out of coal.

After his arrival in Canada, Alfred recovered his health, and over the next two months Henry took him on a tour of Montreal, Ottawa, and Toronto. With Mary they visited New York. The extraordinary gen-erosity to his brother encompassed business as well. "I allowed him to have one-eighth each of my ships *Lotus*, *Rock City* and *Gaspee*," Henry later wrote in his *Reminiscences*. "He was on my hands for several years afterwards, but I had the gratitude of his wife and children for saving him from pestilential Africa."

In Henry, commercial success and charitable virtue breathed the same air. While he enjoyed the comforts and accoutrements of wealth, he felt a keen duty to assist almost anyone who crossed his path. Christ and

Christ's inexhaustible giving haunted his thoughts. Not that he renounced material comforts. Austerity was not his style. He took first-class passage on steamships and railway cars. He took pride in his business profits, carefully listing them in his *Reminiscences*. But he dedicated himself with equal energy to the needy — fellow Baptists, impoverished sailors, and most especially to members of his family, however defective their character. His brothers benefited from his dutiful nature. Alfred, although "a man of good education, great ability, and honest as the sun," Henry observed, "was somewhat arbitrary, very irritable and egotistical." Then there was his brother Sam to whom he'd given money, the same brother who had insulted him in his own house. When Henry expanded his office on St. Peter Street,[8] he brought his youngest brother, Edward, into the firm, despite misgivings about the latter's capacity to make sound judgments.

In 1872, when Edward was in Liverpool, he cabled Henry urging him to buy an interest in an eight-year-old iron sailing ship, *Varuna*. Henry looked up details of the ship in his Lloyd's book. "I saw that she was [a] very long [240 feet], very narrow [32 feet] ship, and therefore dangerous and unhandy. She was [also] over-masted, and would not stand up, even in port, without five hundred tons of ballast." Henry quickly cabled Edward advising him not to put money into *Varuna*. But Edward went ahead and invested a thousand pounds sterling of Henry Fry & Co. funds.

"A most disastrous purchase she proved," wrote Henry.[9] The next winter *Varuna*, on her way from New York with grain, was thrown on her beams by a sea. To prevent the ship from foundering, the captain cut away her main and mizenmasts. A rescue ship seized it as a prize. *Varuna*'s repairs amounted to 80 percent of her value, and she eventually had to be sold at a loss.

"So much for disobeying orders!" acidly observed Henry of his youngest brother's imprudence.[10]

Fortunately, the *Varuna*'s loss came after the most profitable year Henry Fry & Co. ever enjoyed, 1872. "From ships, lumber shipments, commissions and Lloyd's agency combined, I made $50,000" — the equivalent of almost a million dollars today.

Henry was a director of the Quebec Bank at the time. He was pursued by an admiring Quebec Board of Trade, the port city's most prestigious business organization, which wanted him to serve a fourth term as their president. He declined. At a national level, he was already vice-president of the recently formed Dominion Board of Trade, and in line to become that august body's president. The assurance of his succession was reinforced in January 1872 with a solid debating victory by Henry at the Dominion Board's second annual meeting. A dozen directors wanted the board to urge the government to further deepen the St. Lawrence so

Pen-and-ink illustration by Henry Fry, 1891.

A flawed decision: *Looking ahead to the post-wooden age, Edward Fry, defying his brother's orders, bought the iron sailing ship,* Varuna, *in England. On her way to New York,* Varuna *was thrown on her beams by a sea and had to be de-masted.*

that larger and larger transatlantic steamships could reach Montreal at the entrance to the canals. Henry argued that the dredging cost involved would be enormous, and why should the port city of Quebec help to pay for something that would take away business from itself? Not only that, Montreal didn't even have the capacity to handle the shipping it already had ... sometimes ships had to sit at anchor for eight or nine days before they could be loaded or unloaded.

Henry's opponents argued that Quebec was responsible for its own decline as a great natural port, having failed, for example, to increase its grain storage or to build a graving dock for repairing larger ships. But in the end, the Dominion Board, with Henry, voted 18 to 12 not to press the government to proceed in further deepening the river and Lake St. Pierre.[11] Henry's amendment passed. A year later the Dominion Board of Trade elected him its president.

15

1873
Welcoming the Dufferins, and Free Trade

"We respectfully offer our sincere and dutiful welcome on your assuming the important duties of Governor-General of the Dominion of Canada." Grave in demeanor, somewhat puffed up, standing at the speaker's dais, forty-six-year-old Henry Fry, as head of Canada's leading business organization, the Dominion Board of Trade, was reading aloud from a prepared text. The day was January 20, 1873, the place, Montreal's St. Lawrence Hall, which ten years earlier had quietly served as the Confederate Army's northern headquarters during the American Civil War.

Henry had come down to Montreal from Ottawa where he'd presided over the third annual meeting of Canada's first national business association, founded in 1870. The focus of his brief formal oration was Lord Dufferin — astute diplomat, an Irish nobleman favoured in Queen Victoria's court — who had arrived in Canada seven months earlier to serve as the fledgling nation's third governor general. Today was his baptism by Canada's business community, ministered by the Dominion Board of Trade's new president.

"As an organization concerned with the commercial interests of the Dominion," Henry said,

> We beg to direct your Excellency's attention to the great natural resources of our country. Situated as we are geographically, the people of Canada have turned

to whatever natural advantages they possess, under the penalty of being wholly distanced in the race of American progress and prosperity. An extensive canal and railway system has been inaugurated, our rivers have been deepened, ocean steamers have been established, and other means have been taken to make the River St. Lawrence the great natural outlet of the Continent for its ever-increasing Western trade. The route to the Pacific Ocean, through Canada … will connect the Ocean ports on the St. Lawrence with the Northwestern United States by a route shorter than any from American ports.[1]

Henry concluded by offering "our prayer for the health and happiness of yourself and Her Excellency the Countess Dufferin." The governor general's wife — the elegant, adventurous Marchioness of Dufferin and Ava — was in the audience, sandwiching Henry's speech between a morning session of ice skating and an afternoon visit to a Protestant deaf and dumb institution.[2] Dufferin himself had just been photographed so that his face could be reproduced on a new paper dollar.

Four days earlier in Ottawa, the fledgling Dominion Board of Trade had elected Henry as its third president. The board's meeting attracted fifty-four delegates of twenty-two different regional boards, from Nova Scotia to British Columbia (they'd just joined Confederation), as well as government officials. The meeting's complex agenda included discussions of maritime commerce, banking, insurance, public works, and Canada's customs and excise duties.

The Dominion Board was essentially a lobbying organization, and to leave no doubt in anyone's mind whom it was trying to influence, the board held its meeting inside the Parliament Buildings. The delegates debated the deepening of rivers and canals, and the future construction of a 2,700-mile-long trans-Canada railway at the staggering cost of as much as 150 million dollars. As Henry looked on from the Chair, they wrangled over the uncertain outlook for trade with the United States. One delegate found himself saddened by ignorance of Canada to the south. "Once you have left the bordering states," declared L.E. Morin of Montreal, in what would become a familiar refrain, "you seldom meet any person who knows anything about Canada, except its having a terribly cold climate and very thickly wooded country."[3]

The delegates deplored Canada's lack of a direct telegraph from Europe. From Newfoundland, news went to New York, where it was warped to suit American tastes before it reached the Canadian public. "I often feel humiliated by the garbled reports which appear in our newspapers," remarked Henry. "It is a disgrace." The board resolved that the government should be urged to establish independent telegraphic communication between the Dominion, Great Britain, and Europe without the necessity of sending messages through a foreign country or companies (i.e. American) not under the control of the Dominion.[4]

The hottest topic of discussion at the board's Ottawa meeting was the growing pressure for increasing tariffs on goods entering the country from the United States. The Dominion Board of Trade was a traditional defender of the Reciprocity Treaty establishing free trade in "natural" products, primarily agricultural and wood products. But within the board, there was pressure from manufacturing interests to raise tariffs in order to protect home industry from being undermined by cheap products from south of the border.

The board's new president had long favoured free trade. Henry had personally witnessed its benefits. When Victoria came to the throne in 1837, a time when Henry was about to apprentice in the ship and cargo broker's office, tariffs were exorbitantly high and numerous. England had some 1,200 dutiable products, including life necessities such as wheat, sugar, meat, and lumber. The tariff wall was meant to protect home industries not just in Britain, but also the colonies. Excise taxes were numerous and oppressive.

Five years after Victoria mounted the throne, Robert Peel became the reformist prime minister. "He grasped the situation and proposed heroic remedies in the shape of free trade," wrote Henry. "Peel's budget repealed or reduced duties and abolished excise taxes, while introducing a tax on incomes of 150 pounds and up. The success of his measures was almost magical; trade rapidly improved; with [tariff-] free cotton, wool, hemp, flax, manufactures thrived; new mills were built, wages increased, imports and exports mounted up."[5] Not for nothing was Henry an enthusiast of free trade. He had seen it work.

The previous year, in October 1872, Henry and a delegation of the board had travelled to New York, where they met with the president and members of the National Board of Trade of the United States.[6] There was "an almost unanimous resolution in favor of reciprocal trade between the two countries," Henry reported. Commercial union was the means by which Canadians would become a great and powerful people. At least, that was how matters appeared to him and his business colleagues at the beginning of 1873. How his hope for free trade came to disappointment shall be seen. But, first, he wanted to force other issues upon the Dominion Board.

At the top of his game: *When Henry took over as the third president of the Dominion Board of Trade in 1872, it was "Fry-day." He placed high on the board's agenda his concerns over piloting, crimping, and deck loading.*

Notman Collection, McCord Museum.

16

1873
Battling the Crimps

"Friday, 17 January 1873 was certainly *Fryday* for the Dominion Board of Trade," records the maritime historian Kenneth S. Mackenzie. "Henry Fry, perhaps feeling his oats as the newly-elected president of that august body, dominated the day's session with a barrage of resolutions."[1] From his bully pulpit, Henry implored delegates to correct the injustices that had occupied his mind in recent years.

He had already pleaded for quick action on building a graving or dry dock in Quebec so that the port could repair larger ships. "It is not a local, but a national question," Henry insisted. He felt that a dry dock, whether in Indian Cove at Levis or on the St. Charles River, could reverse Quebec's decline as a seaport. As things later turned out, it didn't. To Henry's despair, feuding over the ship-repair dock's location was not resolved for another four years, and the dock didn't become fully operational until 1886.[2]

The graving dock issue, however, was mild stuff compared with Henry's outrage over the "terrible evils" resulting from the desertion of seamen in Quebec. "The crimping system as carried on at Quebec is a scandal and a disgrace not only to that City, but to the whole Dominion," he wrote in a paper presented to the Dominion Board, and prominently featured in the Quebec press. The board, he said, should urge the government to take the most energetic measures to suppress the evil practice.[3]

"The crimps," Henry asserted in his paper, "ply their demoralizing traffic almost with impunity." In 1866, Captain Moore of the ship *Transit* was attempting to prosecute the keeper of a boarding house where crimps were holding members of his own crew. Three crimps savagely beat him in broad daylight in Place d'Armes. Six years later a Danish sailor who refused to desert was murdered on board his own ship. "The murderer has never been caught," noted Henry, "and so the lesson is not likely to have much effect upon his confreres."

Crimping's existence arose partly from the austere, punishing life aboard sailing ships. A sailor or "Jack," wrote Henry, was easily tempted to desert:

> While at sea the law lays its heavy hand upon him. By night and by day, almost without interruption, he is subject to the severest discipline. Any disobedience of a master's lawful commands is met with heavy punishment. To conspire to resist his authority is mutiny. Hence, on his arrival in Quebec, Jack longs for a little unbending, and night's "spree," as he calls it; he is decoyed ashore, poisoned with drugged liquor, and kept in close confinement until he dares not return. Once in the crimp's power, the sailor is helpless. He is hustled on board another ship, often in a state of stupefaction, after having gone through the farce of "signing articles" at the shipping office. The crimp dictates the rate of his wages, often £10, £12 and sometimes £15 sterling per month. One half of this sum is handed over to the crimp, and Jack is dismissed with curses on his lips, often to meet with further punishment at home through his unfitness for duty, as a result of the bad whiskey and other compounds he has imbibed ashore. Often, however, the sailor refuses to desert. His clothes are then stolen, or he is forcibly taken out of the ship. Should he resist, the revolver is brought into play, and often used. Even the Captain and officers of ships are frequently overawed, and compelled to witness the desertion of their crews.

The system results in a heavy tax upon the trade, and, of course, affects the rates of freight.[4]

Crimping thrived partly because of the persistent lack of experienced sailors in Quebec — a town full of carpenters, sail and rope makers, loggers, and leather workers, but few men having sea legs. That wasn't all. As a shipbuilding centre, the port generated a net outflow of ships; fewer trained sailors arrived in Quebec than the number required to crew ships leaving. Exacerbating the shortage, numbers of arriving seaman left the sea to migrate inland and find work in factories and on farms. Thus shipmasters were constantly undermanned and needed help in finding hands. Crimps filled the need. So it was that Quebec officials often turned a blind eye to crimping ... or even defended it. The *Quebec Daily Mercury*, in a personally insulting critique of Henry's opposition to crimping, as well as the dangerous practices of stowing cargoes on decks, went so far as to blame "merchants and ship owners as the culpable parties." The very practices that Henry deplored served his own economic interest and that of his business colleagues, claimed the newspaper. In any event, nothing would be remedied, the *Mercury* wrote, if the legislature did not come up with forceful action.[5]

"Our Governments have never earnestly and sincerely tried to put down the system," Henry admitted. "In 1861, when Sir George E. Cartier was pressed by the Quebec Board of Trade to take steps towards putting it down, he declined, giving it as his opinion that crimping was simply a dispute between ship-builders and ship-owners. The Captains, being only visitors, never combine to resist the demands of the crimps, and are only too glad to get out of a place where they feel they have been plundered."[6] The number of police to combat crimping was pathetically small, declared Henry:

> In a harbour ten miles long and nearly a mile wide, where there may sometimes be seen 250 or 300 ships, not at wharves, but at booms or blocks, or riding at anchor in a strong tideway, just 25 men constitute the whole force! The result is that the law has no terrors for crimps and most of them make large incomes; they keep

out of sight, and if their runners happen to be caught now and then, they can afford to retain the best legal advice, and to pay the very moderate fines imposed.

In Henry's view, the immorality of crimping could never justify its existence:

> These melancholy occurrences have served to bring the question once more before the public mind, and are sufficient excuse for inviting the action of this Board. Is it not a disgrace to our civilization that a handful of lawless men should so long have defied the laws, levied a heavy tax upon a most important trade, demoralised a hard-working and deserving class of their fellow men, and made the very name of *Quebec* a by-word throughout the world? If I could only succeed in waking up the Government to a sense of the importance of the matter, I am satisfied the energetic Minister of Marine and Fisheries would soon find a remedy."[7]

Henry, seconded by R.R. Dobell of Quebec, resolved that "the Crimping system as carried on at Quebec is a scandal and a disgrace not only to that city but to the whole Dominion, that this Board do memorialize the Government to take the most energetic measures for its suppression." J.A. Harding of Saint John, New Brunswick, added an amendment, stating that the resolution ought also to apply to Saint John, which greatly suffered from crimping, "though not, perhaps, to so great a degree as at Quebec." The resolution and the amendment were unanimously passed.

By focusing public attention on the evil, wrote maritime historian Frederick William Wallace, Henry encouraged the passage of legislation to make crimping a penitentiary offence. Unfortunately, the laws had little effect. Good resolutions, Henry was forced to conclude, are often worth scarcely more than the paper they're printed on. As an alternative, he turned to charity. "To offset the lure of drink and questionable delights which the boarding houses offered to deserting seamen," wrote

Wallace, "Mr. Fry raised a fund to pay the salary of a sailor missionary. But neither the good efforts of a seaman's mission nor the law could do much to suppress the practice."[8]

The solution to the problem of crimping ultimately arose from economics. "The decline of shipbuilding did what an army of police could not do," wrote Wallace. "Yearly throughout the 1870s the number of new ships launched became smaller and smaller, and the crimps, finding their occupation gone, packed up and departed for pastures new."[9]

17

1873 and Before:
Battling the Pilots Union

Still feeling his oats at the 1873 Dominion Board of Trade meeting in Ottawa, Henry proceeded to lecture his colleagues on another issue that had irritated him for years: the manner in which pilots were hired to guide ships up and down the St. Lawrence.[1] It led Henry into a controversy that spilled over from merely economic to political, poisoning relations, seldom optimal, between French and English.

To begin with, sailing the St. Lawrence River was a truly risky enterprise, wrote Henry:

> The navigation of a ship from Ireland to New York or Boston is mere child's play compared with the navigation of a ship from Ireland to Montreal. The St. Lawrence from Bic [on the Gulf] to Montreal, a distance of 300 miles, contains a series of sunken reefs, shoals and flats. To make matters worse, the tides do not run true, and the channel is often very narrow. Ships have to contend with snowstorms and ice in the spring and fall, and occasional fog in the summer.[2]

Safe passage, for sure, required that ship's masters hire pilots. The work for the pilots was not easy. No fewer than 133 of them and their apprentices had died in the St. Lawrence River's icy waters between 1819 and 1855.[3]

They laboured at times under vicious weather conditions, competing with one another in sailing out to meet incoming ships to offer their services.

The controversy arose over differences in defining the skills and training of a pilot, how he should be hired, and his fees negotiated. The interminable debate had begun in the 1850s, and it had never ceased. In 1860, the pilots — 250 of them, mostly francophone — had petitioned the Legislative Assembly in the provincial parliament to approve a bill that would allow them to organize their trade on the St. Lawrence, east of Quebec. The arrangement was common in other countries. The pilots claimed that their association would replace senseless, unsafe, clamouring competition with orderly, sensible work allocation. All pilots would "share and share alike" in the earnings of the whole.

Henry opposed the pilots union, and signed on with 98 other Quebec merchants to fight the 1860 bill.[4] One merchant, David Edward Price, who sympathized with the pilots, did not join his colleagues.[5] Price's defection proved critical. When the bill came to a vote, the merchants lost. The pilots were allowed to create a corporation, and all were compelled to join.

The outcome was terribly wrong, Henry complained. "The competent and the incompetent, the sober man and the drunkard, the man who pilots ten ships and the man who pilots but five, are all placed on a dead level and paid alike." In his view, the bill took away all motivation for exertion, and robbed piloting of its best men.

As if to fulfill Henry's loudly proclaimed warnings that the quality of navigation would decline under the new system, the next year he himself became the victim of pilot error in the mooring of his own sailing ship *Lotus*, in the 1861 accident that is related in chapter 8. Had the accident happened a year earlier, before the pilots bill passed and when it wasn't compulsory for a ship entering Quebec to hire a pilot, the outcome might have been different. Under the new law, only the individual pilot, not the pilots' corporation could be sued. Satisfactory redress was hard to find.[6]

Ten years passed, and in 1871 Henry was still warring with organized pilots. On this occasion he came into a head-on collision with Joseph-Edouard Cauchon, prominent journalist and francophone federal Member of Parliament for Quebec Centre. Cauchon intimated that Quebec's merchants were trying to destroy the pilots economically, and that the act allowing the pilots to associate had actually led to reducing shipwrecks on the river. Henry fired back at Cauchon in a March 30, 1871, letter to the *Quebec Morning Chronicle*:

He [Cauchon] asserts that the service is improving in opposition to my assertion that it is rapidly deteriorating. Whether the opinion of one who sits in his editorial chair from month to month, and is so busily engaged in political scheming, is worth more than that of one whose avocation brings him into daily contact with the pilots, and whose business and duty is to watch the working of the system, is a matter of which the public can judge.

His statements that I have forced underwriters to complain ... [and that] I know several owners who tried to defraud the pilots by understating the draft of water of their vessels are unmitigated falsehoods. One would have supposed that his [Cauchon's] long parliamentary experience would have taught him common decency in the discussion of a public question. But it is not so, for he has long indulged in a style of writing that has fairly entitled him to be called a "Red Indian of the Press."

Now, if he has only the moral courage to state in unmistakable terms that I have, at any time, knowingly defrauded any pilot, or the Corporation of Pilots, in any shape or form, directly or indirectly, of one cent, I promise him he shall have an opportunity of proving it in a court of justice, and if he fails, he will stand convicted as the base libeler of his fellow citizens, using the press for the vilest purposes, and disgracing the noble profession to which he belongs.[7]

Beyond the verbal vituperation, the substance of the complaints made by Henry and his fellow merchants was this: Quebec's pilotage system raised the cost of doing business. The next year, 1872, when he was still president of the Quebec Board of Trade, Henry proposed to the Dominion Board, of which he was then vice-president, that it urge the government and Parliament to amend the act incorporating the pilots:[8]

Francophone defender: *Journalist-politician Joseph-Edouard Cauchon defended the right of pilots on the river to form their own union. He clashed publicly with Henry Fry, each accusing the other of falsehoods.*

The law vesting the management of the Pilots Corporation in the hands of six of its own members ... leads
to a lack of discipline and want of proper control on
the part of ship-owners, merchants and underwriters.
Small ships engaged in the Newfoundland, P.E.I. and
West Indies trade are required to pay pilotage fees
almost as great as ocean vessels coming from England.

I am not attacking the pilots, for many of them are
excellent men. It is the system I condemn.

A year later, and now president of the Dominion Board, "without
warning," according to maritime historian Kenneth S. Mackenzie, Henry
introduced at the Ottawa meeting a resolution deploring the unsound
principles and serious evils of pilotage on the St. Lawrence. Specifically,
vessels of less than three hundred tons register should *not* be required
to carry pilots. If the Ministry of Marine and Fisheries were to follow
Henry's resolution, it would almost certainly mean less work and money
for pilots.

To hardly anyone's surprise, except his own, Henry's resolution
infuriated the mostly francophone pilots. Cauchon quickly returned
to the cause. Here was a political opportunity! He pointed his finger
at the pilots' enemy — the mostly English merchants. The English-
dominated business class, led by men like Fry, was rotten, unsupported
by the mass of the people. Fry and the Dominion Board of Trade could
not be more wrong.

Henry was furious. He called Cauchon's charges against Quebec's
merchants "scandalous ... unmitigated falsehoods ... slanders hurled
from a place [Parliament] where we cannot reach him to refute."[9]

Little came of Henry's rant. In the end, the Minister of Marine &
Fisheries intervened and found a compromise. "It blew over," remarks
Kenneth S. Mackenzie, "when an older [Dominion Board] member told
Fry that when he was 'a little older he would learn that to be abused by Mr.
Cauchon was the equivalent of a high compliment.'"[10] Notwithstanding,
Fry was "the grand old man of Quebec shipping," says Mackenzie, "doyen
of Quebec's shipowners."[11]

18

1873
Deck Loading: Triumph of Reform

On January 17, 1873, Henry brought before the Dominion Board of Trade yet one more paper ... the *cause célèbre* that would propel him to a hearing in the Parliament in London the following year, and in his mind to the greatest triumph of his career. It had to do with the overloading of ships, which often caused them to capsize at sea with devastating loss of life.[1] The paper was similar to *Deckloads and Grain Cargoes*, which he'd written a few months earlier for Lloyd's, and which was later republished in America's *Nautical Magazine*.

Henry's effort at reform coincided with a similar effort by the vocal British politician and social reformer Samuel Plimsoll. Fry and Plimsoll — by coincidence both born in Bristol — wrote of the miserable, dangerous lives of seamen, made doubly dangerous by improper cargo loading. Plimsoll, as a Member of Parliament, spoke so intemperately about the evil done by ship owners that he was censured by Prime Minister Disraeli, and his initial reform bill was rejected in the House of Commons in 1872, although it was eventually realized in 1876. Plimsoll's name became famous in nautical history: the line inscribed on a ship's hull is called a Plimsoll line. If the water rises higher than the Plimsoll line, a ship is determined to be carrying too heavy a cargo.[2]

Henry, unlike Plimsoll, was specifically concerned with the greed-driven, deadly practice of ships crossing the North Atlantic in winter with extra cargo on their decks, making them top-heavy. In 1872, deck loading had been the principal factor in the catastrophic loss of seventy-one ships and the pathetic drowning of more than 250 seamen, claimed Henry, to say nothing of four million dollars of lost cargoes. And that was only one shipping season! Hundreds more sailors had died before. Thousands more would die in future if something were not done to prevent unscrupulous ship-owners from aggressively seeking more profit by piling more squared timber on deck, claimed Henry:

> Fully three-fourths of all the losses of wood-laden ships in the North Atlantic in the Fall of the year may be traced directly or indirectly to the practice of carrying deck loads. Most ships engaged in this trade are necessarily second-class ships, many of them having seen their best days. They are peculiarly unfitted for deck loads. [They] are weak in their upper works from decayed iron fastenings, and defective frames and beam arms. As soon as the ship begins to roll in a heavy sea, she strains and leaks, and the deck load causes her waterways to open; if the pumps are good and the crew can stand at them,

Pen-and-ink illustration by Henry Fry, 1891.

On the way to Parliament: *In November 1873, intent on reform, Henry boarded the steamship* Sarmatian *in Quebec and crossed the North Atlantic to England. There he pleaded with members of Parliament and House of Lords to enact legislation banning deck loading of ships, a practice fatal to seamen.*

she may possibly escape; but far more frequently when the pumps are most needed they are least available; a sea breaks on board, the deck load gets adrift, the sailors get their limbs broken, or they are killed by loose logs in trying to get them overboard; or the pumps are broken off at the deck by loose timber washed about, and thus rendered useless; the ship becomes waterlogged, provisions and fresh water are destroyed, and the unhappy crew take to the rigging or the tops, there, alas! too often to perish amid the horrors of starvation, cold and delirium.[3]

It was not as if the evil were unknown. In 1840, Canadian legislation prohibited North Atlantic deck loads leaving North America between September and May. "It saved the lives of thousands of seamen," Henry declared. But the act had been repealed in 1862. Now, in 1873, he was urging Ottawa to restore its provisions. What applied to the safety of ship passengers, after all, ought to apply to the safety of seamen manning cargo vessels, he said:

Mark how carefully the Government insists on the inspection of emigrant ships before they are allowed to sail, and of all steamships before they are permitted to carry any passengers. In various ways all civilized governments seek to protect their subjects from the consequences of the wilful carelessness, neglect, or greed of their employers. Ask any intelligent seaman what he thinks about deck loads, and he will reply, "Ships are not built to carry deck loads, and it would be a good thing if they were prohibited by law; but if So-and-So carries one, I must do so, or I shall probably lose my situation." This is a very mistaken view of the matter. Who will pay the four millions of dollars lost in 1872? Not the underwriters ... they are not a medium for collecting a tax from the fortunate for the benefit of the unfortunate; not the shipowners, for in most cases they are fully insured. No, the loss will be borne either by the producer of what we export or the consumer of what we import. Whatever is paid in increased cost of insurance or freight must come out of their pockets.[4]

Every Canadian farmer and every Canadian lumberer, continued Henry, was thus affected by deck loading's unfair imposition of hidden costs, particularly late in the year, near the end of the shipping season, when storms whipped the North Atlantic. Henry had little sympathy for ship-owners or underwriters. "The former owe their losses to their own cupidity, whilst the latter, by a single line inserted in their policies, could prohibit deck loads altogether."

Blaming ship-owner cupidity was something about which the *Quebec Daily Mercury* could agree with Henry. But, as with crimping, the newspaper gave him no support. Shipwrecks in the fall, opined the *Mercury*, were just as frequent now as before when deck loading was not permitted. It blamed bad stowage in ship holds, not top-heavy deck loading, for the wrecks — stevedores working too hastily and under pressure.[5] The wreckage and sinkings also were a consequence of the inferior, aging ships — sometimes called sailors' coffins — used in the wood trade.[6]

For Henry, though, deck loading was an abuse that must be ended:

> I plead for this law in the name of humanity; in the name of the thousands of poor sailors who are bound by rigid legal instrument to stick to their ships and do their duty, though death stares them in the face; and who, once having signed articles, have no right to object to any amount of deck load that may put a few pounds in the ship-owner's pocket. I plead for it in the name of the hundreds of widows and orphans, who are deprived of their natural supporters, and cast upon the world in poverty and wretchedness for lack of the protection which every sailor has a right to expect in his perilous calling.[7]

In conclusion, Henry moved that the board urge the government of the Dominion to enact legislation to put an immediate stop to the practice of carrying deck loads between Canada and Europe between September 1 and May 1, "as being destructive to human life, and materially increasing the cost of insurance." No one objected. The resolution passed unanimously, and within a few months Parliament assented to a regulation, drawn up by the federal Department of Marine and Fisheries, which was slightly watered down from Henry's proposal. No timber could be carried on deck to Europe between November 15 and March 15, and limits were placed on the height of deck cargoes in the West Indies trade.[8]

Passage of the Deck Load Law earned an enthusiastic editorial in the *Quebec Morning Chronicle* of May 14, 1873. The newspaper praised Peter Mitchell, the minister of Marine and Fisheries, for guiding the legislation. Mitchell had mentioned Henry in his speech before Parliament. The *Chronicle* echoed the minister: "Mr. Fry, not only in this country, but in Great Britain has advocated the abolition of deck loads."[9]

In October 1873, Henry informed the Dominion Board that he had to go to England on "important business."[10] The business was ship-loading reform. In November he sailed out of Quebec on the steamship *Sarmatian*, taking with him his wife, daughter, four sons, and a nursemaid for a six-month sojourn in Bristol. He rented a house for the family on Clyde Road near his mother and his sister Lucy. Sons Henry, Willie, and Arthur attended private school.[11]

Having got the family settled in Bristol, Henry travelled in early 1874 to London. There he laid the fatal facts about deck loading before Lloyd's, which at once appointed a subcommittee to investigate the subject.[12] Lloyd's discovered that deck loading had led to a 30 percent increase in property loss and a forty percent increase in loss of life on the North Atlantic during winter.

Armed with these facts, Henry appeared before the Royal Commission on Unseaworthy Ships. Arthur Wellesley Peel, Speaker of the House of Commons and son of the former prime minister, stated that Mr. Fry's evidence had convinced him of the great danger of deck loads. Soon afterward, Parliament passed what was essentially a copy of the Canadian act. "It was the most important and successful of my efforts in public life," Henry later recalled. "I have no doubt that it saved hundreds of sailors' lives."[13] Two years later, Parliament passed the more famous 1876 Unseaworthy Ships Bill promoted by Samuel Plimsoll.

Neither act succeeded in totally eliminating the evil practice. Greed inevitably overpowered reform. "Unscrupulous men found ways to sidestep the law," lamented maritime historian Thomas E. Appleton.[14] Ships properly loaded in Montreal and Quebec could take on additional and cheaper coal in Nova Scotia, where no port wardens were available to prevent overloading. Even if caught, a ship master was subject only to a forty-dollar fine, which was little compared to the profit to be made from transporting extra cargo. Sailing ships, more than iron steamships, were more likely to encounter disaster from excessive loading. As with crimping, the dangers of deck loading lessened as large, cargo-carrying wooden ships went out of commission, and the age of sail drew to an end.

19

1874
Britain or America, Which to Favour?

Although a fervent free trade believer and promoter, Henry Fry, like many Canadians, worried that the complete tariff-free exchange of goods across the country's southern border might ultimately erode the young nation's sovereignty. He had other misgivings as well. He'd witnessed unwillingness by the United States to enforce trade reciprocity after it had agreed in principle to lower tariffs — an hypocrisy that led him to doubt American sincerity.[1] Finally, why should Canada favour U.S. goods over those from Britain, a great nation and imperial power, whose navy and armed forces defended Canada at no cost?[2]

On the other hand, how reliable was Britain as a trading partner? It had interests in Europe, India, and the Far East to consider. How much could Canada rely on Britain for favourable trading arrangements in the years ahead? Canada might be loyal to her mother country, but would Britain reciprocate?

America or Britain: Was favouring one a disfavour to the other? Such was the conflict in Henry's mind.

Following his success with deck loading reform before Parliament, on March 18, 1874, he was invited to speak to the Associated Chambers of Commerce of the United Kingdom. Henry began somewhat discordantly with a complaint about a topic unanticipated by his audience — lighthouse fees — perhaps leaving the organizers wondering why they'd invited the Dominion Board of Canada's president to speak:

Canada is in proportion to its population the largest
ship-owning country in the world. In actual tonnage she
stands fourth if not third. Why then should Canadian
ships have to pay for the lights that keep them from running aground at night when navigating England's coast?
Canada charged nothing to the world's ships for the lights
it erected along the entire 700 miles of the Gulf and the
river St. Lawrence, as well as the shores of Nova Scotia
and New Brunswick. But Canadian ships visiting Great
Britain pay for every beacon they pass. It was unjust.
Canadian ship-owners are first taxed to support their own
lights, and again taxed upon arrival in Britain. If Canada
can afford to maintain her lights and buoys free of charge
to all the world, a wealthy country like Great Britain may
well follow her example.[3]

Responding, Britain's Chancellor of the Exchequer, Sir Stafford
Northcote, who was in the audience, asked Henry, "What is the practice
in the United States?"

"They light their whole coast from Freeport, Maine, to Galveston,
Texas, free of charge to all the world," Henry answered.

"And how do the general charges on ships in ports compare to
Britain's?" asked Northcote.

"All Canadian ports are free. The local charges in British ports are
very heavy."[4]

To this criticism, Henry's hosts made no response. But they did
invite him to a grand dinner at the Westminster Palace Hotel across from
Westminster Abbey. There, glasses were raised and a toast made to representatives of the "Colonies" attending the meeting of the Associated
Chambers. Henry responded to the toastmaster. He told of the progres-
sive leaps forward that had occurred in Canadian banking. Moreover,
Canada since Confederation had experienced a 75 percent increase in
imports. A large part of the imports were from Britain. Yet not so long
ago, said Henry, Canadians sensed British government indifference to
its former colonies, doubtful even that they should be allowed preferred
trading status. "They [Britain] seemed to say, 'You may go if you like,

or you may stay if you like; you have become a burthen to us, and we are indifferent to what course you take.'" Now Henry raised his voice, speaking with fervour.

"That is not a way to build up a great empire!" he cried. "I say that though these may be the sentiments of a small political clique, it never was, and never will be, the feeling of the great mass of the English people!"

Here! Here! Loud cheers greeted Henry's words. Encouraged, he continued:

> While the legal tie between Canada and Britain is slight, much stronger is the real tie of honest affection. [In Canada] we are proud of our equal law, under which English and French, Protestants and Catholics can live together in peace and harmony. I don't believe that Great Britain can ever be indifferent to the allegiance of such a people, and I trust the day is far, very far distant when the link which now so happily binds us together, shall be severed!

As Henry sat down, the assembled diners cheered loudly. He had clearly scored with his speech. Two nights later he was invited with the Associated Chambers group to a grand banquet in the magnificent Georgian town palace, Mansion House, in the heart of London's financial district, the City. With Henry's earlier remarks perhaps on their minds, the delegates resolved in future to affiliate more closely with Colonial and foreign chambers of commerce such as Canada's Dominion Board, whose president had appeared in their midst.[5]

Having spent six months in England, Henry returned to Canada with his family in May of 1874. In July, he travelled to New Brunswick to attend the semi-annual meeting of the Dominion Board of Trade. As a result of his having been abroad, he'd missed the meeting in January. The main topic of discussion at the summer meeting was the proposed Reciprocity trade agreement with the United States — a kind of NAFTA without Mexico. It would eliminate, by 1877, the tariffs on almost all products crossing the border. A *New York Times* correspondent in Canada observed that the proposal was being eagerly and earnestly discussed "wherever businessmen congregate in the saloons of river steamboats, in hotel halls and smoking rooms."[6]

Most Dominion Board members were less than enthusiastic about the proposed treaty. Henry himself initially welcomed it, at least in principle: "No one can rejoice more than I do at the prospect of a measure to facilitate trade between Canada and the United States. Whether we look at the magnitude of the interests involved, or at the length of time the Treaty is to remain in force, it deserves the calmest deliberation from businessmen, uninfluenced by political feelings."

Henry then cited the words of an American friend: the proposed treaty should be "just, liberal and comprehensive."[7] However, the draft treaty looked to Henry to be neither just nor liberal toward Canada. Indeed it brought fear into the hearts of Canadian manufacturers. Tariff removal would open Canadian markets to surplus U.S. manufacture, while the Canadian government estimated it would result in losing duty revenue of four million dollars annually.[8] The country was already suffering from inequities in its maritime trade. As an example, when Britain had repealed the Navigation Laws in 1851, Americans were the first to

Art by Robert Dudley, 1872, from Eileen Marcil's *Charley-Man*.

The Canada Timber Dock: *Merchants like Henry each winter travelled to England to book orders for millions of varied pieces of timber. Here, at a specially named dock in Liverpool, ships delivered their Canadian cargoes the following summer.*

benefit. Their ships began to enjoy the opportunity to compete equitably with British and Canadian ships all over the world. But the Americans didn't return the favour.

"If you go to Bombay," said Henry, "you find American ships competing with British ships in carrying merchandize [sic] to Liverpool. If you go to Australia, you find American ships loading for London; and to come nearer home, I suppose, there is no port in the British Empire where competition with American ships has been found so severe as in this city of St. John." But when it came to Canadian shipping in the United States, reciprocity often didn't exist. It was unfair:

> Supposing I send a ship to New York, and I want to go from there to California, I am not allowed to carry a ton of freight, because from New York to San Francisco is considered coasting trade. Or if I have a ship in Baltimore or Philadelphia, and want to send her to New York, I am obliged to pay for stones to ballast her, because I am not permitted to carry freight. Now, I ask, is that reciprocity? Americans can take freight from London to Australia, but we cannot carry any from New York to San Francisco.[9]

Henry worried about still another item in the draft treaty: a commitment requiring Canada to deepen its canals. "We think it unwise for our government to pledge this country to deepen our Canals and the River St. Lawrence to twelve feet within a limited time, and at a cost practically unknown. Suppose that at the end of five years we have failed to carry out this provision of the Treaty, in what position would this country find itself?" While Americans could bring their barges by canal up to Ottawa, Canadians could not travel via the Champlain Canal down the Hudson all the way to New York City, but rather had to discharge their cargoes at American ports on Lake Champlain.

While he was an ardent free-trader, Henry had no problem with the U.S. levying duties on Canadian raw wood products. "With regard to the lumber trade," he told the board, "I am of the opinion that it is no matter to us in Canada whether the United States admit lumber free, or charge five or fifty per cent duty. The Americans must to a very great extent have our lumber. The duty they impose on it they themselves have to pay." Indeed the duties actually might have the effect of reducing demand for wood too cheaply priced, the wasteful use of a resource. Henry was sensitive to the ruinous cutting of trees that had been taking place in Canadian forests. His wish for renewable woodland gave an interesting twist to his reasoning.

"Instead of opening up new markets for our lumber, my policy would be to preserve our forests. The less timber we cut the more profitable our forests will be. We have been wasteful in our use of them in the past; and it would now be better to preserve them, rather than seek new markets." Henry could number himself among Canadians with an early awareness of the need to conserve and renew the country's natural resources.

Finally, the draft Reciprocity Treaty involved a twenty-four-year commitment, which Henry regarded as far too great. "We are taking a leap in the dark. A shorter time, and a shorter notice of abrogation would be more prudent." Unless the treaty were to be substantially amended, Henry opposed its approval by Parliament, and so did the Dominion Board at its 1874 summer meeting.

In Parliament, the Liberals seemed mostly against it, too. The Conservatives under John A. Macdonald were mutely opposed. The reality was that Canada, which lacked an income tax, needed high customs duties to finance the building of roads, canals, and railways. Macdonald conveniently believed that the revenue-generating duties should be designed to protect Canadian producers and manufacturers who needed the protection.[10]

In the end, the Reciprocity Treaty not only never saw the light of day, but tariffs actually rose steeply in the years ahead.[11] For this Henry came to blame the United States.

20

1874-1876
Prosperity, but Hard Lessons

Henry celebrated his forty-eighth birthday on June 5, 1874. Now at the apex of his career, seemingly clear of mind and full of vigour, he was serving on the boards of a dozen organizations ranging from the Bible Society to the Quebec Bank. In the previous two years he'd made more than a hundred thousand dollars (as much as two million dollars today) from lumber shipments, owning ships, and from commissions and work associated with his Lloyd's Agency. While in England earlier in the year he'd sold his beloved, sturdy *Mary Fry* for 75 percent of her original cost, realizing an immense profit on a single ship that had generated thirteen years of income transporting, among other things, guano from Peru to Hamburg and teak from Rangoon to England.

In May he returned from England with his entire family — wife Mary and now seven children, plus nurse — aboard the Allan Line's two-year-old steamship *Polynesian*. It took eleven days to cross the North Atlantic from Liverpool. For three days the four-hundred-foot steamship was slowed by dense fog off the Newfoundland coast. Arriving in Quebec, Henry saw men and tugboats working furiously to clean up the wreckage in the port caused sixteen days earlier by a sudden breaking of the ice bridge upstream.

"A perfect orgy of destruction," is the way Quebec historian James MacPherson Lemoine described the scene on the river, arguably the most destructive such disaster that ever struck the port.[1] Coming on an ebb tide, an immense volume of ice had jammed a hundred ships and barges against one another. Some were stove in, filled with water, and sank, leaving only their bows and masts above water. The deluge smashed and carried away wharves and piers.

After the family disembarked from *Polynesian* and ascended to their house on the terrace, Henry could peer at the floating wreckage from his bedroom window.

Returning home, Henry was acutely disappointed by news of the failed enactment of the Canada-U.S. Reciprocity Treaty aimed at stimulating commerce across the 5,500-mile border. Worse, not only had the treaty failed to be ratified, but customs barriers were being aggressively raised. Each country was finding reasons to punish the other. And worse, two extraordinarily prosperous years of rising prices and profits were being followed by an economic tsunami. In September of 1873, panic seized the stock markets of New York and Europe. Banks and railways failed. There was a sense of impending peril, not only in Quebec, but throughout the commercial world inhabited by merchants like Henry.

"In 1874 came the inevitable reaction, and very severe it was," Henry wrote in his *Essays*. Deflation was extreme. "Wood fell by 30 to 40 percent in price. Homeward cargoes [from Canada to England] were sold for freight and charges. 1875 and 1876 were years of depression, falling prices, and heavy losses."[2] So severe were the depression's effects that they would linger in Canada for another twenty years.

Henry himself lost forty thousand dollars in 1874 on wood and goods carried over from 1873, his stock unsold while prices plummeted. The year 1877 proved bad too. Banking and business in Montreal, Canada's financial capital, were close to collapse. However bad the conditions, though, the Canadian banks managed to perform modestly better than their U.S. counterparts (as in the crash of 2007–08).

By coincidence, or as a result of shrewdness, Henry's liquidity was strong. He had accumulated some thirty thousand dollars of insurance premiums, "and was flush of cash," he reported.[3] From 1855 to 1877 he had loaded more than four hundred cargoes of wood destined for Europe and Buenos Aires. In the twenty-year period, he'd netted $330,000 in profits as a merchant and from underwriting. After accounting for expenses, he was $216,000 wealthier than he'd been in 1855. He knew, because he accounted fastidiously for details of his spending. The family's household expenses and his "private expenditures" had eaten up $80,000. He'd generously given away about $30,000 to the church and various charities, to his mother, an aunt, sisters, and brothers. Then there was the $4,000 he'd given in 1858 to his betrothed Mary Dawson as a condition of their marriage.[4]

There's nothing in family papers to suggest that Henry's and Mary's marriage was a symphonic love match. Perhaps it was. Or perhaps it was more like a solid, institutional union, in which the partners play out the role of commanding, successful husband and procreative, efficient wife. Mary, though, was far more than a child-bearing machine. For one thing, she was a canny businesswoman. From the beginning, the couple had established a contract specifying who owned what, and who owed whom. If the marriage fell short of triumph, it certainly was not because it lacked solid contractual underpinnings. Were he to die, Mary would receive all Henry's "household furniture, pictures, horses, carriages, plate and all household effects," as well as inheriting all of the capital improvements he'd made in the Dufferin Terrace row house belonging to Mary.[5]

As for the rest, the executors of Henry's last will and testament — his brother-in-law Sam Dawson and his shipbuilding crony Dinning — would oversee the sale and distribution of it [the proceeds] to wife, children, and relatives.[6]

By today's accounting, Henry was a millionaire several times over. In his own travel and personal expenditures, he did not skimp. Crossing the Atlantic was always in first-class cabin. In the summer, going by boat or train down the St. Lawrence to Rivière-du-Loup, he enjoyed his beloved Cacouna cottage, next door to two of Canadian Protestantism's eminent prelates. Up on the lawn, holding his spyglass in hand, Henry might glimpse one of his sailing ships moving upriver on a favourable tide. His children romped on the lawn in front of the cottages. The family could descend by steep stairs down a cliff, walk through a wheat field, and onto the stony beach, where their toes and occasionally entire bodies were immersed in the icy water. The air was sweet with the aroma of salt water and wildflowers.

To be in Cacouna was to withdraw from a troubled world. In the summer of 1874, politically defeated Sir John A. Macdonald retreated to his cottage a few miles west of Henry. "When summer came," writes Donald Creighton in *The Old Chieftain*, "he [Macdonald] went off to Rivière-du-Loup for a long holiday, from which the importunate appeals of his followers failed to drag him."

In the fall of 1874, business dragged Henry back to Quebec, where the children resumed school and the social season was in full swing. Quebec was proving attractive to the new governor general, Lord Dufferin, and his vivacious Irish wife, the Marchioness, who found it a convivial and more sophisticated place than the remote, new capital on the Ottawa River. They were treated to endless receptions and obsequious celebrations of the British Empire. Their presence between 1872 and 1878 caused tens of thousands of schoolchildren, nuns, native Indians, factory workers, insane asylum occupants, and citizens of all stripes to don their best finery merely to see them.[7] Henry, who worshipped the Empire even more than the governor general did, joined in the enthusiasm. Indeed the Fry house was located on the terrace that would be named for the immensely popular Dufferin when he left Canada in 1878.

Above and west of the family's house, on Cove Field next to the Plains of Abraham, a golf course had opened, the second in North America.[8] One of its founders was James Stevenson, Henry's banker and future father-in-law of his oldest son. Henry himself was not a sportsman, but his brother Edward belonged to the Quebec Yacht Club, dedicated to promoting yachting and to running regattas on the St. Lawrence River. Edward was also a keen curler. These were pleasures the younger man could enjoy, in part because his job as Henry's junior partner enabled him to afford the extracurricular activities. The two men had more time now for leisure. Their office on St. Peter Street was a less bustling place.

"I was now reduced to two ships and one-sixteenth of a third," Henry wrote. "I could not afford to buy costly iron ships. I ought to have dropped wooden ships forever then, but I looked out for a couple of good second-hand ships suitable for my own lumber trade, as my hobby was far too strong to give up ship owning."

In March of 1875, he travelled down to Boston to inspect the *Gaspee*, built by one of the best American shipbuilders, John Currier of Newburyport. The 170-foot-long, 993-ton *Gaspee* had just arrived from Calcutta. "She was a very handsome model, and although sixteen years old, was sound, in good order, and had recently had new masts, spars, and rigging," noted Henry.[9] He bought her for 23,000 dollars. Soon *Gaspee* was making voyages to Britain carrying deals of wood, and to New Orleans to pick up cotton. "To my eye, she was 'a thing of beauty and a joy forever,'" recalled Henry when he wrote his *Reminiscences* in 1891, "but her day was over,[10] and with these fine sailing ships departed much of the poetry of sea life."

His next ship purchase worked out less favourably. It also roused in him a resentment of Americans, sequestered in the angrier reaches of his mind. It happened this way. In January 1876 he made his customary trip to England to spur business and find cargoes for the coming year, sailing out of ice-free Portland, Maine, on the steamship *Sardinian* to

From Reminiscences of a Retired Ship Owner.

Charting his wealth: *Henry wrote a summary account of his profits and expenditures between 1856 and 1876.*

Liverpool. Before he returned, he saw that a ship he knew, the 1,078-ton, 175-foot *Tirrell*, was for sale in London. Though the *Tirrell* was twenty years old, built originally in Portsmouth, New Hampshire, she had been fitted with new decks, masts, and rigging. Henry later wrote his recollections of the *Tirrell*.[11]

> Captain Morgan, her owner had sailed her from the first, making large sums of money in the East Indian teak trade. I went on board and examined her cursorily. I was so struck with her likeness to my favourite *Sunbeam* [see chapter 11] that I bought her for the low price of 3,300 pounds sterling. When the purchase was completed I gave old Morgan a dinner, and asked him all about her. He assured me that he knew nothing wrong about her … that she made no more water than any such a ship may be expected to make.
>
> Both statements were barefaced falsehoods. I sent her to Quebec in ballast. On her way [across the Atlantic] she made a great deal of water. I got my friend, John Dick, the Port Warden, to examine her carefully, and we found that the cunning old Yankee had perpetrated a gross fraud upon me. A close examination shewed that her breasthooks and knees had been working badly, but all the evidence of it had been very carefully concealed by thick plaster, putty and paint. We found that the timbers round both bows were quite rotten. I had to give her virtually a new bow, breasthooks, and some knees.[12]

The repairs of *Tirrell* cost more than what Henry had paid Morgan. "It was the worst bargain I ever made. I had always been in the habit of treating men as honest until I found them out to be rogues, but in dealing with a Yankee it is necessary to act upon the opposite principle."

A hundred years after America left British rule, Henry looked south and saw in his former brothers a distinctly different people. The Yankee trader seemed aggressive and amoral in business dealings, scornful of the minor players to the north. The appearance was aggravating and aggrieving to Henry. He was unlike bankers and merchants who can piously be found in their pews on Sunday, and on Monday at their offices cold-bloodedly calculating enrichment at the expense of the poor. Each day for Henry included bible reading and church affairs. Business decision-making could not be separate from Christian practice. A trading transaction should never violate ethical standards. And if he saw a Christian obligation that could be met out of his influence as a merchant, he did not shirk from taking it on. What might look like an unreasonable business risk to his colleagues was worth doing for the good it might accomplish.

21

1877
The Great Ship *Cosmo*

One day in the fall of 1876, Henry arrived at a decision that would lead to the shipbuilding triumph of his life. It happened a few months after he'd crossed the North Atlantic on the steamship *Abyssinia* in April, following one of his regular visits to England. Arriving in New York and viewing lower Manhattan from the deck, he could see the first sky-scrapers, including the new 230-foot-high Western Union building and the eleven-storey mansarded Tribune tower.[1]

The city's bustle appealed to Henry, but on this occasion he didn't linger long in Gotham, and quickly boarded a northbound train to Canada. Back in Quebec, one of his first actions was to extend his partnership with his brother Edward in the operation of their shipping business, Henry Fry & Co., increasing Edward's salary to $166 a month.[2] Within a year, however, his confidence in his brother's business acumen would be shattered, and his own life radically transformed.

Financial stress played a role. A worldwide economic downturn, which had started with the financial crisis of 1873, was underway. Prices were depressed, banks distressed. In the fall of 1876, Henry's friend and collaborator Dinning asked to meet with him. The shipbuilder disclosed that he faced the next winter totally without money to construct a ship: "Some two hundred decent men at Cap Blanc are dependent on my yard for work. Without it, fully a hundred poor people will starve." Dinning implored Henry, "Give me a contract for a new ship, and I will build her cheaply."

It was the last thing Henry needed. He was sitting on a heavy inventory of wood, with no spare cash. Yet perhaps there was still something that could be done to create work for the Cap Blanc shipyard workers. He talked with Abraham Joseph, the Jewish head of the Stadacona Bank and a fellow director of the Dominion Board of Trade — a man whom Henry liked and admired. Three years earlier, when the Stadacona Bank failed, Joseph had used his own money to repay investors and depositors.[3] The banker said he was more than willing to help Henry finance a ship built by Dinning.

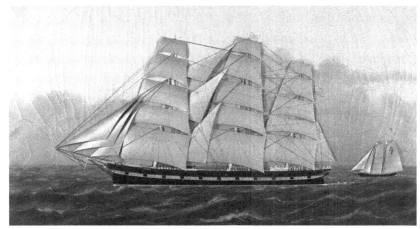

Mixed media, owned by the author, photographed by Doug Abdelnour, Bedford Photo-Graphic.

Unique art: *Upon the launching of his greatest ship, Henry commissioned marine artist Thomas H. Willis of Connecticut to make this masterful portrayal of* Cosmo. *Sea and sky are painted, the hull, sails, and rigging, as seen on the back of the work, are stitched. The full colour image,* Willis' Cosmo, *appears on the cover of this book.*

Henry also talked with James Stevenson, general manager of the Quebec Bank, who said that "he would be only too glad to lend me the money." Henry thus had the support of the port city's leading bankers. Yet he went into the deal reluctantly. He merely "felt that [he] should do it as an act of mercy." He agreed to pay Dinning $39.50 per ton for a 1,200-ton ship … or $47,400, an amount he would advance in weekly instalments so that the workers could receive the pay they desperately needed.

Henry immediately found himself absorbed in the details of the new ship's construction. So focused was he on the design that he didn't travel to England in the winter of 1877. He involved himself in the minutiae of its assembly, starting with the laying-out of the ship's plans in the moulding loft and the setting of the keel on the sloping beach of Dinning's yard. "I superintended her construction all winter, chose her dimensions and model," he wrote.

Henry decided to give the ship the name *Cosmo*, the barque on which he'd first sailed from England in 1853. The original had been named for the illustrious Florentine merchant prince Cosimo Medici. For the jutting wooden figurehead of the new *Cosmo*'s bow, Henry ordered a carved representation of the fifteenth-century potentate's head and torso.

The specifications for the three-masted ship were stringent. The keel and planking to the unloaded waterline were to be of the finest rock elm. "Tamarac frame, beams and planking," Henry wrote. "Double diagonal ceiling (giving great strength), locust and elm treenails, and iron lower masts and bowsprit." Tamarac, or red spruce, had the best combination of strength and durability for shipbuilding, in Henry's opinion. Tamarac-built ships were "sound and tight when … even forty years old."[4]

Weighing 1,220 tons, the *Cosmo* measured 200 feet overall, with a 37.3-foot beam. She was typical of Quebec-built sailing ships launched after 1854. The captain's and mate's quarters were in the stern, while the crew was housed forward. The galley was between. Sometimes there was a wheelhouse, but more often the man at the wheel was at the mercy of the elements and, in a storm, lashed to the wheel. Over a quarter-century, a total of 349 such large square-rigged ships were built in yards along the St. Lawrence and the St. Charles rivers. Virtually all of them were basically simple containers with a single deck, suited to carrying huge loads of timber — the world's most cost-efficient freighters at the time.

Cosmo, though, was far more than a container. "When she was launched," wrote maritime historian Frederick William Wallace, "Lloyd's surveyor stated that the *Cosmo* was the finest ship ever constructed in Quebec. The foremast, mainmast, and lower bowsprit were of iron. Her cabins were beautifully finished in ash and black walnut."[5]

Lloyd's rating of the ship *Cosmo* was 9A 1, indicating a first-class vessel whose rating would hold good for nine years.[6] A project to help the poor had produced a masterpiece!

A proud, excited Henry commissioned the marine artist and craftsman Thomas H. Willis in Connecticut to portray the ship. Willis, twenty-seven years old at the time, was in his ascendancy as the master of a unique kind of ship art. On a canvas thirty-one inches wide by eighteen inches high, Willis painted sea and sky. He fashioned the *Cosmo*'s hull from embroidered velvet, made the rigging with silk thread, the masts of woven string, and the sails of silk or cast paper — all of it stitched onto the oil-painted canvas and placed in an ornate frame.[7]

Photo by the author.

On view today: *A large-scale model of* Cosmo, *rescued from a waterfront bar, now hangs in Quebec's Morrin Centre, in the library of the Literary and Historical Society, Canada's oldest such institution.*

Nor was Henry finished with commemorating the apex of his career as a ship-owner. Something far larger had to be made. Henry paid one of the master carpenters in Dinning's yard to build a handsome nine-foot model of *Cosmo*. The model was likely mounted and displayed initially in Dinning's yard. Then it became something of a white elephant, finding its way around Lower Town, in taverns and hotels along the waterfront. Each move led to damage. One summer night in 1927 a Norwegian skipper, Captain Jarlsen, who was in port, eyed the oversized, beaten-up *Cosmo* model in a pub in Ancienne-Lorette.

"Where did you find that?" Jarlsen asked the barkeeper.

"Would you like to buy it?"

"No," replied Jarlsen, "but I may know someone who would."

The next day, Jarlsen called on his friend Edmond Lecouvie, who, in addition to his vocation of police constable, was a skilled model ship-builder — among the best in North America.

"See, Lecouvie, I don't want to buy the ship," declared Jarlsen. "But you should see it. It's very old. It could be valuable."

Jarlsen and Lecouvie visited the bar and examined the nine-foot model. "It was in a terrible state," Lecouvie later recalled. "Her spars were all gone, and her rigging too. The bowsprit was broken, her hull stove in. But I knew she meant something. She was original."

After intense bargaining, Jarlsen bought the *Cosmo* for "a paltry sum," and presented it to Lecouvie. "You can make her fit again," he told his friend. Lecouvie did. After restoring the giant model, he later sold it to the Literary and Historical Society. (Visitors to Quebec can view it today in the Morrin Centre, home of the society's library.)

Lecouvie's involvement with the *Cosmo* didn't end. In the fall of 1951, Princess Elizabeth visited Canada with her handsome husband, Prince Philip Mountbatten, who had served in the Royal Navy. The prince was a keen collector of model ships. During the visit, Quebec officials told his secretary that the city would like to present Philip with the gift of a model sailing vessel built in the port. Was there a particular ship the prince would like? Evidently Philip or his aides asked Lloyd's for advice, because the answer came back: the prince would like a model of the *Cosmo*, once declared by the London-based insurance group as the finest ever built in Quebec.

"Dear M. Lecouvie," wrote the Duke of Edinburgh's private secretary on December 18, 1951. "His Royal Highness has asked me to write and say that he would very much like to have a model of the *Cosmo*, which he would place in his study. I do not know what size you make these models, but I am sure that anything under two feet in length would be readily acceptable."

Immediately, Lecouvie began work, taking more than eight hundred hours to carve by hand at least a thousand tiny pieces assembled into a thirty-inch long model of *Cosmo*. Finished, the exquisitely crafted ship model was transported across the Atlantic aboard the *Empress of France*.[8]

"Dear M. Lecouvie, I know that you will be very happy to hear that the *Cosmo* arrived safely in London," wrote the duke's private secretary on June 20, 1952. "You will be interested to hear that this model will take a high place of honour amongst the other models in His Royal Highness's possession." (It can be seen today in Buckingham Palace.)

Photo courtesy of Gaston Dery.

Prince Philip's gift: *A small model of* Cosmo, *by master craftsman Edmond Lecouvie, is in the private Lecouvie/Déry Collection. A similar thirty-inch model, given to Prince Philip, Duke of Edinburgh, when he and Princess Elizabeth visited Quebec in 1951, is today in Buckingham Palace.*

The editor of the *Quebec Chronicle Telegraph*, on June 2, 1952, heaped on more praise:

> With the building of the two-foot model of the good ship *Cosmo* for Prince Philip, the three-masted timber ship becomes one of the most storied of the sailing ships built at Quebec during the nineteenth century. In the annals of the Ancient Capital, it has its rightful place among the legends and stories of history that have added to its fame over three hundred years. It signaled the end of the prosperous era of the wooden ships that wrote *finis* to the importance of the French-Canadian woodsmen whose skill with wood and the axe was legendary. It was said that a Quebec ship carpenter could split a playing card edgewise with the adze. This skill was consolidated … in the *Cosmo*.

Still, Lecouvie was not finished with *Cosmo*. He made yet another model, a copy of the one given to the prince, for his own collection, which includes forty-two miniature ships carved from Canadian walrus ivory. Acquired by Gaston Dery of Quebec, it is today part of his private Lecouvie-Dery Collection.

As for the real *Cosmo*, she (or should one say *he* for Cosimo?) splashed into the St. Lawrence on Wednesday, June 27, 1877: "Mr. Dinning yesterday launched a splendid ship of 1,250 tons, named the *Cosmo*, built under contract for Mr. Henry Fry," reported the June 28 edition of the *Quebec Daily Mercury*. No description of the launching exists, but it almost certainly followed the ritual of ship launching described by Captain Joseph Elzear Bernier in *Master Mariner*, and by Eileen Marcil in *The Charley-Man*, her definitive history of wooden shipbuilding in Quebec:

> After the winter's work came the great day of launching. The workmen were required to be on hand before dawn. On his arrival each man was served a stiff drink of Canadian whisky. At dawn the work of removing blocks was begun. Just before the key was knocked out,

a final drink was served to the men. Then a final blow knocked the key out. As the ship started down the ways, her godmother, standing on a platform, broke a bottle of Madeira or port against the bow. The ship slid gracefully down the ways into the water amid thundering cheers. The workmen and the guests gathered around long narrow tables loaded with sandwiches, cheese and biscuits, ale and spruce beer. On launching day, every workman was given a full day's pay.[9]

Often ship launchings in Quebec were an occasion for pomp and ceremony, the music of military bands, and steamboats blowing their horns. But in the latter years of wooden shipbuilding, launchings became so commonplace and the reporters' clichés so worn that only a cursory announcement would appear in the paper. Such may have been the case with *Cosmo*. On the other hand, the launching might have been a glorious affair. Such was the recollection of an eighty-six-year-old Quebec fire inspector, Moses Murphy, in 1952. Murphy told the *Quebec Chronicle Telegraph* that as a teenager he "trod the deck the day she was launched [and] worked the hook to load her first cargo of timber. It drew the biggest crowd of any ship launching in Quebec.[10] The bells of the city rang out, the cannon of the Citadel fortress thundered, and the gaily garbed brass band blared *Britannia Rules the Waves*. The shout raised by the crowd as she took to the waves could be heard for miles."

Murphy's description of the launching can't be found in newspaper accounts of the time. In his attempt to reconstruct in his mind an event that happened seventy-five years earlier, he probably conflated *Cosmo*'s launching with the beginning of her maiden voyage on Monday, July 2, 1877, when Dominion Day was celebrated.

It would have happened this way: *Cosmo* must have been fully masted and rigged and virtually ready to sail after she went down the ways, because within five days she was fully loaded with wood, including 308 pieces of oak, 2,758 pipe staves, plus elm and red and white pine — destined, Henry believed, for certain sale in England. Under the command of Captain Alex Laverick, *Cosmo* hooked up to the steam-powered towboat *Conqueror 2*, ready to move downriver that rainy morning.[11]

It was no ordinary day, though. The day before, July 1, was the first time that Dominion Day (now Canada Day) had fallen on a Sunday since Confederation ten years earlier. There was no precedent. What to do? Would it not be unseemly on a church-going day to wave flags and trumpet martial music, and fire off cannons in honour of the young nation's founding? At some higher level of authority, or of wisdom, it was determined that Dominion Day should be celebrated the following day, Monday. "The national holiday having fallen on Sunday," reported the *Quebec Daily Mercury* of Tuesday, July 3, "yesterday was fixed upon for its observation. Two principal retail stores of the Upper Town … were closed. The banks and Custom House were open as usual, and business in the Lower Town was in full blast. In honor of the day, flags were displayed at the various public buildings, and B Battery fired a salute of twenty-one guns at noon."

As it happened, *Cosmo* left her mooring on the morning of Monday, July 2. The noontime 21-gun salute likely coincided with her going down the river. All that noise, crowds, and flag-waving would have impressed Murphy. Looking back seventy-five years, he may have recalled, not the *Cosmo*'s launching day, but rather her maiden voyage six days later when Quebec's citizenry were loudly celebrating Canada's tenth birthday. The ship and the holiday merged in his mind.

What is known for certain is what happened to *Cosmo* and to her builder, Dinning — and the misfortune that entered Henry's life not long after the great ship was launched.

22

1877
In the Wake of the *Cosmo*

The *Cosmo* made her maiden voyage in July of 1877 to Liverpool, where Henry received an offer from a firm to buy the ship at a price equal to her cost. "It would have been well if I had accepted, but I could not foresee events," recalled Henry about the desperate struggle soon to unfold in his life.

In Liverpool dry dock, the bottom of *Cosmo*'s sleek hull was coppered to protect it against worm and marine weed, and the ship sailed with a cargo to New Orleans. Over the next dozen years, she crisscrossed the world's oceans, carrying kola nuts to China and nitrate from Chile. In 1883, *Cosmo* came to be owned by Quebec tycoon James Gibb Ross. When Ross suffered a bankruptcy, the ship was taken over by a Norwegian. "She made remarkably fast passages," wrote Henry, "but times were very bad, steam was everywhere cutting out the sailing ships." In 1889, sailing out of Savannah, Georgia, bound for Hamburg, Germany, *Cosmo* disappeared over the horizon, never to be seen again.[1]

At the time of *Cosmo*'s launching, in the same yard, shipbuilder Dinning — "with his usual lack of judgement," commented Henry — borrowed money to construct a similar ship, the *Lorenzo*, named for another Medici. Dinning soon found himself bankrupt … again. "Contrary to my oft repeated advice," wrote Henry, "he persisted in building too many new ships with borrowed money, about 49 or 50 in all. He never seemed to learn wisdom from experience."[2]

Dinning's *Lorenzo* was the last Quebec square-rigger to be built on the north shore of the St. Lawrence below the Plains of Abraham. For a while after the *Cosmo*'s and the *Lorenzo*'s launchings in 1877, Quebec's yards remained open, the coves holding wood, building the occasional steamboat or barge, and repairing ships. But gradually the yards were abandoned. Landfill and asphalt took their place under what is now Champlain Boulevard. Looking down today, nothing is left to suggest to a visitor's eyes the vast, teeming yards of half-built ships and coves full of logs that enveloped the whole of the shoreline below the city during the nineteenth century.[3]

Dinning's declining fortunes coincided with those of Quebec. The former gateway to North America had failed to build grain elevators and dry docks. Ships now steamed past the city upstream to Montreal, where cargoes were transferred into shallower draft boats to go up the canals to the Great Lakes. In the other direction, Montreal became the transfer point for grain and wood destined for Europe.

Quebec's success as a shipbuilding centre began and ended with wood. To be a player in the iron and steel era required large amounts of financial capital. Quebec's businessmen did not step up to the plate. In Philadelphia, by contrast, a joint stock company in 1872 raised a half-million dollars to build iron ships. Belfast, after Glasgow, became one of the world's greatest builders of steel steamships. One Belfast yard alone employed ten thousand men.

It could have happened in Quebec, Henry believed.[4] Steel plates, angle iron, beams and rivets could be imported from England in ten days, although Henry didn't mention the fact that such supplies could not reach icebound Quebec by ship in winter. Still, Quebec had the yellow pine and the carpenters with skills to make decks, fashion staterooms, and fit interiors. There were mechanics capable of repairing the engines of the largest steamships. The cost of labour was low. The opportunity and resources were there, Henry insisted, but no leader had appeared with the vision and corporate skills to raise the immense capital needed. True, the Davies shipyard at Lauzon began small steamship construction; but by 1912 that family-owned company declared that it would give up if the government did not come to its assistance.[5]

"If the late Senator James Gibb Ross were alive," Henry later wrote in 1895, "he would certainly start a steel shipbuilding company in Quebec, and make it a success."[6] But by then tycoon Ross was dead, and entrepreneurs and merchants resembling him were mostly gone. They'd moved back to England, or to Montreal, where they operated out of offices on St. James Street and dwelt in mansions on Sherbrooke Street.

Henry recorded in his *Reminiscences of a Retired Shipowner* that "the building of *Cosmo* led to a most unexpected result." When the great sailing ship arrived in Liverpool in July 1877, no one was waiting to purchase her cargo. Edward, his brother and business partner, had "failed lamentably to carry out my instructions as to sales of wood. He came back from England in the spring [of 1877] with most of my heavy stock unsold. For the first time in my life, I feared financial trouble."[7]

Edward's failure was undoubtedly linked to the decline in wood sales and lower prices, both of which resulted from the worldwide economic depression that had begun in 1876 and lasted until 1879. The combination of the two hit Henry hard. Forced to ask the bank to renew existing loans, he became so worried that, combined with other heavy responsibilities and obligations and the intense heat of summer, "it affected my health, and robbed me of sleep."[8]

He visited the office of Henry Fry & Co. on Rue St. Pierre less often in the summer of 1877. Recriminations against Edward strained their relationship.[9] After lunch one day Henry climbed the hill toward his house. Streaming down past him on Sous le Fort were labourers ending their day's work preparing the foundations of the new parliament buildings. Atop the hill, reaching the Place d'Armes, he turned west past the old Château Haldimand, which in fifteen years time would be razed to make way for a giant new hotel. A pathway led on to the level lawn, in a few weeks to be named Dufferin Terrace in honour of the departing governor general.

Past the Governor's Garden containing the Wolfe-Montcalm monument, which he'd restored, he reached the family's handsome three-storey home. Inside, the house was decorated in subdued opulence, the walls covered in mauve damask, the windows densely curtained. A gas lamp with chimney shade illuminated the cloak room. Oil cloth covered the floor. In the sitting room hung ten oil paintings, three of which Henry had purchased from Cornelius Krieghoff, master painter of Quebec's early rustic charms. He climbed the stairs past the drawing room, on whose shelves rested a history of the Baptist Church next to Goethe's autobiography. In the bedroom, he lay down on the great mahogany bedstead under a framed engraving of the adoring, worshipful Dante and his beloved Beatrice.[10]

And there in the house, excepting occasional visits to his office and a trip to his summer home at Cacouna on the lower St. Lawrence, Henry mostly remained for the next three months. He was dimly aware that his morose condition mirrored his mental crisis of 1851, although to friends and family it seemed new and mysterious in origin.

Many people carry within themselves the potential for mental illness. An event may trigger an inherited disposition to be depressed or elated. Like plant seeds that germinate only when certain combinations of soil, moisture, and sunlight arise, the seeds of depression sprout when certain circumstances combine in our lives. Seemingly out of nowhere, depression flowers like an exotic weed. And so it was with Henry. The *Cosmo* cargo loss had triggered in him a galloping melancholy. He slept little. He ate less and less. He complained constantly of feeling ill.

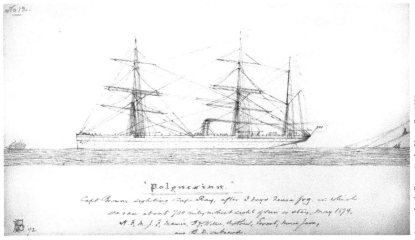

Pen-and-ink illustration by Henry Fry, 1891.

Final eastward crossing: *In February 1877, Henry made his last transatlantic crossing to England on the steamship* Polynesian, *leaving his business and his home behind. Wooden sailing ship construction was near its end in Quebec.*

At first his wife, Mary, was impatient, believing brisk Victorian encouragement was all that was necessary to cure him. "Henry," she said, "you should do as I do. If something is worrying you, just don't think about it."[11] But he would think, and as the weeks passed, Mary realized that her husband's condition was worsening. The episodes of melancholy became more frequent and intense. By late summer Mary decided they should travel to England to seek medical help. On an overcast September day the couple, with two of their sons — Arthur, eleven, and Fred, nine — descended with their luggage to the docks below their home and boarded the *Polynesian*, headed for Liverpool. The steamship accelerated down the St. Lawrence aided by an ebb tide, and a following wind filling her auxiliary sails. Henry stood in the *Polynesian*'s stern, gazing back at the dwindling shipyards. He sensed his life, like his beloved city, left behind, in unavoidable decline.

In quitting Quebec, Henry was leaving his brother Edward in charge of the business. Once in Bristol, the Canadians moved into the house of Henry's sister Lucy and her husband, Charles Clifft. The two boys attended school in Bristol. After a year, though, Mary determined that her sons should go back to Quebec, and Edward was summoned to accompany them on the voyage home.[12] Edward arrived in Bristol in May 1878. During his brief visit, he and Henry discussed the business. Edward contended that he was doing all the work, yet he owned only a quarter of Henry Fry & Co. It was agreed that he would have a half-interest, and Edward sailed back to Quebec with the two boys.

In Bristol Henry was living amid the familiar environs where he'd been raised, educated, apprenticed, and received employment until age twenty-seven. He described the city of his birth in his handwritten *Notes on England, Wales and Scotland*. Bristol's population in the 1880s was about the size of Montreal's, he wrote. Above the docks on breezy downs were the suburbs of Clifton, Redland, and Cotham, strewn with the villas of Bristol's wealthier citizens.

> The scenery in every direction is exquisite. Clifton Down is a favourite of geologists, many beautiful specimens being found in the limestone rock. Below, the picturesque little Avon is spanned by a fairylike suspension bridge.

The City is famous for the quality of its manufactures, especially for its leather, floorcloth, stoneware, glass and lead. In Bristol may be seen five great orphan asylums; noble asylums for the blind, the deaf, and the dumb; a large Grammar School; a university, a fine art academy, Zoological Gardens; a music hall seating 3,000; hospitals, fine hotels, Gothic churches and a Catholic Cathedral.[13]

The pleasant surroundings notwithstanding, Bristol failed to release Henry from the thrall of his episodic depression. Nor did his religion; nor the doctors whom he saw. It did not help either to brood over Edward's missteps in the *Cosmo* affair. Edward was now managing Henry Fry & Co. Henry's business involvement was desultory at best. In the late summer of 1879, he and Mary re-crossed the Atlantic. Entering New York Harbor, they could see the massive stone towers and cabling of the Brooklyn Bridge, under construction at the time.[14] The couple quickly transferred to a train — bound not for Canada, but for Connecticut.

23

1878-82
Despond

Late in the morning of a crisp, cloudless autumn day in 1879, Henry Fry was still abed, his head lolling on a down pillow. Through a window the branches of a towering elm cast soft wavering shadows over the linen sheets and the white walls of his room. From the Connecticut River came the hoarse honk of a tugboat. It was a restful place, restorative as it was designed to be. Near the new campus of Trinity College, the thirty-five acres of verdant high ground surrounding the Hartford Retreat for the Insane had recently been laid out by Frederick Law Olmstead and Calvert Vaux, celebrated designers of New York City's Central Park. Beds of chrysanthemum and late-blooming roses lined the lawn. The autumn had been pleasantly warm … an Indian summer.

Henry had come here in August, accompanied by his wife, Mary, after they'd crossed the Atlantic by steamer from Liverpool to New York, followed by a train trip to Hartford. A carriage met them at the station.

"You the people for the Retreat?" inquired the driver. Without awaiting an answer, he lifted Henry's steamer trunk onto the carriage roof, lashed it down, and the horses proceeded with the driver and two passengers to the Retreat. At the entrance to the turreted main building, Henry's brother Edward, down from Quebec, awaited the couple. They were escorted to the admissions office where an assistant physician interviewed Henry.

"Patient came voluntarily with wife and brother," records the Retreat log on August 25, 1979. "He has been traveling abroad of late and has consulted many eminent men. He thinks he is utterly unable to digest nearly all articles of food."[1] Such was the terse entry record for the new patient, a British merchant whose home was in Quebec. A bustle of paperwork, readings and ink signings followed, and Henry was officially admitted. Mary, Edward, and Henry climbed the stairs to his room.

"You will be comfortable here, dear, I'm sure," said Mary to her husband. Henry, not responding, sat on the edge of the bed, face down, staring blankly at the floor, despondent.

"The carriage is waiting, and I must go," she said. It was done. From Hartford she and Edward caught the next train north to Quebec.

The following morning, Henry was examined by Dr. Henry Stearns, Superintendent of the Hartford Retreat for the Insane, where as a private patient Henry was paying a pricey three hundred dollars a month.[2] Founded in 1822, the Retreat (in 1931 it became the Neuro-Psychiatric Institute, then in 1941 the oddly named Institute of Living) was one of the first mental health centres in the United States. It was emphatically not an asylum for the deranged poor. And it was located in Hartford, one of America's wealthiest cities.

"We have in our snug retreat," once wrote the *Retreat Gazette*'s editor, "all sorts of characters and condition of men — priests, elders and deacons, merchants, tinkers, and tailors — generals, colonels, captains and corporals — editors, printers, politicians, and other characters."[3]

Patients were regularly treated to concerts, lectures, readings, and exhibitions.[4] Boredom was to be avoided at all cost. Assistant physicians made rounds throughout the day seeing the 130 patients. Henry had bought his way into the nineteenth century's version of the McLean Hospital outside Boston where the ultra-wealthy go, or where their relatives send them to dry out or be purged of neuroses.

During the Civil War, Stearns — a burly man with large silvery side whiskers, studious and blessed with a benign, generous temperament — had had ten thousand patients under his care and a hundred surgeons under his command.[5] He'd borne profound witness to emotional distress and mental illness among soldiers. A friend of General Ulysses Grant, the doctor after the war turned to caring for the insane. Now he was concerned about the safety of his new patient, whom attendants described as "suicidal." He noticed Henry Fry gnawing compulsively on his raw fingers. Self-inflicted scratches marred the man's neck.

Photos by the author.

Retreat: *Melancholy and depression, exacerbated by misapplied narcotics, caused Henry to spend almost a year in Connecticut's Hartford Retreat for the Insane. Up-market patients resided in smaller cottages. Among the retreat's patients were "editors, politicians, priests, merchants, generals, tinkers and tailors, and other characters." The 1875 art hangs today in the Hartford Institute for Living.*

Details of Henry's execrable mental and physical collapse are chronicled in The Hartford Retreat's records, entered between the end of August 1879 and the end of July 1880.

> *Aug. 29.* Very despondent. Wishes to remain in bed nearly all the time. Thinks he is feeble, but general health is good. Has been out to ride on two occasions.

> *Sept. 15.* Has had the electricity several times. [A mild galvanic current applied to the head as a treatment for dementia and melancholia]. Thinks he cannot live long. Feels much better after getting up and exercising.

> *Oct. 9.* Is very despondent and unwilling to get up in the morning. Talks continually about himself and condition — how happy he used to be, and how miserable he is now. Likes company and someone to talk to. Has taken electricity several times and milk punch [a brandy-laced sedative] on going to bed.

> *Nov. 12.* Was visited by his brother-in-law [Samuel Dawson], but seemed no better.

> *Feb. 20.* Is "dying" this morning. Mr. Fry's wife has been to see him.

> *Mar. 18.* Does not sleep and had red streaks around his neck. He appeared to be under some excitement. His attendant [has been] instructed to leave him as little as possible to himself, and to leave his door open at night.

> *Apr. 1.* Have been injecting 1/8 gr. Morphine into his arm twice daily to be gradually increased.

> *April* [no date]. Morphine increasing gradually, no improvement noticed, and it was discontinued.

> *June 8.* Does not improve.

At the time of his admission, Henry was described as "probably" suffering from "melancholia," or depression. The cause? "Overwork," claimed the patient. The *Cosmo* affair had so worried him, insisted Henry, that "it affected my health and robbed me of sleep."

The wild fluctuations in the shipping trade, the nerve-racking ups and downs of his own wealth, and the tensions with his relatives who worked for him undoubtedly had contributed to triggering Henry's illness. He was almost certainly vulnerable genetically. At Hartford he admitted to doctors that his father, George of Bristol, had suffered periodically from depression, possibly linked to a business failure when Henry was young. Henry himself suffered a mental collapse that had caused him to flee England in 1853 (see chapter 3). He was not incurious about what might have caused his depression. In his library was the first book of psychiatry, Robert Burton's 1621 multi-volume *The Anatomy of Melancholy, What It Is: With All the Kinds, Symptomes, Prognostickes, and Several Cures of It.*[6] Burton's work is surely one of the most amazing pieces of English literature — like *Tristram Shandy*, an *omnium gatherum*. When it was republished in 1927, the book's jacket described *The Anatomy of Melancholy* as "a compendium … of poetry, medicine, morbid psychology, philosophy, old wives' tales, philology, wars, theology, morals, history, climatology, travel, food, art, politics" and more. One can only speculate that Henry read all of it … 1,036 pages in the modern version, including a fifty-page index.

On July 20, 1880, Henry left the Retreat: "Patient has left for the seashore, and will probably not come back. Discharged." During ten months the Retreat's doctors had not only failed to cure Henry of his illness, there's reason to believe they had worsened his condition through over-medication, cannabis and bromides, and the misapplication of electrotherapy and morphine.[7] He may have become addicted to the injected morphine — commonly overused by doctors in the 1880s. If so, he would have suffered withdrawal symptoms, such as anxiety, depression, insomnia, aches, and pains.[8] Whatever … Henry had recovered sufficiently — at least, in his own mind — that he exited the Retreat.

A week after his leaving Hartford, the Retreat office received a letter from an "attendant," saying that Mr. Fry was "doing well and is benefited by the change." He was in Maine breathing the fresh, cool sea air, away from the inland summer heat. He appears also to have journeyed north in order to spend time ensconced in his beloved Cliff Cottage at Cacouna, breathing the remedial breezes of the broad St. Lawrence. An 1881 Canadian census listed him, statistically at least, as a household member in Quebec City living with his wife and seven children. When winter came, he may have gone to New York. His illness would not leave him, though. By June of 1881 Henry had returned to Connecticut, this time to the town of Cromwell, where he came under the care of Dr. Winthrop Hallock.

Hallock was the pioneer of *The Cottage System for the Insane* — not housing the mentally ill in a large asylum, but rather in smaller dispersed, more humane buildings. An admirer described Hallock as having "an earnest, kindly spirit and quiet strength imparted to all those about him." He envisioned a group of two-storey houses, segregating patients by sex and by acuteness of mental illness. To hold down costs, patients would volunteer to clean halls, make beds, and serve food. His system would be far superior, in Hallock's view, to the "utter inadequacy" of the mental hospital system prevalent in America and Europe, where the insane, without money, were horribly treated. At the same time Hallock claimed that he wasn't concerned with caring for the rich, who were able to pay for places like the upmarket Hartford Retreat. "What they prefer and need does not concern us here," he wrote.[9] Perhaps not, but affluent Henry Fry, ironically, would become his patient.

By 1877, Hallock had translated his dream into physical reality. His family owned thirteen acres of meadows, woodland, and several buildings and homes at Cromwell, Connecticut. He called the place Cromwell Hall. The land sloped eastward, and early in the morning the rising sun painted the sky in pink. His patients could look down on the Connecticut River and glimpse ships travelling between Long Island Sound and towns upriver. There was even a tennis court. Hallock's own home was a comfortable, spacious Victorian on the periphery of the land.[10]

Hallock had converted existing bungalows into dormitories for thirty-three men and women. The main building contained a dining hall and sun room. (A dozen years later, Toronto's principal hospital for the insane opened a branch built on the Cottage System.) The Treatment House was equipped with electrical apparatus, a colonic table, and recreation room.[11] Henry's treatment probably was intensified with morphine injections if his later testimony in a court hearing is to be believed.

Dr. Hallock occasionally served as an expert witness in legal cases where mental illness had to be defined or affirmed. So it was that he and Henry, at the end of May 1882, travelled to Quebec City where they had an appointment to appear in Superior Court.

24

1882-89
Miracle and Mystery

Henry and Dr. Hallock arrived on June 2, 1882, in Quebec, where Mary, Henry's wife of twenty-four years, was petitioning the court to declare her husband incapable of handling his affairs. Mary had come down from Montreal where she was living. She appeared grim during the reading of her petition for interdiction — a legal restraint imposed on someone judged incapable of managing his estate due to mental incapacity.

> To my honorable Judge of the Superior Court the petition of Dame Mary Jane Dawson respectfully showeth that for some time past her husband Henry Fry has been and now is suffering from mental disease and is quite incapable of transacting his affairs. He has been for a long time in an establishment under treatment, but there has been no improvement in his condition. The petitioner asks that the court interrogate Henry.[1]

The man who now came before the court bore a pitiable resemblance to the vigorous merchant who'd once walked Quebec's corridors of power. Henry's hair had turned grey and disordered, his face appeared sallow, his hands raw and red, his eyes dead. He shuffled into the courtroom. On the stand, he responded in a wavering, despondent voice. He was asked where he had been living.

"I have been residing partly in New York and partly in the village of Cromwell," answered Henry. "At an hotel and private house."

"Have you not been in bad health? What was the cause?"

"My health has not been as good as usual … more from absence of my home and friends, but I attribute the original trouble to the doctor's mistake. Being a sensitive man, he gave me narcotics, which I think was a mistake."

"You consider that you cannot yourself manage your affairs?"

"Though being necessarily absent, I consider myself able to do so. My brother is very competent to do that. He is my partner."

"Where do you intend to reside in future?"

"I do not know. They give me narcotics every night. It stupefies me."

So stupefying that the court recorded, "the said Henry Fry goes on speaking in incoherent manner."[2]

Dr. Hallock was summoned to the stand, where he deposed.

> I, Winthrop B. Hallock of Cromwell, Connecticut, have devoted much attention to insanity and to the various forms of mental illness. Henry Fry of Quebec has resided with me under my immediate care and treatment for about one year. I came with him from Cromwell to Quebec this week. The form of mental illness under which Mr. Fry has been suffering would be classed as monomaniacal hypochondria: an inability to talk or think except for a short time about any subject but his own bodily and mental state. When not in the presence of others, he will talk and laugh to himself. He gnaws his fingers, keeping them constantly raw; he wakes from sleep in a half-delirious state, he cries and moans imagining he is going to die. I have no hesitation in saying that he is insane and quite unfit to attend to his affairs.[3]

Hallock's expert testimony was supported by two Quebec physicians and surgeons — Colin Sewell and James Arthur Jewett. By two o'clock in the afternoon the interdiction of Henry Fry was complete. With the approval of Henry's son Henry Jr., his brother Edward, his brother-in-law Samuel Dawson, the banker James Stevenson, and his Cacouna neighbor Andrew Thompson, Henry's wife was appointed curator, or curatrix, as the court noted. She was to take charge of her husband's "person and to administer his property."

For the forty-six-year-old mother of seven children it was a heavy, unenviable burden. Worse, with it came the shame of Henry's official listing as an interdicted person in Quebec. "Notices of said interdiction must be transmitted to the Notaries of this District of Quebec in order that no person be ignorant of the said interdiction." In short, Henry was publicly declared unable to transact business in the city over whose Board of Trade he'd once ruled, where he'd built great fully rigged sailing ships, kept families from hunger, founded the YMCA, served as school commissioner, fought crimping, saved the lives of sailors imperiled by faultily loaded cargo, and guarded the St. Lawrence River and thousands of ships traversing its dangerous waters. The city he loved had formally rejected him.

To wind down Henry's affairs, Mary gave wide powers to the Quebec merchant Richard Reid Dobell. By November her oldest son, Henry Fry Jr., joined Edward Fry as a partner, and the two undertook to manage the business of Henry Fry & Co. The partnership lasted about two and a half years. At the end of April 1885, Edward took over for himself the business that had been launched by his oldest brother in Quebec thirty years earlier.

Mary, gathering cash from the sale of bank shares, moved permanently to Montreal. For income she had loans outstanding to no fewer than nine people, who were paying her interest rates between 5.5 percent and 7 percent, secured by their real estate and insurance policies on their houses. She owned properties herself.[4] Shrewd in finance and real estate, Mary saw that there was enough money for her husband's care. But he was no longer the man whom she was once married to. Lovell's 1887 Montreal Directory lists her as "Mrs. M. Fry, widow."[5] In December 1877 she bought a house at 66 McTavish Street, conveniently located across the street from the McGill campus. Convenient because twenty-five-year-old Henry Jr. was studying law at the university on his way to becoming a well-known Montreal notary.

Photo courtesy of Dick Avison.

The matriarch: *In 1886, Mary Dawson Fry, then fifty, was living in her own house in Montreal across from the McGill University library, separated from her husband, Henry, who was living southeast of Montreal in the region known today as Estrie.*

As for Henry Fry Sr., he likely travelled from Quebec with Dr. Hallock back to Connecticut, where he remained for a while under his care. How long is unknown.[6] At some point Henry moved to the town of Farnham in the Eastern Townships (Cantons de l'Est, or Estrie). Hallock, perhaps sensing that Henry wished to go back to Canada to be nearer to his family, may have referred Henry to Dr. George F. Slack, a Farnham physician. Slack was known to use a pioneering treatment for mental patients.[7]

At the same time, the family appears to have wanted him in Montreal. In October 1888, Mary gave Henry Jr. $10,800 to buy a stone cottage on Fort Street, then in Montreal's west end. Henry Jr. said he "acquired the property for his father."[8] Did Henry actually come to live in the cottage? Wherever he lived, it was clear that Mary didn't wish him to reside with her on McTavish Street. The wounds of his mental illness had not totally healed. The discordant qualities of restlessness, fretting, and irritability are the hallmarks of depressives, with whom even the most patient and tolerant of humans have difficulty co-habiting.[9]

In 1889, however, Henry reappears, suggesting that he'd partially recovered. It was in writing. Henry's own writing. Something of a miracle had occurred.

A Fresh Beginning

In the summer of 1889 in Quebec, the city where seven years earlier he'd painfully demonstrated his stultifying mental illness, Henry wrote an exquisite tribute — highly literate in the quality of its expression — to his dearest male friend, the Baptist minister David Marsh, who had just died. The next year he completed more than three hundred pages of *Essays* on trade, tariffs, and U.S.-Canada relations, which a hundred years later would find their way into the stacks of the Thomas Fisher Rare Book Library at the University of Toronto. The *Essays* were "written for, and dedicated to my children," who now ranged in age from the unmarried and sickly twenty-nine-year-old only daughter Mame to sixteen-year-old Ernest, youngest of his six sons.

For two of his sons, Henry and Arthur, he completed the book *Reminiscences of a Retired Shipowner*, accompanied by twenty-three flawlessly executed pen-and-ink illustrations which he made of ships that he'd owned. He wrote *Notes on England, Wales, Scotland, Ireland and Paris*, a 183-page travelogue to educate "a young Canadian." He made pen-and-ink drawings, with captions, of ships from Columbus's square-rigged *Santa Maria* to the 1890 steamer *Empress of India*, including barques, brigs, fore- and aft-rigged schooners, and combined sail and paddlewheel ships.

The sheer volume of Henry's writing in such a short period suggests activity almost manic in its intensity, a man who slept little. All the while he was researching and writing his final and most researched work, *The History of North Atlantic Steam Navigation*, which would be published in London in 1896 — a work written, he confessed, "during a period of enforced leisure from ill health."

"Enforced leisure"? What did it mean to Henry? Leisure enforced by doctors to enable his cure? Leisure time available to write because his interdiction barred him from working again as a merchant? Or self-enforced leisure because he was cured, clear of mind, and quite able to manage his time?

Sons and daughter: *Children of Henry and Mary Fry circa 1885, left to right: Arthur, William, Henry, Mamie, Frederick, Alfred. Ernest in foreground.*

Throughout his worst bouts of depression and self-doubt, Henry never totally lost the temporary capacity to think normally and clearly, and to write intelligibly. From moments those episodes extended to mornings, then to whole days of essay and letter writing, drawing ships, and research.

The 1891 Census of Canada clearly records Henry as living in the bustling town of Farnham, with a woolen mill and tannery, on the main rail line between Montreal and Vermont. He was renting a room or rooms in the house of Joseph Massicotte, a tinsmith with a wife and four children under the age of ten. He was living two doors away from his physician, Dr. Slack, who owned several properties in Farnham, possibly including the Massicotte house where Henry was residing. Henry's granddaughter says that he was under the care of Dr. Slack for a long time, and Slack remained his primary physician until the day Henry died.[10]

The 1891 Census contained a column indicating whether the subject suffered from "Infirmities." The Henry Fry entry suggests the information was provided when he was absent, by someone in the household who recorded whatever Dr. Slack had once dictated.[11] Henry was listed as a person "unsound of mind," and the enumerator takes the unusual step of entering what appears to be the word *insomnia*. That he suffered from insomnia would hardly be surprising, given the immense volume of work Henry was doing at the time of the census — countless hand-written words, scores of illustrations.

The census was outdated by the time it was published. Henry, apparently sound of mind, had transferred his powerful mercantile energies into intense, studious research, and thousands of words and hours of writing. They reveal the thought of a nineteenth-century Victorian in Canada, loving his Quebec home, suspicious of Americans, assumptive of Anglo-Saxon superiority, vocally proud both of Canada and the Empire of which, in his mind, Canada was an indissoluble part.

25

1889-94
A Mind at Work

Industry is the enemy of melancholy.
— WILLIAM F. BUCKLEY, JR.

The writing of a tribute to a deceased friend requires the author to blend biographical accuracy with sentimental warmth. When the writing is superb, the reader not only sees the deceased's life in factual perspective but the heartstrings are tugged at. The work cannot be the product of a disordered mind. The author must be in command of his faculties. And so they were for Henry Fry when, in 1889 in Quebec, he wrote a tribute to Henry Marsh, the simple, eloquent Baptist pastor who'd been his friend almost from the first time he'd arrived in the river port city as a young merchant thirty-five years earlier:

> He never attempted to fathom the profound mysteries of life, nor to soar in rhetorical flights. It was only talk, but what beautiful talk! His profound humility, his simple, yet touching language, the tenderness with which he alluded to the suffering of any of his flock, and the earnestness with which he pleaded for all ranks and conditions of men were, to my mind, infinitely superior to the best of liturgies.

In private intercourse he was remarkable for his great tenderness and suavity of manner, his sweetness of temper, his charity towards all men, and his love of children. Nothing could ever provoke him to say an unkind word of any living creature. He seemed to live in an atmosphere of love and tenderness.[1]

The writing was fluid, keen, even enthusiastic, patently not emanating from an unsound mind.[2] Nor was his tribute to Marsh a singular effort. About the same time, Henry began writing 289 pages of handwritten *Essays* on how business cycles impact international trade, on tariff reciprocity and the merits of free trade over protectionism. He completed the work in March 1890.[3]

His writing was clear, occasionally acerbic. He wrote so much in such a relatively short time that it's imaginable, if not a fact, that he slept little. Enforced leisure had become willingly self-enforced labour.

Several of Henry's *Essays* focus on Canada's trade relations with its powerful southern neighbour. The United States, having climbed out of the ruins of the Civil War, was asserting its economic dominance over North America. To merchants like Henry, tariff barriers between Canada and the United States were undesirable. But unfettered free trade between the two countries, or commercial union, was something else … and far worse, in Henry's view, was what it might lead to: political union.

Canadians are not fools, nor do they forget the past. Are the men … who induced Lord Palmerston in 1848 to repeal the British Navigation Laws under a promise of complete reciprocity, and then refused to open their coasting or California trade; the men who in 1863 made Canada pay to the cent for the St. Alban's raid by their own people; the men who refused to admit a Canadian barge into the Erie or Whitehall Canal while enjoying the use of our own … are these the men to control the tariff and destinies of this free, happy country? God forbid! The U.S. have an intense longing for Canada, and some think that the latter might add to her material prosperity by [a] union; but Canadians detest the political methods of the U.S.; have no love for their extreme protection theories, and cling fondly to the institutions of Britain.[4]

At the time of Henry's writing, tariffs, protectionism, and commercial union shaped the battleground of Canada's 1890–91 election campaign. The Liberals under their new leader, Wilfrid Laurier, were willing to negotiate with the United States to dismantle tariff walls, a policy favoured by Canadian farmers. The aging Conservative leader Sir John A. Macdonald opposed. Macdonald attacked anything that smelled of commercial union, almost tantamount in his mind to annexation.

"Every American statesman covets Canada," declared the prime minister.[5] "The greed for its acquisition is still on the increase." It was a view that helped propel Macdonald to victory in the election of 1891.

The real situation — it should not be a surprise — was neither as simple nor as unequivocal as politicians portrayed it. For one thing, the Canadian government depended on income from duties to pay for its operations. For another, many Canadian businessmen, even if they favoured free trade, were suspicious that the United States would fail to reciprocate with tariff reductions of their own. Their suspicion was not unfounded, suggested Henry: "No one doubts that perfect freedom of trade in certain articles would be a mutual blessing, but the Americans will not agree to any treaty unless they are quite sure that they have the best of the bargain." He recalled the reasons for the Canadian grudges:

> We admitted their vessels to the Welland, St. Lawrence, Ottawa and Chambly canals on the same terms as our own vessels. How many of ours did they admit to the Erie and Whitehall Canals? Not one! Who repealed the materially beneficent Canadian American Reciprocity Treaty of 1854? Not Canada. Americans have ruined their own fisheries through greed. Now they complain because we object to their ruining ours.[6]

Henry could have been writing about U.S. barriers to Canadian timber in the aftermath of the North American Free Trade Agreement

(NAFTA) a century later. Free trade, or commercial union, Henry feared, would inevitably lead to a U.S. takeover of Canada. It would fulfill the dream of Americans who looked forward to "manifest destiny," the political union of all of North America in a republican democracy. For Canadians like Henry, however, Manifest Destiny would be the equivalent of military defeat. In his mind, Canada's destiny was to remain tied to Britain's. Sir John A. Macdonald had echoed Henry's deepest sense of his own identity in 1875 when he famously proclaimed at a dinner in Montreal, "I am a British subject, and British born, and a British subject I hope to die."[7]

One man, in particular, became the focus of Henry's fear and hatred of annexation: Erastus Wiman, a businessman and promoter, a Canadian who'd made a small fortune on New York's Staten Island, running a ferry service and developing real estate. Wiman wrote pamphlets and gave dozens of speeches in Canada and the United States advocating commercial union. While he hadn't openly advocated political union, Wiman, in Henry's mind, was aiming at nothing less — tantamount to annexation. It would start innocently with tariffs administered by a joint commission. But the majority serving on such a commission inevitably would be Americans. "By the minority of her population Canada would have little or no influence in the regulation of the [tariff] amounts," wrote Henry.

"Mr. Wiman knows perfectly well that if ever this [preferential U.S. tariffs] were accomplished (may God forbid) it would immediately involve Canada in trouble with England." Henry then exploded:

> This bastard Canadian [Wiman] is deliberately plotting to bring about trouble between Canada and Britain and to involve us in such a position that we shall alienate the sympathy and help of our brethren, only to fall into the hands of a set of grasping, selfish, unscrupulous Yankees. This is how the renegade traitor insults his native land, and works against the Great Empire to which he, nominally, still owes allegiance.
>
> At present we lean upon England's great Navy, the real defense of Canada, saving the enormous cost of a standing army, navy, ambassadors, consuls, and more.

> Now could we ask England to defend us while we were
> discriminating against her manufactures in favor of
> the U.S.?[8]

Here was Henry back in full swing. Here again was the Henry intel-
lectually outraged by perceived injustice. Here again was the Henry
who'd attacked the greedy practice of deck loading ships making them
unseaworthy, who'd condemned the criminality of crimps kidnapping
innocent seamen. He was astride his high horse once more.

The prospect of U.S. annexation especially aggrieved him. "The second objection [to union]," he wrote, "involves the principle of taxation
without representation, the very principle against which the Americans
themselves rebelled in the last [eighteenth] century. How long would
five millions of free people submit to be taxed by a foreign legislature
where they would be under-represented? We know enough of American
selfishness to realize that the interests of Canada in such [a] union would
have no weight."

With tariffs, Henry found himself floundering in contradiction. As
president of the Quebec Board of Trade and of the Dominion Board of
Trade he had praised the economic benefits from eliminating punitive
tariffs. But now he found himself defending tariffs, for what appeared
at the time to be an inescapable reason. Without the revenue from
duties levied on imports, the Canadian government would be close to
inoperable. Canada imported far more in quantity and in value than
did the United States — about twenty-two dollars per capita, the U.S.
only about twelve dollars. Commercial union would lead to "the loss
of seven million dollars now received on imports from the U.S., and
at least five million more on imports from Britain," wrote Henry. "To
make up these twelve millions, heavy direct taxation would have to be
substituted." God help Canada if it were ever to impose an income tax
on its citizens! "Canadians have an inveterate prejudice against this
form of taxation," he remarked.

Henry feared too that a collapse of tariffs would destroy much of
Canada's manufacturing, a worry that would echo a hundred years later
when Canadians debated the effects of NAFTA. Initially, as Henry saw it,
Canada would benefit from its agricultural exports rising, and from the

lower prices of manufactured goods coming in from the United States. But down the road the Dominion would pay dearly for the benefits. Canadian industries would be "crushed," wrote Henry. "We should be at their mercy and pay dearly in the future for a temporary reduction in prices. It is a choice between freedom with some sacrifice, and slavery with dollars. Neither Britons nor Frenchmen will hesitate one moment when they fully understand the case."

Henry was not mistaken in anticipating French Canadian support of continuing strong ties with its conqueror. If you were a people accustomed to the rule of kings, monarchist Britain was a more comfortable fit than the republican United States. And there was religion. The idea of political union with dominantly Protestant America, which would wait another seventy years to elect its first Catholic president (John F. Kennedy), was anathema to Quebec's Roman Church. When it came to possible American annexation, the British could count on the support of those whom they'd once defeated to be militant in their opposition.

Henry found still direr consequences were Manifest Destiny realized. In his mind, the Civil War had not resolved the issues separating North and South, where "whites are set against blacks." Manifest Destiny would mean union with a country whose politics, in his opinion, were morally bankrupt. "There are in the U.S. plenty of men as honourable, as high-minded, and as liberal as any on Earth, but they count for nothing under their wretched system of government."

Henry's view seems to have been prejudiced by his reading American newspapers, or excerpts from them in Canadian papers. The *New York Post*, he observed, "says that great city is ruled 'by murderers, pugilists, gamblers and saloonkeepers, and many of the state legislators are admittedly not much better.' The *Boston Herald* says that U.S. Senatorships are bought with money.

"Canada, on the other hand," wrote Henry, "is better governed, has more real liberty, less crime, more respect for law, and a higher tone of religion and morality. There is not a city in the U.S. that for order, quiet, Sabbath observance, education and progress equals the City of Toronto!"

In the twenty-year period 1867–1887," reflected Henry, "Montreal and Toronto doubled their populations; Winnipeg, Regina, Calgary and Vancouver have risen from fur trapping posts to thriving cities. It is to be hoped that our Government ... will carefully guard the interests and the perfect freedom of our happy country. With her vast resources; the abundance of good land, of lumber, minerals and coals; the rapid increase of population and railways; the deeper canals; and backed by the cheap money and the power of Great Britain, there is a future for Canada unsurpassed, if not unequaled by any country on the face of the globe."[9]

Henry was anticipating what Wilfrid Laurier would tell Ottawa's Canadian Club a dozen years later in 1904: "The nineteenth century was the century of the United States. I think we can claim that it is Canada that shall fill the twentieth century." Henry shared Laurier's errant forecast since it is routinely acknowledged that the twentieth century, in quantitative terms at least, belonged to America not Canada. While Henry could boast about the doubled populations of two Canadian cities, Canada's growth came nowhere near matching the economic and population growth below its southern border after the Civil War. Between 1861 and 1900 the U.S. population grew by 138 percent, compared with Canada's 49 percent. While a million-and-a-half immigrants flooded into Canada, two million people left Canada for greater opportunity in the United States.[10]

Better than political union with its neighbour to the south, wrote Henry, would be Canadian membership in something bigger and better: a permanent union with beloved Britain. The idea of a Commonwealth of Nations — which is to say, the British dominions and protectorates — was already in the air, and would be formalized in 1917. In 1890 Henry called it "Imperial Federation, the founding of a great Anglo Saxon Empire with a population of 320 millions. That the multifarious affairs of such an Empire could be managed by a council sitting in London is a dream.... A *free trade league* would be an immense advantage. Representatives [from the dominions] might sit in the houses of the Imperial Parliament."[11]

Other Writings

When he wasn't working on his *Essays*, Henry was researching his future history of steamships. As well, he wrote for his sons, now in their twenties, a travel book and reminiscences of his life as a ship-owner. The author seems at times to be writing almost for the mechanical sensation of doing so. In 1891, he penned 209 pages of *Notes on England, Wales, Scotland and Paris for a Young Canadian, with Sketches of Typical Sailing and Steamships*. Much of it seems derived from personal observation. Some of it reads as if it were copied from travel guides. Henry describes everything from English municipal and real estate law to the dialects of the people and the port of Glasgow. He writes enthusiastically about the glories of the British Isles. He advises his sons, if at all possible in crossing the Atlantic, to land in Southampton not Liverpool in summer, so that they may experience the beauty of the English Channel and the scenic train trip to London. Once in London, though, "the roar of the street traffic from four in the morning to midnight is terrible."

Henry advises "the young Canadian" which newspapers to read and the best ports in Ireland to visit. Travel to France is recommended. The orderliness of Paris contrasts with unruly London: "Everything is regulated by a strict paternal government. Abandoned women are not allowed to patrol the streets as they are in London; everything that can offend the eye or ear is prohibited. The politeness of the lower classes is so different from the same class in England ... or the U.S."

Finally, "the Young Canadian" should above all be aware of his or her good fortune to be linked to England:

> The Young Canadian may well pause and admire this cradle of his forefathers, its wonderful people, and the great Empire to which he belongs. This island, smaller than Quebec, controls an empire of about ten million square miles of territory, 320 million people speaking 150 different languages, with 200,000 ships and steamers protected by 367 powerful ships of war ... an empire founded on just laws, human freedom, and the fear of God! Happy youth! To be the heir of such inestimable privileges and participator in such a glorious history![12]

In 1891 his children were demonstrably on his mind. In two leather-bound, handwritten books, works of painstaking labour, Henry penned his recollections of owning and operating ships. The edition for his eldest son, Henry, was simply entitled *Reminiscences of a Retired Shipowner*. It includes twenty-five pen-and-ink illustrations with intricate details of rigging and spars, descriptions of what happened to every ship he owned, an accounting of his wealth, the dates and passages of his transatlantic crossings, and of shipwrecks caused by deck loading. The second version, *There Go the Ships*, for his third son, Arthur Dawson Fry, repeats the information about his own ships, with added research on shipping that became part of *The History of North Atlantic Steam Navigation*.

Folio from *Reminiscences of a Retired Ship Owner*, by Henry Fry.

Merchant-turned-writer: *Henry by 1890 was engaged in writing essays on trade and politics, business cycles, the misfortunes of sailors, a travelogue, magazine articles ... and a book of reminiscences.*

Henry's artistic skill yielded a dozen illustrations of ships that he gave in 1892 to his eldest son, Henry, for his thirtieth birthday, calling them *Leaves of My Life*. He'd either been a passenger on the ships, or had dealt with them as Lloyd's agent. The annotation written below each illustration is a brief account of his experience with each ship. On the *Canadian* in 1856 Henry witnessed the First Officer tragically washed overboard. The *North Briton* is seen steaming out of Portland, Maine, carrying newly married Henry and Mary to Liverpool. The *Polynesian* in May 1874 emerges from the fog to sight Cape Ray after running seven hundred miles without sight of sun or stars, with Henry, wife, four children, and a nurse on board.

In another booklet Henry outlined the history of ships from the earliest seafaring days of the Egyptians and Phoenicians. He drew on his own library, brought from Quebec, or books in the library of the Literary and Historical Society, on whose board he once served. He'd become a writer and an historian. He was no longer a travelling, deal-making merchant, gregarious community and business leader, no longer a married head of household. He'd left his family, or at least they appear to have chosen to dwell apart from him. He was living singly as a researcher and author.

26

1894-96
The History of
North Atlantic Steam Navigation

Henry Fry's life was certifiably Victorian in chronology as well as spirit. Born seven years after Queen Victoria's birth, he died seven years before her death. He lived to witness and worship the triumphant ascendancy of the British Empire during the Victorian age. England's colonies and dominions were linked by massive numbers of war and merchant ships, a development which allowed Henry to profit as a participant, and which he chronicled as an historian. He lived to see sail give way to steam, farm to factory, and protectionism to open trade. In 1890, he wrote about the changes that had transformed the civilized world during his lifetime.

> The bottom of the sea has been explored. The heavens have been photographed. The earth has been weighed and the distance of the sun measured. Within the memory of men now living there were no railroads, no telegraph, no ocean steamships; no Lucifer matches, no photographs, no postage stamps. Now electrical lights have turned night into day and doubled the work done in 24 hours. Greenwich has flashed a message to Montreal in three quarters of a second time. It often took four months to exchange messages between Europe and America.

Cargoes of grain are now bought in Montreal and sold in Britain within two hours. The first regular Atlantic steamship in 1838 charged $250 for a cabin passage; the rate is now $40 to $100, the accommodation is superior, and you go in half the time. During the Irish famine of 1847, it cost 54 cents to carry a bushel of wheat from New York to Liverpool by sail. It now carries by steam for 6 cents.[1]

What had caused such a revolution in transportation economics? For Henry, it was a triple-headed technological revolution. First was the mass building of iron ships — stronger, more economical, faster, and more enduring than wooden hulls and cloth sails. Second, the screw propeller had replaced the paddle wheel, dramatically lowering costs. And third, the compound engine dramatically reduced the amount of coal needed to drive a ship across the Atlantic.

Within Henry's lifetime, steamships replaced sailing ships in carrying cargoes on even the longest ocean voyages. With a smaller crew the screw-propeller steamship came to make three voyages for every one made by a sailing ship. The opening of the Suez Canal in 1869 further doomed sail.

"The beautiful 'White Wings' of old are fast disappearing before the dirty, ugly 'Machines' of our day," wrote Henry.[2]

He knew whereof he wrote. As he was penning his *Essays* recalling the economic progress that had occurred during his lifetime, he was compiling information for his book *The History of North Atlantic Steam Navigation*. The Farnham and Sweetsburg post offices must have experienced a torrent of letters going out and coming in as Henry pursued his research.

In the beginning, his history was to be a work circulated privately among a "few old friends" in the shipping and shipbuilding business. The few old friends — including his Cacouna neighbour Andrew Allan, chief of the Ocean Steamship Company — urged him to arrange for the work's publication. *The History of North Atlantic Steam Navigation* went on press in London in 1896 — a 325-page book with more than fifty illustrations that is still referenced by maritime historians today.[3]

THE HISTORY

OF

NORTH ATLANTIC STEAM NAVIGATION

WITH SOME ACCOUNT OF EARLY SHIPS AND SHIPOWNERS

BY

HENRY FRY

EX-PRESIDENT OF DOMINION BOARD OF TRADE OF CANADA
AND LLOYD'S AGENT AT QUEBEC

"They that go down to the sea in ships, that do business in great waters; These see the works of the Lord, and his wonders in the deep. For he commandeth and raiseth the stormy wind, which lifteth up the waves thereof. . . . He maketh the storm a calm, so that the waves thereof are still. Then are they glad because they be quiet, so he bringeth them unto their desired haven."—*Psalm* cvii. 23-30.

WITH OVER FIFTY ILLUSTRATIONS OF SHIPS
AND PORTRAITS OF OWNERS

LONDON
SAMPSON LOW, MARSTON AND COMPANY
LIMITED
St. Dunstan's House
FETTER LANE, FLEET STREET, E.C.
1896

A major reference work: *Henry's crowning literary achievement,* The History of North Atlantic Steam Navigation, *was published in 1896, the year of his death. The book, reprinted as recently as 2008, is still in use by maritime researchers.*

Never one to back away from controversy, Henry, in the book's first chapter, "Early Navigators," resumes the argument about who discovered North America (see chapter 2 of this book). Relying on the writings of Sebastian Cabot, the son of John Cabot, Henry concludes that the Cabots not only discovered the Gulf of St. Lawrence thirty-eight years before Jacques Cartier, but that they were the first to explore the eastern shore of what would become the United States, a place that Columbus never saw. In effect, Henry was thumbing his nose at both French Canadians, for whom Cartier is a virtual patron saint, and at Americans — Italian or not — who annually celebrate Columbus's discovery of their country. Henry's failure is that later researchers found Sebastian Cabot to be an inveterate fibber, a boastful exaggerator of his own and his father's explorations.[4]

Henry, however, was accurate in another matter — the historical claim that the U.S.-built *Savannah* was the first steamship to cross the Atlantic. It was. But in 1819 the *Savannah* crossed mostly under sail, the engine powering her paddlewheels for only eighty hours of the twenty-nine days it took her to reach England. "As an Atlantic steamship, she was a complete failure," concludes Henry, a merciless critic of the *Savannah*'s alleged accomplishment.

The honour of building the first ship to make a trans-oceanic voyage entirely under steam belongs not to the United States, wrote Henry, but to Canada. In 1831, the wooden-hulled *Royal William*, 364 tons and 160 feet long, was launched in Cape Cove under the Plains of Abraham in a crowd-drawing ceremony headed by the governor general, Lord Aylmer, and his wife. Its engines were built and installed in Montreal. Carrying 330 tons of coal for fuel, the *Royal William* steamed out of Quebec port in August 1833, re-coaling in Nova Scotia and the Isle of Wight in the English Channel, before reaching Gravesend, London — twenty-five days at sea wholly propelled by steam.

One man impressed by the *Royal William*'s achievement was Samuel Cunard, born of a family of Empire Loyalists who'd left Philadelphia after the American Revolution and moved to Halifax. Cunard bought a share in the *Royal William*, convinced that steam was the future of ocean navigation. "The Cunard Line and its Competitors" forms the longest chapter in *The History of North Atlantic Steam Navigation*. Henry writes about "the most remarkable and successful shipping line the world has ever seen."

The first Cunard "liner," the 210-foot wood-hulled *Britannia*, equipped with Napier engines, in 1840 crossed from Liverpool to Halifax and Boston in two weeks time, consuming thirty-eight tons of coal per day. Fifty years later, Cunard was operating monster steamships — "floating palaces" — crossing the Atlantic in five and a half days, carrying as many as two thousand passengers with sumptuous accommodations for first-class ticket holders. So efficient was the mail service facilitated by high-speed liners that a letter posted in London on a Monday would reach its New York addressee the following Monday, only twice the time now taken for airmail.

The discipline and punctuality of the Cunard service awed Henry: "To anyone who, like the writer, was in the habit of sailing these ships … never was seen discipline more perfect, or order more complete."

The captains on the bridge were the very *crème de la crème* of the British mercantile service, he wrote:

> Brave, bold, watchful, cautious, and stern, they were also, with perhaps one or two exceptions, accomplished gentlemen. Punctuality was always a marked feature of the management, and justly very highly prized. Cunard ships sailed not only to the day and hour, but to the minute. Before eight bells were all struck the lunch or dinner bell was heard; and for many years the British public looked for their American and Canadian letter on Monday morning as regularly as those by an express train.

Henry especially admired Cunard's practice of not allowing safety to be compromised by speed. Other shipping lines were neither as prudent nor as lucky. In the lower St. Lawrence reefs, ice and fog, fatally combined with poor piloting and lack of navigational aids, wrecked vessels. Compasses may have been affected by large deposits of iron ore on the north shore of the Gulf, not discovered and mined until the twentieth century. In *North Atlantic Steam Navigation*, Henry chronicles the history of tragic ship sinkings that occurred during the last half of the nineteenth century in North Atlantic crossings. The year 1854 alone saw the loss of as many as eight hundred lives, more than half the number who would go down on the *Titanic*.

In 1860, the steamship *Hungarian*, in a gale, misinterpreted a light off Cape Sable, Nova Scotia, and ran ashore; not one of the 237 people aboard survived. During its first years in the 1850s, the Allan line lost eight ships in eight seasons. In thick weather in March 1873, the White Star Line's *Atlantic* ran ashore off Halifax with the loss of 560 souls, mostly in steerage; in November, that typically storm-ridden month when Henry first crossed the Atlantic on the sailing ship *Cosmo*, the French steamship *Ville de Havre*, outward bound from New York, collided with an iron sailing ship, resulting in the loss of 226 lives. A year later, in 1874, the Inman Line's *City of Glasgow*, with 480 persons on board, left Liverpool for New York and was never heard from again. In September of the same year, the Collins Line's *Arctic* collided with another ship off Newfoundland, drowning all but 35 of the 368 passengers and crew. In fog in the Scilly Islands off England's southwest shore in May 1875, the Eagle Line's *Schiller* was wrecked, causing 331 passengers to drown.

All of these tragedies occurred during a twenty-three-year period when Henry made eighteen round trips by steamship from North America to England, usually during the worst weather between November and February.[5]

The loss of life and injury from shipwrecks was devastating for the crews aboard and for their families. British and Canadian governments did little to provide for retiring merchant seamen in their old age, or in sickness or, in the case of their drowning, for their widows and orphans. The social injustice predictably angered Henry, who uses a chapter of *North Atlantic Steam Navigation* to express his outrage:

> What is the fate of the aged or infirm [merchant] seaman? When he is unfit for further sea service, either by age or by accident, or by his dread enemy rheumatism, he is the most helpless being alive. There is nothing left for him but the parish "workhouse" with all its horrors, and a pauper's grave. Should the seaman die as a result of an accident or drowning at sea, his widow and children are thrown

helpless on the world, to eke out a miserable existence as best they can. It is not only the "man before the mast" who thus suffers. Scores of respectable old shipmasters may be seen in the leading seaports, who accept a guinea a week or even less, as night watchman on idle ships; and when this fails, driven to despair by want, a few of them take the final plunge into the river or the dock. This is no fancy picture. The author has seen it all in real life and vouches for its truthfulness.[6]

In his *Reminiscences*, he describes voyages in which he experienced terrifying gales, near-collisions, iceberg sightings, and dense fog.

Even though each trip he took was potentially perilous, nothing in Henry's writing suggests fear. Repeatedly he expresses confidence in the skilled seamanship of the masters and crews. "The numerous fatal accidents described in this work may create the erroneous impression as to the perils of the sea," he observes in the final chapter of *The History of North Atlantic Steam Navigation*. Especially after 1880, the incidents of tragic losses declined in relation to the volume of ships and passengers.

"Many predicted that increased speed must produce increased loss of life," writes Henry. "The record of the past few years does not bear out this opinion." In the 1880s, a 43.6 percent traffic increase was accompanied by a 28 percent decrease in lives lost. In 1890, 200,000 cabin and 372,000 steerage passengers crossed from New York to various European ports without a single fatality.*

In the fifty years from 1840 to 1890, the speed of Atlantic steamships trebled, from eight to twenty-three knots. Reaching as high as twenty-seven miles an hour, ship speed was unlikely to go much higher, predicted Henry in 1896. Even so, he did not see faster travel as a necessity. "There is a craze among passengers for speed, which amounts to a mild form of insanity." With the fast communication made possible by cable, there was no longer a real necessity for speed, he reasoned.

---

* Sixteen years after publication of *The History of North Atlantic Steam Navigation*, in 1912 the *Titanic* collided with an iceberg and sank, with 1,517 lives lost. Henry was not alone among experts in failing to predict the possibility of such a steamship disaster. But two years after the *Titanic*, he would not have been surprised by an almost comparable disaster on the St. Lawrence River near Rimouski, when the luxury liner *Empress of Ireland* collided with a Norwegian vessel on a foggy night, May 29, 1914, and sank, with the loss of 1,012 lives.

Indeed he anticipated the future of steamship travel. "A long sea passage is desirable, both on the score of health and enjoyment," he wrote. Today the world's largest passenger ship, Royal Caribbean Cruise Lines *Allure of the Seas* typically moves across the water not much faster than steamships did at the time Henry was writing *The History of North Atlantic Steam Navigation*. Modern passengers are not paying thousands of dollars to shorten the time to their destination, but rather for leisurely enjoyment and health, as Henry anticipated.

Notman Collection, McCord Museum, MP-0000.25.932.

Warning to the government: *In 1892, Henry wrote a letter to future prime minister Wilfrid Laurier, warning about the Conservative government's potential folly of subsidizing a non-Canadian company's operation of a weekly high-speed steamship service on the treacherous St. Lawrence River.*

Nevertheless, in the late nineteenth century the craze for speed drove operators of packet ships to inflate promises of the service they could provide in return for government-subsidized, trans-oceanic mail carrying. Henry was wary. In 1894, he took time out from writing *The History of North Atlantic Steam Navigation* to write a letter to Liberal Party chief Wilfrid Laurier, the opposition leader in Ottawa. The reigning Conservative government was entertaining a bid from the Australian steamship operator James Huddart, who claimed that in return for a subsidy of three-quarters of a million dollars annually, Huddart could provide weekly steamship service between England and Canada at a speed of not less than twenty knots. The Australian's promise, he told Laurier, was full of "fearful risk for a very doubtful advantage." The St. Lawrence River is one of the world's most treacherous ship passages — in places "a succession of sunken reefs, shoals and flats, to say nothing of snowstorms, ice and fog. Mr. Huddart knows nothing from personal experience of the St. Lawrence, or of the difficulties and dangers of its navigation. He resides some 9,000 to 12,000 miles from the scene."[7]

Huddart's bid, though, received a sympathetic hearing in Ottawa, which had recently hosted the Colonial Conference aimed at encouraging trade among Australia, New Zealand, and Canada. Huddart's Canadian-Australian Steamship line already operated a subsidized service between New South Wales and British Columbia. From there a person could travel by train to Canada's east coast, and board a liner for England, proving it possible to traverse the western continent without stepping on American soil. It was a transportation concept chauvinistically appealing to the Conservatives, whose 1891 election victory under Macdonald was partly based on public fear that U.S. trade dependency could lead eventually to political annexation. Laurier, on the other hand, entertained no such fear. He saw robust north-south trade with the United States as healthy for Canada.

While Henry applauded the fostering of Canadian trade with Australia, New Zealand, and the Far East ("It will add to the prestige of Canada, and promote the unity, security and prosperity of the whole Empire"), it didn't follow in his mind that Canada should subsidize the Australian to operate the service from Montreal and Quebec to England. Rather it should be entrusted to an experienced Canadian operator like the Allan Line that was familiar with St. Lawrence navigation and pilots. The government five years earlier had foolishly rejected an Allan bid. By default, New York picked up Quebec's loss of traffic. In the end nothing came of the Huddart bid, and the drain of traffic to New York continued.

Laurier, whose riding was Quebec East, presumably appreciated Henry's letter confirming his own views about the Conservatives' errant judgment. Two years later, he became prime minister when the Liberals narrowly won the 1896 election. Henry would not live to witness the triumph of his fellow Quebecer.

27

1896
Voyage End

A head-and-shoulders photograph of Henry made on July 19, 1892, shows a man gazing, if not at a physical horizon, at a sober or defining scene present in his mind.[1] After sixty-six years his beard has gone from black to silvery white; it has thinned since William Notman photographed him twenty years earlier in Montreal. His broad sloping forehead is bald, but the crown has lost little of the hair that grew in 1872. He is wearing a high-lapelled jacket buttoned at the top, his neck adorned with a cravat, something between a modern tie and an ascot. His lips are pursed, the jaw and mouth expressing determination.

Two months previously, Henry's eldest son, Henry Jr., had married Laura Stevenson of Quebec in the city's Holy Trinity Anglican Cathedral. The *Daily Mercury* of May 2, 1892, recorded "a large gathering of the elite of Quebec society to witness the nuptials of Henry Fry, the son of Mr. Henry Fry, formerly a lumber merchant of this city, and Miss Laura, youngest daughter of Mr. James Stevenson, General Manager of the Quebec Bank. Mr. Stevenson gave his daughter away." William Fry, twenty-eight, the groom's brother, was best man. Among the invited guests were the Honourable H.G. and Mme. Joly de Lotbinière, he the former premier of Quebec, and Mr. and Mrs. W.M. Price of the illustrious lumber and paper mill–owning family.

Neither Henry, the father of the groom, nor Mary, the mother, are listed as present at the nuptial. Why absent? In their minds may have been the memory of Henry's interdiction ten years earlier from transacting business in Quebec, and the fact that the interdiction technically had never been lifted.

Quebec City, in any event, had become a place of the past. The year before the wedding, Mary gave up renting out the family's three-storey row house on Dufferin Terrace, and sold the property for $6,218.63. She'd owned the building since 1861. Today it's a small hotel wonderfully located on the cliff above a point on the river where cruise ships dock in the summer months, disgorging thousands of tourists into Lower Town.

The contents of the house — silverware, china, chests, sideboards, dining table, piano, sofas, a chess and card tables, a barometer, numerous engravings, and ten oil paintings, several by Krieghoff — were dispersed to the children who'd grown up in the house over a twenty-year period.[2] Possibly the books found their way to the cottage on Fort Street in Montreal, or down to the Eastern Townships where Henry was living.

Sometime between 1892 and 1894 occurred what may have been the happiest event in Henry's life. He and Mary reunited. After a painful separation of at least a dozen years, a tranquility of spirit, a peace of mind, had returned to Henry. His terrible turmoil was ended. Mary, sensing it, looked for a place where the couple could live, not distant from Henry's physician, Dr. Slack.

Sweetsburg is part of Cowansville today, but at that time it was a separate municipality, a rail centre, possessing a courthouse that was the judicial centre for Missisquoi, Brome, and Shefford counties. In Sweetsburg, twenty-seven years earlier, three Fenians captured in an 1866 cross-Vermont raid had been sentenced to die by hanging.[3] There was a bucolic charm to the area, with lovely vistas of the Eastern Township hills. A.Y. Jackson of the renowned Group of Seven painters lived in Sweetsburg, where he composed the oil *The Edge of Maple Wood* in 1910.

One of the town's leading citizens, Frederick T. Hall, in 1880 built himself a mansion to which he gave the august name Belmont. It was a three-storey building, less distinguished architecturally than other homes built by Sweetsburg's wealthier residents, but sturdy and functional. The rooms had twelve-foot ceilings, and were heated by coal on grates in grey marbled fireplaces. By 1885 Mr. Hall's wife made part of it into a school for young ladies.

When Hall died in 1892, Belmont was sold to J. Robertson of Montreal. Mary and Henry may have known Robertson, who offered the building's spacious rooms for rent, and so the couple took up lodging at Belmont House.[4]

Life was almost back to normal. The stigma of his psychiatric problems, which might have attached to his reputation, was gone. Society saw again a man in full — a retired successful merchant and an internationally acknowledged authority on maritime history. Henry wrote an article on Quebec shipbuilding for the May 1895 issue of the *The Canadian*. The two-year-old monthly magazine about politics, science, art, and literature was a *Walrus* or *Saturday Night* of its day, publishing articles "descriptive of various portions of the Dominion, and dealing with their scenery and resources, from the pens of travellers and well-known and graceful writers." In the same issue as Henry's piece on Quebec shipbuilding were an article on the Underground Railroad for escaping slaves during the Civil War; an article on early Canadian artists in which Krieghoff is dismissed as a minor if popular painter; essays on the work of Robert Louis Stevenson; and a half-dozen short stories and poems.[5]

By the end of March 1895, Henry completed the writing of *Lloyd's: Its Origin, History and Methods* (see chapter 5). With a possible prod from his brother-in-law Sam Dawson, Dawson & Co. published it as a twenty-eight-page booklet, and *The Gazette* in Montreal positively reviewed it on June 28, 1895: "Mr. Fry, who was in charge for Lloyd's of the St. Lawrence River from Sorel all the way to the Gaspé, gives a vivid account of the business methods of Lloyd's [the system of registration, rewards for saving lives, salvaging rules, and more].... Those who read it, however experienced they may be," kindly observed the newspaper, "will certainly know more of Lloyd's history and methods than they ever knew before."[6]

In 1896, the British publisher Sampson Low, Marston and Company, St. Dunstan's House, London, published Henry's *The History of North Atlantic Steam Navigation, with Some Account of Early Ships and Shipowners, with Over Fifty Illustrations of Ships and Portraits of Owners*. The *Montreal Gazette* in January 1896 gave the book a two-thumbs-up review:

The task of writing the history of one of the most important developments of an age fertile in inventions and discoveries fell to one who was admirably fitted for it, both by innate gifts and leanings, and a life's experience in the Maritime business. For many years the author was the agent of Lloyd's at Quebec, while his election to the office of President of the Dominion Board of Trade bears witness to the high opinion of his knowledge and judgment entertained by his leading fellow citizens.[7]

The editorial praise came just in time for the author to savour. A few weeks after it appeared, Henry Fry died in Sweetsburg. The date was February 27, 1896. It was the end of a life of nearly seventy years stretching across a momentous period of economic growth derived from the huge expansion of trade between Europe and North America across the North Atlantic, which Henry himself had fostered and chronicled.

No cause of death was given.[8] Henry's body was transported to Montreal, and was buried on a stormy winter's day in the Mount Royal Cemetery.[9] The cemetery then, and now, is the most imposing in Montreal. It first opened in 1852, designed with winding paths, trees, bushes, and ponds — "more like a park than just a burial park," writes Quebec historian Rod McLeod. "The living were welcomed to picnic and stroll through its leafy glades. In imported New England fashion, it was Montreal's first park."[10]

Mount Royal Cemetery's topology somewhat mirrors the social stratification of the mostly anglophone community whose remains lie under its gravestones. The loftier the family, the higher its members are buried in the cemetery, just as in life the higher their homes had been on Westmount Mountain. The Fry plot is a modest three-quarters of the way up to the highest point. And there Henry resides to this day.

Among the debts listed in his estate at the time of his death was one of $117.50 to Dr. George Slack. Having cared for him when he first arrived in Farnham, Dr. Slack was still serving as his doctor when Henry died in 1896. It was not a year Slack was likely ever to forget. At age forty-nine, he'd decided to take a byway out of medicine and run for Parliament as a Conservative in the riding of Missisquoi. Four months after Henry's death, he was defeated in the June 1896 election by a margin of 261 votes, earning a respectable 46.5 percent of the electorate's approval. It was perhaps a blessing for Missisquoi citizens, to say nothing of Henry, had he been alive, that Slack didn't make it to Ottawa. Later in the same year, he was arraigned in court, accused of forging his sister's name on a power of attorney. On November 27, reported the *New York Times*, despite the pleadings of friends and relatives, the judge sentenced the good doctor to twenty-three months in prison.[11] Henry's physician was placed in a Montreal communal jail where he served out his term administering to the sick in the infirmary. He died in 1918.

Joyous as Mary's and Henry's late-in-life reunion should have been, misfortune continued to dog them. Their only daughter, Mame, now thirty-six years old, had long suffered from tuberculosis. For a time she had been treated at the famous TB sanitarium at Saranac Lake in the Adirondack Mountains of northern New York State, where Robert Louis Stevenson was a patient. Henry and Mary decided to bring Mame to live with them in Sweetsburg. After Henry's death, Mary accompanied her daughter to Montreal. On the night of their arrival in the city, May 8, 1896, Mame passed away in the Windsor Hotel. Within two months, Mary had been battered by the tragic loss of her only daughter and of her husband of thirty-eight years.

At the time of Henry's death, Mary had $755.87 in cash at the Eastern Townships Bank in Cowansville. She was a modestly wealthy woman. She owned the cottage at Cacouna, and the Montreal house at 66 McTavish Street, which she was renting out for fifty-four dollars a month plus taxes while she was living in Sweetsburg. She had loaned money to Henry Jr. to buy the adjoining property at 64 McTavish. She owned at least two more homes, plus property-secured, interest-bearing loans that she had made to acquaintances.

Her relations with her brother-in-law Edward Fry, her husband's former business partner, remained strained.[12] In 1885 Mary had released Edward from claims relating to the business of Henry Fry & Co. while she took from him rights in the government-leased cove at Sillery known as Fry's and Bowen's Cove — thirty-six acres, including wharves, piers, tenements, and other buildings. Richard Reid Dobell, who had operated the cove, acquired Henry's interest.[13]

When Henry's mind had collapsed, his eldest son, not Edward, was put to work settling his father's affairs. Henry Fry Jr. took a year off from his notarial studies at McGill to go to Quebec to conduct the work. After Henry's death, Justice Lynch ordered that Henry Fry Jr., notary, and Arthur Dawson Fry, clerk, be appointed trustees for the estate of Henry Fry. Edward C. Fry was removed as a trustee. There's not much question that Mary was behind the legal action.

She was at that time back in Montreal, where she would spend the remaining thirty-five years of her life. The city was booming. Her brother Sam Dawson captured the scene earlier: "Montreal seems to know no barriers to progress. They are tearing down what is left of the old town. The hand of the Philistine is heavy. Landmark after landmark is gone or has suffered the last indignity of restoration."[14]

Mary continued to summer in Cacouna. As a dutiful widow, she wore black, as had her Queen Victoria after the death of Albert, Prince Consort. Even in the summer heat, Mary was clothed in a long black dress covering her shoes. The author's cousin Mary Dawson Fry recalls as a child lifting the hem of her great-grandmother's dress to confirm that she indeed possessed feet.

Eventually Mary moved to an apartment on Montreal's Sherbrooke Street West across from the Museum of Fine Arts. From her art collection, she gave to the museum the Cornelius Krieghoff oil *Indian Hunter in the Forest*, painted in 1856.[15] Children and grandchildren, even great-grandchildren, came to visit over the years.

"She was a true Victorian matriarch," wrote a grand-niece, "generous and affectionate, although strong in her likes and dislikes. She was blessed with a philosophical outlook, perhaps developed from necessity."[16] Afternoon teas in her Montreal apartment were formal, recalled her grandson Edmond. Conversation comfortably dealt with the outward appearances of things. Deeper, disturbing issues did not belong in the colloquy. By the time she was ninety, she'd lost her oldest son, Henry, and two grandsons to accidents and suicide. Tragedy dogged her, but she didn't allow it to scratch the surface of a life of good manners and good deeds. Finally, at the age of ninety-six, this talented woman — skilled in business, mother to seven children, bearer of sorrows — died in Montreal on April 10, 1932. Her remains were reunited alongside Henry's in the Mount Royal Cemetery, where they lie today.

Conclusion

The rise and fall of Henry's fortunes almost exactly followed the trajectory of wooden shipbuilding in Quebec. After his arrival there, the volume of new ships built in Quebec yards soared from 25,791 tons in 1855 to a peak in 1864 of 54,714 tons — sixty of the ships being of more than a hundred tons. These were years of prosperity and intense industry. But after 1864 the construction of wooden vessels began to decline. By 1877, when Henry fell ill, the amount of ships built in Quebec, including the *Cosmo*, had fallen to as little as 17,908 tons. By the time he died, the industry too had died. The last wooden ship of more than a hundred tons built in Quebec, *White Wings*, slipped into the water in 1893,[1] three years before Henry's death. Most of what was left of Canadian wooden shipbuilding continued into the twentieth century in the Maritime provinces, where schooners were built for the coastal trade. But in Quebec, as Henry wrote in 1895, "Wooden ship building is dead beyond recall; the yards are deserted; and every trade in the Ancient City feels it deeply."[2]

Henry Fry was a member of a small, prosperous crowd of Victorian bankers and merchants who reigned economically over Quebec, a major seaport of the world in the nineteenth century during a brief unique period in the city's history when it was not dominantly francophone. The ships, the yards, the offices, and all the accessory industries of which he was a part have vanished along with the men who built the great wooden ships and filled their holds with cargo to be sold abroad. They long ago fled, leaving Quebec a place of government, education, and tourism. A Canada whose primary fealty was to the British Crown is today as nonexistent as the great billowing sails that once made the St. Lawrence River's surface glitter like silver.

Henry's nineteenth-century business success serves as a reminder that Britain's eighteenth-century victory on the Plains of Abraham was not a conquest of destruction, but rather presaged a recovery from the economic ruins of French colonial rule. The nineteenth-century economic stimulus for Lower Canada came from men like Henry with close mercantile ties to England. Their eyes remained fixed eastward across the Atlantic, while tens of thousands of immigrants coursed through the portal of Quebec, their eyes turned westward to an alternative future.

Henry correctly foresaw that the Canadian economy would be driven by U.S. trade relations. He anticipated the possibility of economic domination from the south and feared it could lead to Canada's annexation. That did not happen, but another kind of fusion, which might be less kindly described as a cultural miscegenation, took place. Canada's ties to the mother country withered with the decline and collapse of the British Empire in the first half of the twentieth century. It was followed in the second half of the century by the collapse of the spiritual pillar of Quebec culture, the Roman Catholic Church. Into the resulting void poured, like a tsunami, a wave of U.S. consumer products and culture. A brutal architecture of hotels and commercial structures came to scar the skyline of the city that once was Henry's beloved home, while mail-order Levittown houses grew like a rash in its suburbs. Laws aimed at protecting Quebec's francophone heritage proved a frail barrier against the pervasive, powerful conquest by secular materialism from the south, an infection of film, music, fast food, and big-box store shopping that engulfed not just Quebec but the rest of the world. Religiously inspired philanthropy, both Catholic and Protestant, was replaced by government agencies to aid the indigent and ill. Henry's generous, paternalistic, ad-hoc charity in rescuing the city's unemployed poor seems quaint by comparison.

He was in some ways a caricature of the popularly derided anglophone who dominated business and the technical professions of Quebec until the 1970s. Impersonal corporations — at least half of the largest

having their corporate headquarters in Ontario and the United States —
have mostly supplanted the nineteenth century's wealthy merchants. Men
like Henry were profoundly and intimately engaged with the community,
compared to the remote control of owners in Toronto and New York.
His influence was not *in absentia*. He dwelt in Quebec, and cared deeply
about the welfare of the people and the city that had embraced him when
he first arrived from England. He worried to his dying day about the fate
of Canada in North America, and his knowledge of ships and the St.
Lawrence River is securely woven into the nation's history.

Henry's depression in the 1880s may have been exacerbated by
his doctors' misguided use of narcotics. It's easy to speculate that his
collapse could have been prevented, or at least mitigated, by expert
twentieth-century pharmacology. No doubt his illness would have
been less of a social liability today. Bipolar disorder and depression are
no longer secrets demanding concealment by families.

Henry Fry's life serves as a reminder that success can be a hair's-
breadth distant from ruin, yet a life once in ruin may end exultantly.

Notes

Preface

1. Frederick William Wallace, *Wooden Ships and Iron Men* (London and Toronto: Hodder and Stoughton, Ltd), 4; also see page 271 of Henry Fry's *The History of North Atlantic Steam Navigation* (London, Sampson Low, Marston & Company, 1896) for leading ship-owning nations in 1894, when Canada was fourth in sail and ranked sixth overall.
2. Mason Wade, *The French-Canadian Outlook: A Brief Account of the Unknown North Americans* (Toronto: Macmillan, 1955), 39.
3. The second battle, the Battle of Sainte-Foy, took place in 1760, a year after the better known Battle of the Plains of Abraham.
4. Census Report of Canada, 1861, City of Quebec.
5. Eileen Marcil, "A Project to Write a Biography of Henry Fry," 1991.
6. Wallace, *Wooden Ships and Iron Men*, 97.

Chapter 1

1. Narcisse Rosa, *La construction des navires à Québec et ses environs, grèves et naufrages* (Quebec: Éditions Léger Brousseau, 1897). *Le contre-maître donne d'abord ordre d'enlever les clefs qui retiennent le navire et celui-ci*

n'étant plus retenu par rien, descend sur les lisses et coule majestueuse-
ment sur les flots. Alors les ouvriers font retentir les airs de leurs hourras,
et ils se rendent à une table servie sur le chantier mêm pour y déguster le
fromage assaisonné d'un peu de bière et de propos joyeux.

2. Eileen Marcil, email to the author, November 23, 2011.
3. Eileen Marcil, *The Charley-Man: A History of Wooden Shipbuilding at*
   Quebec, 1763–1893 (Kingston, ON: Quarry Press, 1995), Appendix B.
4. Henry Fry, *Reminiscences of a Retired Ship Owner* (handwritten book
   in the possession of the author), 1891.
5. Portraits of Henry and Mary Fry by Notman are viewable online at
   the archive of Montreal's McCord Museum: *www.mccordmuseum.*
   qc.ca.
6. Frederick William Wallace, *In the Wake of the Wind-Ships* (Toronto:
   The Musson Book Company Limited, 1927), 101.
7. Eileen Marcil, *The Charley-Man*, definition of burden, 365.
8. The model of the *Cosmo* can be seen today by visitors to Quebec's
   Morrin Centre, home of the Literary and Historical Society. The art
   presently hangs in the author's home, with the *Cosmo*'s hull created
   from wool, the sails of paper, the lines of silk, against a painted sea
   and sky.
9. Henry Fry, *Reminiscences*.
10. Ibid.
11. "Proceedings at the Semi-Annual Meeting of the Dominion Board
    of Trade, Saint John, New Brunswick, July 1874."
12. Undated photocopy of article in *Quebec Mercury*, supplied by
    Kenneth S. Mackenzie.
13. Henry Fry, *Essays on Free Trade and Protection, British Statesmen,*
    Lloyd's, Cycles in Trade, Commercial Union and Reciprocity (papers
    placed in the Thomas Fisher Rare Book Library, University of
    Toronto, 1890).
14. Henry Fry, *Reminiscences*. The book contains a list detailing (dates of
    departure and arrival, name of ship and line) of every North Atlantic
    crossing the author made.
15. Edward married Elizabeth Marsh, a daughter of the Reverend David
    Marsh.
16. Henry Fry, *Reminiscences*.

Chapter 2

1. Samuel Eliot Morison, *The European Discovery of America* (New York: Oxford University Press, 1971).
2. Henry Fry, *Notes on England, Wales, Scotland, Ireland & Paris (for a Young Canadian) with Sketches of Typical Sailing & Steamships*, 1891, 58–63. Copy of handwritten book owned by the author.
3. Description based on the author's one-week visit to Winscombe and Somerset in 2004.
4. White's map of Barton in Winscombe Parish in 1792.
5. *Liber Albus* (White Book describing the laws and customs pertaining to the cathedral).
6. Christopher Fry, *Can You Find Me: A Family History* (New York: Oxford University Press, 1978).
7. Francis Knight, *Heart of Mendip*, first published 1915, re-published 1970.
8. Early in the seventeenth century, the Fry family dropped the *e* from its name. Henry had a forebear born Frye in 1593, but by the time the man died in 1665, having lived through Cromwell's abolition of the monarchy, his will is under the name of George Fry, yeoman. It would suggest he was a minor farmer cultivating his own land, belonging to a class of English freeholders below the gentry. George bequeathed the family's Barton property in Winscombe parish to his son William, and a half-century later, in 1716, the son of that William left to his children properties which included a dwelling house, orchard, and garden in Winscombe, and four and a half acres in nearby Loxton. Sources: Christopher Fry, Frances Knight, Maria Forbes, and Norman Davies.
9. The same coat of arms is etched on the forks, knives, and spoons of the author's silverware, transported to North America and replicated by a Montreal silversmith. Much about the Fry family origins are not included here. At the Society of Genealogists in London, according to Somerset historian Margaret Jordan, are nine boxes of Fry records, plus thirty-two bound volumes containing Fry parish records. The greatest authority on the family's history is the late Norman Davies of Newbury, England.

10. Genealogical information furnished to the author by Norman Davies of Newbury, England, and by Maria Forbes of Maxmills, Barton.

11. In the Bristol rolls, Number 2 Prince's Street was listed as a dwelling house and shop belonging to Andrew Goss and occupied by George Fry, value twenty-four pounds.

12. *www.brigstowe.pwp.blueyonder.co.uk/riots.htm.*

13. Henry Fry, *Reminiscences.*

14. Donald Creighton, *The Young Macdonald*, 15.

15. *A Cyclopaedia of Canadian Biography*, a biography of Edward Carey Fry (Toronto, Rose Publishing Co., 1888).

Chapter 3

1. Henry wrote that the honour of being the first ship to cross the Atlantic under steam belonged to the Quebec-built paddle-wheel-equipped *Royal William* in 1831, although the ship had to shut down its engine from time to time to clean its boilers. The U.S.-built *Savannah* crossed in 1820 with an engine but mostly powered by sail (see chapter 26 of this book); see also John Maxtone Graham, *The Only Way to Cross.*

2. Henry Fry, *History of North Atlantic Steam Navigation*, 38.

3. Ibid., 41.

4. Confession to the Baptist Church of Christ at Broadmead, 1855, furnished from the church's records by Dr. Roger Hayden of Bristol.

5. Ibid.

6. Henry Fry, *Essays.*

7. Isambard Kingdom Brunel and the Great Western Railway, *www. historynet.com/isambard-kingdom-brunel.*

8. Henry Fry, *Reminiscences.*

9. Ibid.

10. Henry Fry, *Essays*, 273.

11. Henry Fry, *Reminiscences.*

12. Basil Greenhill and Ann Giffard, *Westcountrymen in Prince Edward's Isle* (Halifax: Formac Publishing Company Limited,

2003). Nicholas De Jong and Marven Moore, *Shipbuilding in Prince Edward Island, 1787–1920* (published by Canadian Museum of Civilization).

13. Henry Fry, *Reminiscences.*
14. Ibid.
15. Janet Browne, *Charles Darwin: The Power of Place* (New York: Alfred A. Knopf, 2002), 236.
16. *Diagnostic and Statistical Manual of Mental Disorders, Third Edition* (American Psychiatric Association).
17. Henry Fry, *Reminiscences.*
18. Ric Burns, *New York: An Illustrated History* (New York: Knopf Doubleday, 2003).

Chapter 4

1. Henry Fry, "Shipbuilding in Quebec City," *The Canadian Magazine*, May 1895.
2. Charles Dickens, *American Notes for General Circulation* (1842).
3. Michael George Mulhall, *Industries and Wealth of Nations: Canada*, 316. Over the frontier to the United States proceeded 1,310,000 people, while 1,115,000 remained in Canada.
4. William Wood, editor-in-chief, "Unique Quebec," in *The Storied Province of Quebec*, vol. 1 (Toronto: Dominion Publishing Company, 1931), 167.
5. Eileen Marcil, *The Charley-Man.*
6. Arthur M. Lower, *Great Britain's Woodyard: British America and the Timber Trade* (Montreal and London: McGill-Queen's University Press, 1973).
7. William Wood, *The Storied Province of Quebec*, vol. 1, 172.
8. Eileen Marcil, *The Charley-Man*; Wallace, *Wooden Ships and Iron Men*; Baron of Renfrew, Wikipedia.
9. George Gale, *Historic Tales of Old Quebec*, 148.
10. Eileen Marcil, *The Charley-Man*, 44.
11. Louisa Blair, *The Anglos: The Hidden Face of Quebec City*, vol. 2, 22.
12. Eileen Marcil, *The Charley-Man* (Appendix), 363.

13. Rev. John Alexander, *Biographical Sketch of the Late Rev. David Marsh*, 1888.

14. Henry Fry, tribute to Henry Marsh, 1889.

15. P.L.Gauvreau, *Navigating the Lower Saint Lawrence in the 19th Century*. Furnished to the author by Gilbert Bosse, Métis.

Chapter 5

1. Henry Fry, *Reminiscences*.

2. Henry Fry, *History of North Atlantic Steam Navigation*, 121.

3. Henry Fry, *Reminiscences*.

4. Ibid.

5. Ibid.

6. Confession to the Baptist Church of Christ at Broadmead, 1855, furnished from the church's records by Dr. Roger Hayden of Bristol.

7. Henry Fry, *Reminiscences*.

8. Art Cohn, Lake Champlain Maritime Museum. Email to the author, October 30, 2008.

9. Henry Fry, *Reminiscences*.

10. Henry Fry, *Lloyd's: Its Origin, History and Methods* (Quebec: Dawson & Co., 1895).

11. Eileen Marcil timeline.

12. For example, 1871, *Princess of Wales* wreck; 1872, *Pride of England*. Marcil timeline.

Chapter 6

1. Quebec did not serve long as the capital. The following year, 1857, Queen Victoria chose Ottawa as Canada's permanent capital.

2. Henry Fry, *Reminiscences*.

3. Eileen Marcil, *The Charley-Man*, Appendix B.

4. Testimony of David Gilmour before the Inspector and Superintendent of Police, Quebec, October 18, 1856.

Office of the Inspector and Superintendent of Police, Quebec, 18th October, 1856. Sir,— His Excellency the Governor General having had his attention called to the letter of Henry Fry, Esq., Lloyd's Agent at this port, published in the London "Times" in September, complaining of outrages committed by crimps at Quebec, has directed me to investigate these charges, in order to ascertain, for the information of His Excellency, how far they can be verified by the condition of things at this port.

I beg therefore to request that you will have the goodness to communicate to me, in writing, at your earliest convenience, all that you know on the subject of such outrages.

I have the honor to be, Sir,
Your most obedient servant,
[Signed] J. Maguire,
Inspector and Superintendent of Police

5. Judith Fingard, *Jack in Port* (Toronto: University of Toronto Press, 1982), 200.
6. Editorial, "The Crimping System: How It Is Fostered," *Quebec Mercury*, May 28, 1857 (copy to the author from Gil Bosse of Métis, Quebec).
7. Ibid.
8. Henry Fry, *Essays*, 277.
9. Henry Fry, *Reminiscences*.
10. Ibid.
11. Henry Fry, *Reminiscences*, "My Atlantic Voyages." Sources for wrecks: Henry Fry, *History of North Atlantic Steam Navigation*; *www.cimorelli.com*, "Shipwrecks in the North Atlantic, 1841–1978."
12. *Dictionary of Canadian Biography*.
13. *www.measuringworth.com*, GDP deflator.
14. Marriage contract between Henry Fry, Esquire, and Miss Mary Jane Dawson. December 1858, document #4148.

15. Email exchange, May 2011, of Liz Avison and Sheila Yeoman, assistant curator, History Collection, Nova Scotia Museum.

16. Later in life, writes Lucy Fry Webster in her short biography of Henry, he carried in his back pocket a small oval portrait of Mary, a miniature reproduction of Havell's painting.

17. Information furnished by Liz Avison, Barrie, Ontario, a great-granddaughter of Mary Dawson Fry.

Chapter 7

1. Henry Fry, *History of North Atlantic Steam Navigation*, 32, 47.

2. Robin Craig, *The Ship: Steam Tramps and Cargo Liners, 1850–1950*, vol. 5 (National Maritime Museum, Great Britain). Preface by Basil Greenhill to a book commissioned by the National Maritime Museum and Her Majesty's Stationery Office.

3. Eileen Marcil, *The Charley-Man*, 316, 356n5.

4. Henry Fry, address to the Associated Chambers of Commerce of the United Kingdom, London, 1873.

5. Eileen Marcil, *The Charley-Man*, 315.

6. Henry Fry, *Reminiscences*.

7. Ibid.

8. Eileen Marcil, timeline for Henry Fry, S.C. 1454.

9. Henry Fry, *Reminiscences*.

10. Eileen Marcil, *The Charley-Man*.

11. Henry Fry, *Reminiscences*.

12. William Wood, editor-in-chief, "Storied Quebec" (chapter 17), in *The Storied Province of Quebec*, vol. 1, 243.

13. Ian Radforth, *Royal Spectacle: The 1860 Visit of the Prince of Wales to Canada and the United States* (Toronto: University of Toronto Press, 2004).

14. Special correspondent, *New York Times*, August 16, 1860. Dateline, Russel House, Quebec.

15. Henry Fry, *Notes on England, Wales, Scotland, Ireland and Paris, for a Young Canadian*, 30. Copy of handwritten book owned by the author.

16. Ibid.

17. Henry Fry, *David Marsh*. Copy of typed transcript, from Eileen Marcil.

Chapter 8

1. Susan Mann, *The Dream of Nation*, Carleton Library Series (Montreal and Kingston: McGill-Queen's University Press, 1982), 103.
2. Henry Fry, *Essays*, 1890.
3. Henry Fry, *Reminiscences*.
4. Hearing in court, Quebec, July 19, 1861, Honourable Henry Black presiding. Suit brought against the ship *Lotus* owned by Henry Fry, Mark Whitwell, and John Allward to recover damages arising out of a collision with the ship *Washington* in the harbour of Quebec.
5. Henry Fry, *Reminiscences*.
6. Note from Liz Avison to Eileen Marcil, emailed to the author March 5, 2007.
7. Eileen Marcil, Henry Fry timeline. Lease for five years from January 1, 1962, building belonging to the estate of James Gibb.
8. Eileen Marcil, Henry Fry timeline. "Purchase by William Walker, Henry Fry, and Jas Bowen of Cove for 11,571 pounds. To pay 1,000 pounds each year, and balance of 6,571 pounds to Commissioner of Crown Lands. Notarized by A. Campbell, 1/28/61"; see also chapter 27, footnote xii, in this book.

Chapter 9

1. Henry Fry, *Reminiscences*.
2. Edwin G. Burroughs and Mike Wallace, *Gotham: A History of New York City to 1898* (New York: Oxford University Press, 1999), 874.
3. Henry Fry, *Reminiscences*.
4. Ibid.
5. Jacques Bernier is a specialist in socio-economic history of Quebec, 1760–1867. He is particularly interested in the social history of medicine and the history of the area of Quebec.
6. Lucy Fry Webster, *A Short Biography of Henry Fry Sr.*

7. Henry Fry, *Reminiscences*.
8. Drawn from a seven-page list of the contents of the Fry house on Rue des Carrières prior to its rental in 1882.
9. Ibid.

Chapter 10

1. Shinplaster was a common name for paper money of low denomination circulating widely in the frontier economies of the nineteenth century. According to the *Oxford English Dictionary*, the name comes from the quality of the paper, which was so cheap that with a bit of starch it could be used to make papier-mâché-like plasters to go under socks to warm shins.
2. Henry Fry, *Reminiscences*.
3. Henry Fry, letter to the editor, *Quebec Morning Chronicle*, January 19, 1861.
4. Letters to the editor, *Morning Chronicle*, January and February, 1861.
5. Henry Fry, letter to the editor, *Morning Chronicle*, January 19, 1861.
6. Letter to the editor, *Morning Chronicle*, January 28, 1861 (signed by "A Practical Stevedore").
7. Letter to the editor, *Morning Chronicle*, February 7, 1861 (signed "A Merchant").
8. Eileen Marcil, *The Charley-Man*, 66.
9. Henry Fry, "Shipbuilding in Quebec," *The Canadian Magazine*, May 1895.
10. Eileen Marcil, *The Charley-Man*, 79, 80, 139, 200.
11. Census Report of Canada, 1861, City of Quebec.
12. Henry Fry, letter to the editor, *Morning Chronicle*, January 19, 1861.

Chapter 11

1. *www.measuringworth.com*.
2. Edwin G. Burroughs and Mike Wallace, *Gotham: A History of New York City to 1898* (Oxford, New York: Oxford University Press, 1999), 877.

3. Henry Fry, *Reminiscences*.

4. The illustrations are in *Reminiscences of a Quebec Ship Owner*, dedicated to Henry Fry Jr., and owned today by the author.

5. "The Custom-House Destroyed," *Morning Chronicle and Shipping Register*, September 12, 1864.

6. Eileen Marcil. *The Charley-Man*, 380–81.

7. "The Dinner at Quebec," *Saint John Morning Telegraph*, October 24, 1864.

8. Donald Creighton, *John A. Macdonald: The Young Politician*, 371–80, contains a lucid, detailed description of the political manoeuvring at the Conference on Confederation in Quebec, which lasted from October 8 to 27: "Russell, the proprietor of one of the biggest hotels in Quebec, had been persuaded to keep his establishment open much later in the season than was usual … and the Canadian Cabinet had planned a long series of dinners, *dejeuniers* and balls."

9. "The Dinner at Quebec," *Saint John Morning Telegraph*, October 24, 1864.

10. Henry Fry, *Reminiscences*.

11. Henry Fry, *History of North Atlantic Steam Navigation*, 278.

12. Documents from both Eileen Marcil and Lucy Fry Webster contain a detailed list of the organizations in which Henry Fry served as president and director.

13. The school closed in 1941 with the retirement of its headmaster — known as the Rector — F.T. Handsombody. It was wartime, and the masters were joining up, and there was no chance of getting replacements. Source: Ronnie Blair, Quebec.

14. Aileen Kennedy Fyfe, *Industrialized Conversion: The Religious Tract Society and Popular Science Publishing in Victorian Britain* (Cambridge, UK: Jesus College of Cambridge, 2000).

15. Henry Fry, *History of North Atlantic Steam Navigation*, 122.

16. Henry Fry, *David Marsh*, 1889.

17. Edwin P. Conklin, *The Storied Province of Quebec*, vol. 1, 551.

18. Alan Calcutt, *Faith in the Midst of Struggles* (McMaster Divinity College, August 8, 2001): "The history of the Quebec Baptist Church is one of constant struggling. Its vitality is directly dependent upon the vitality of the English-speaking community in Quebec City. The

church serves a minority group and depends fully on their presence for survival. In the Quebec City region, the proportion of the population made up of English-speakers declined from 39 percent in 1871, to 15 percent in 1901, to 3 percent in 1981. Even though Quebec City has a total population of more than 600,000, and the English-speaking population is between 14,000 and 15,000, there are only between 7,500 and 8,000 permanent (anglophone) residents, of whom 26.4 percent are 55 years of age and older. This means that a major part of the permanent (English-speaking) residents will soon be leaving this world for their eternal destination."

19. Henry Fry, *David Marsh*, 1889.

Chapter 12

1. Richard Rice, "Shipbuilding in British America, 1787–1890" (doctoral thesis, University of Liverpool, December 1977), 1,274; W.S. MacNutt, *New Brunswick: A History, 1784–1867* (Toronto: Macmillan, 1963), including quote from an issue of the *Saint John Chronicle* in 1837 (chapter 5). Investment in labour represented the main charge in the cost of getting the timber down to ports principally in Quebec. The money was advanced by credit by British merchants. The levels of wages, prices, and profits were extremely sensitive to swings of the trade cycle. The credit structure tended to exaggerate the fluctuations. "Little wonder then that the psychological traits of mania and despair were so identified with the timber trade. 'A breath had made it,' remarked the *Saint John Chronicle* in 1837, 'and a breath might take it away.'"

2. Henry Fry, *Reminiscences*.

3. William Henry Atherton, *Montreal, 1535–1914* (Montreal, Chicago: S.J. Clarke). Quebec, Montreal, and New York were first linked by telegraph in 1847.

4. Henry Fry, *Reminiscences*.

5. In October 1865, Rivière-du-Loup contractor Joseph Martin wrote to Henry Fry that for $175 Henry could have the fourth lot, causing Martin to believe that the entire four-acre site of the four Cliff

Cottages could be worth $700. Martin had architect's plans that would enable him to build a house for £1,475. In a letter to Martin, dated August 17, 1865, Henry wrote that his wife liked the proposed site for the house and that he had "no objection to taking a fourth share of the property for $175…. As I am taking my wife to England next summer," Henry wrote, "I do not feel disposed to enter into any building arrangements just now." Henry did not make the trip to England in 1866, however. Mary in the interim had become pregnant, and bore their third son, Arthur, November 26, 1866. Subsequently, Martin reported that Henry visited Cacouna again, and evidently took on the obligation to build a cottage. *Lettre de Joseph Martin, carpentier de Cacouna, 14 Fevrier, 1866.* "The four buildings are up and being roofed." *Lettre de W. Smyth, 8 Novembre, 1866.* "The houses will be finished in a fortnight" (*deux semaines*).

6. Samuel Dawson, *Handbook of the Dominion of Canada* (Montreal: Dawson Brothers, 1884), 26.
7. Henry Fry, *Reminiscences.*
8. Henry Fry, *History of North Atlantic Steam Navigation.*
9. Henry Fry, *Sir N.F. Belleau: A Biographical Sketch.*
10. Henry Fry, *Reminiscences.*
11. Ibid.
12. *Quebec Gazette.* Monday, March 9, 1868, page 2, Col. 3C. Obtained through Gilbert R. Bossé of Métis-sur-Mer, QC.
13. Ibid.
14. Eileen Marcil, *The Charley-Man*, 236, Col. 2.
15. Kenneth Mackenzie, letter to the author, November 2011.

Chapter 13

1. A version of this chapter appeared in the November/December 2009 issue of *Quebec Heritage News*, under the title "Obelisk Encore," by John Fry. About the same time, by chance, Parks Canada made the decision to tear the monument down and rebuild it with new stone.
2. René Villeneuve, *Lord Dalhousie: Patron and Collector* (Ottawa: National Gallery of Canada, 2008). Dalhousie kept a close eye on the

monument's construction. The agreement between the committee and the master mason, John Phillips, on April 22, 1828, specifies the use of Montreal greystone. This bluish-grey form of limestone was being used to build Notre Dame Church at the time, and it had caught the imagination of people in the capital. It seems, besides, that the Neuville quarries had been exhausted, and those at Deschambault were not yet in operation. Montreal limestone is harder than that found in the Quebec City region.

3. Letter to the editor, *Quebec Morning Chronicle*, September 12, 1864 (signed "Quebec").
4. Contract between Henry Fry and Henry Hatch, master builder, before the notary Henri-Charles Austin, August 6, 1869, #4745, uncovered by Eileen Marcil.
5. "The Corner Stone Re-Laid," *Quebec Chronicle*, September 9, 1969.
6. Alfred Hawkins and John Charlton Fisher, *Hawkins's Picture of Quebec: With Historical Recollections* (Quebec City: Neilson & Cowan, 1834), 265.

Chapter 14

1. J.M. LeMoine, *Picturesque Quebec* (Montreal: Dawson Brothers, 1882). Sixtieth anniversary history of the Quebec Young Men's Christian Association (YMCA), 1930. Over 132 years, the YMCA was located in several buildings throughout the city. The Quebec branch finally closed in 2002.
2. Henry Fry, *Essays*; May 26, 1870, and other 1870 issues of the *Quebec Morning Chronicle* about Fenian raids can be found online at *http://collections.banq.qc.ca*.
3. Henry Fry, *Reminiscences*.
4. "A Decade of Turbulence: Withdrawal of British Troops from Canada," *Canadian Military History Gateway*, *www.cmhg.gc.ca/cmh/page-507-eng.asp*.
5. Henry Fry, *Reminiscences*.
6. Lynda Dionne and Georges Pelletier, *Cacouna, les randonees du passe* (Quebec City: Editions Continuité Inc., 1995).

7. Henry Fry, *Reminiscences*.

8. Eileen Marcil, Henry Fry timeline. In 1871, Henry Fry & Co. took a three-year lease for the middle flat of two-storey stone house on the south side of St. Peter Street for fifty dollars a year.

9. Henry Fry, *Reminiscences*.

10. Ibid.

11. "Proceedings of the Second Annual Meeting of the Dominion Board of Trade Held at Ottawa, January 17–20, 1872" (Montreal: Gazette Printing House), 13–27 (Wm. McGiverin, Esq., President; Henry Fry, Esq., Vice-President); Kenneth S. Mackenzie, "The Quebec City Graving Dock," *Seaports and the Shipping World*, January 1987, 36, and "The Settlement Up the Creek," paper presented to Canadian Historical Society, 1991: The rivalry between Montreal and Quebec City was a vicious, unproductive battle "that many times saw the participants cutting off their noses to spite their faces, right up to the present day. Watch the angst/glee when Montrealers face the fact that the newest generation of container ships will off-load at the 'Ancient Capital.'" The river deepening proceeded anyway. The graving dock, built around 1886, was Quebec's compensation.

Chapter 15

1. "Address of Welcome to his Excellency the Governor General, Summary Report of the Dominion Board's Third Annual Meeting in the Proceedings of the Fourth Annual Meeting."

2. Marchioness of Dufferin and Ava, *My Canadian Journal*, entry for January 20, 1873 (London: John Murray, 1891), 58.

3. "Proceedings of the Third Annual Meeting of the Dominion Board of Trade, January 16, 1873."

4. Ibid.

5. Henry Fry, *Essays*.

6. *New York Times*, October 16, 1872.

Chapter 16

1. Kenneth S. Mackenzie, "The Pilotage Question to 1873," *Seaports and the Shipping World*, September 1987, 40.
2. Kenneth S. Mackenzie, "The Quebec City Graving Dock, Steam Operations on the Lower St. Lawrence to 1914," *Seaports and the Shipping World*, September 1987.
3. Henry Fry, paper presented at the third annual meeting of the Dominion Board of Trade, January 17, 1873.
4. Ibid.
5. Copy of *Quebec Daily Mercury*, 1873, editorial furnished by Kenneth S. Mackenzie.
6. Henry Fry, paper presented to Dominion Board of Trade, January 1873.
7. Ibid.
8. Frederick William Wallace, *In the Wake of the Wind-Ships* (Toronto: The Musson Book Company Limited, 1927), 120–21.
9. Ibid.

Chapter 17

1. Kenneth S. Mackenzie, "The Pilotage Question to 1873, Steam Operations on the Lower St. Lawrence to 1914," *Seaports and the Shipping World*, September 1987.
2. Henry Fry, *History of North Atlantic Steam Navigation*, 145; see also chapter 26, page 211, of *A Mind at Sea*.
3. Jean Leclerc, *Les pilotes du Saint-Laurent, 1762–1960*, 225.
4. "Petition to the Legislative Assembly of Canada Regarding the Incorporation of Pilots," *Morning Chronicle*, April 27, 1860. See also "Pilots Again," *Quebec Morning Chronicle*, Monday, April 20, 1863: 2, Col. 5C: "That the first section of the said Bill provides that every branch pilot who shall have charge of a vessel of more than six hundred tons, within the present limit of pilotage below Quebec, shall be entitled to claim and receive six dollars for every one hundred tons above six hundred tons, over and above the

amount at present fixed by law, for piloting such vessels; That your petitioners are of opinion that this enormous demand upon the shipping interests and the trade of the country, is caused by the unsatisfactory working of the Act 23 Vic. Cap. 123, entitled 'An Act to incorporate the pilots for and below the harbour of Quebec,' which provides, that the net income of the corporation shall be divided equally among the members thereof, irrespective of the amount of work each member performs; That the natural result of such division of income has been greatly to diminish the earnings of the active and efficient pilot, and to place him on a footing with the indolent and incompetent."

5. Evan Price, *History of the Price Family*; Jean Leclerc, *Les pilotes du Saint-Laurent*.

6. Gilbert R. Bossé, maritime researcher, Métis.

7. Henry Fry, letter to the editor, *Quebec Morning Chronicle*, March 30, 1871 (written from Bristol, England). Henry says that he is responding to recent letters in the *Chronicle* "that appear to be very bad translations from the *Journal de Quebec*. The style of these articles at once reveals their author. No one but Mr. Cauchon would have had recourse to personal abuse, willful misstatements, and attempts to traduce the private character of his fellow-citizens for a political object." At about this time, Cauchon defeated Quebec's wealthy, powerful James Gibb Ross, the anglophone independent Conservative candidate in the 1872 federal election for the constituency of Quebec Centre. The Cauchon versus Gibb electoral contest "degenerated into a bitter campaign centered around racial and religious differences," according to Ross's biography in the *Dictionary of Canadian Biography Online*, written in collaboration with Kenneth S. Mackenzie.

8. "Proceedings of the Second Annual Meeting of the Dominion Board of Trade, 1872."

9. "Report on Meeting of the Quebec Board of Trade," *Quebec Mercury*, August 5, 1873.

10. Kenneth S. Mackenzie, "Steam Operations on the Lower St. Lawrence," *Seaports and the Shipping World*, September 1987.

11. Ibid.

Chapter 18

1. Henry Fry, "Deck-Loads on Sea-Going Vessels," paper presented to the third annual meeting of the Dominion Board of Trade, Ottawa, January 1873.
2. The international load line or Plimsoll line on the starboard side of a vessel indicates the maximum safe draft resulting in minimum freeboard. The water line varies with cargo, season, and whether salt or fresh water.
3. Henry Fry, "Deck-Loads on Sea-Going Vessels."
4. Ibid; also Kenneth S. Mackenzie, "Canadian Shipping and Imperial Legislation," *Seaports and Shipping World*, February 1988, 48.
5. Editorial, *Quebec Daily Mercury*, 1873, furnished by Kenneth S. Mackenzie.
6. Arthur R.M. Lower, *Great Britain's Woodyard: British America and the Timber Trade 1763–1867* (Montreal: McGill-Queen's University Press, 1973), 237.
7. Henry Fry, "Deck-Loads on Sea-Going Vessels," paper presented to the third annual meeting of the Dominion Board of Trade.
8. Thomas E. Appleton, *Usque ad Mare: A History of the Canadian Coast Guard and Marine Services* (Ottawa, Department of Transport: Queen's Printer, 1969).
9. *Quebec Morning Chronicle*, May 14, 1873, 2, Col. 1C.
10. "Proceedings of the Fourth Annual Meeting of the Dominion Board of Trade, Ottawa, February 24, 1874," cites Henry Fry letter of October 30, 1873: "Urgent private affairs compel me to leave for England immediately. My apologies for my absence."
11. Lucy Fry Webster, *A Short Biography of Henry Fry Sr.*
12. Eileen Marcil, Henry Fry Timeline; also Henry Fry, *Reminiscences*.
13. Henry Fry, "British Seamen," in *Reminiscences of a Retired Ship Owner*.
14. Thomas E. Appleton, *Usque ad Mare: A History of the Canadian Coast Guard and Marine Services.*

Chapter 19

1. See chapter 25, page 195, of this book.
2. Henry Fry, *Essays.*
3. The Associated Chambers of Commerce of the United Kingdom report of Henry Fry's remarks in the *Quebec Mercury*, March 1874, photocopy furnished by Kenneth S. Mackenzie.
4. Ibid.
5. Ibid.
6. "The Reciprocity Treaty: What Is Thought of It by the Large and Small Manufacturers — Its Advantages and Disadvantages — Protection More Desirable," *New York Times*, September 21, 1874.
7. "Proceedings at the Semi-Annual Meeting, Dominion Board of Trade, at Saint John, New Brunswick, July 1874."
8. "Proceedings at the Semi-Annual Meeting of the Dominion Board of Trade, July 1874"; Henry Fry, *Essays.*
9. Ibid.
10. Donald Creighton, "The Forked Road," in *John A. Macdonald: The Old Chieftain* (Toronto: Macmillan, 1955).
11. Richard Pomfret, *The Economic Development of Canada, Second Edition* (Scarborough, ON: Nelson, 1993), 73.

Chapter 20

1. George Gale, *Historic Tales of Old Quebec* (Quebec: Telegraph Printing Co., 1923); James MacPherson Lemoine, *Picturesque Quebec*, vol. 2, 250.
2. Henry Fry, "Cycles in Trade," in *Essays*, 279–80.
3. Henry Fry, *Reminiscences.*
4. See chapter 3 of this book.
5. The contents of the house were detailed in 1882 when Mary rented the place to Edward Spaulding, a New Yorker who moved to Quebec. A photocopy is in the possession of the author.
6. Henry Fry will of 1866, Archives Judiciares, Palais de Justice, Quebec.
7. Marchioness of Dufferin, *My Canadian Journal*, 115–19.

8. Horace Hutchison, *Famous Golf Links*, 182–88.
9. Henry Fry, *Reminiscences*.
10. Henry Fry, *Reminiscences*, written for his son Arthur. *Gaspee* had a leak "caused by a cheap contractor in Liverpool, who to save a little trouble, when re-coppering her, omitted to move the blocks, and so could not properly calk her. Moral: avoid cheap tradesmen unless you know them well."
11. Ibid.
12. Ibid.

Chapter 21

1. Edwin G. Burroughs and Mike Wallace, *Gotham: A History of New York City to 1898* (New York: Oxford University Press, 1999), 943.
2. Eileen Marcil, Henry Fry timeline.
3. *www.jewishvirtullibrary.org.*
4. Eileen Marcil, *The Charley-Man*, 227.
5. Eileen Marcil, *The Charley-Man*, 320, 323, 326; William Wallace, *Wooden Ships and Iron Men*, 217. Wallace may have derived his Lloyd's information from Henry Fry's *Reminiscences of a Quebec Ship Owner*.
6. *Cosmo*'s Bureau Veritas rating was a superior 3/3 for ten years. Just before *Cosmo*, the Lloyd's surveyor rated the ships *Belstane* and *Batavia* 10A.
7. The piece hangs today in the author's home in Katonah, New York. Several of Willis's works can be found in Connecticut's Mystic Seaport Museum and Boston's Peabody Museum.
8. Lucy Fry Webster, *A Short Biography of Henry Fry Sr.*
9. Eileen Marcil, *The Charley-Man*, 346, 347 (image), and 351.
10. *Quebec Chronicle Telegraph*, June 2, 1952. Moses Murphy was fourteen years old when the *Cosmo* was launched.
11. *Quebec Chronicle Telegraph & Shipping News*, July 4, 1877.

Chapter 22

1. Bård Kolltveit, *Wilh. Wilhelmsen, 150 Years: 1861–2011: History and Stories* (Lysaker, Norway: Dinamo Forlag/Wilh. Wilhelmsen, 2011).

2. Henry Fry, *Reminiscences.*

3. Eileen Marcil, *The Charley-Man*, 123.

4. Henry Fry, "Shipbuilding in Quebec," *The Canadian Magazine*, May 1895.

5. Eileen Marcil, *Tall Ships and Tankers: The History of the Davie Shipbuilders* (Toronto, McClelland & Stewart, 1997), 130.

6. *The Canadian Magazine*, May 1895.

7. Henry Fry, *Reminiscences.*

8. Ibid.

9. Henry's disappointment with his youngest brother's performance is recorded on page 52 of his handwritten *Reminiscences of a Retired Ship Owner*, dedicated to his eldest son, Henry Fry Jr. with Christmas greetings in 1891. His disappointment and criticism are missing from what is virtually the same writing in *There Go the Ships: Reminiscences of a Retired Ship Owner*, dedicated to Arthur Dawson, Henry Fry's third son. Possibly Henry did not wish to give lasting offence to that branch of his descendants. Also, see chapter 27, note 3, of this book.

10. Contents of the house on Rue des Carrières, lease of 46 Rue des Carrières, fully furnished by Henry Fry Jr., as attorney for his mother, Mary Dawson, living in Montreal, to Edward B. Spaulding of New York, for one year, with inventory including list of books, March 3, 1882.

11. Lucy F. Webster, *A Short Biography of Henry Fry Sr.*

12. Ibid.

13. Henry Fry, *Notes on England*. 1891.

14. Edwin G. Burroughs and Mike Wallace, *Gotham: A History of New York City to 1898* (New York and Oxford: Oxford University Press, 1999), 937.

Chapter 23

1. Hartford Hospital and the Institute of Living. Medical Record of Henry Fry, a patient at the Hartford Retreat, 1879–80. Obtained August 22, 2003, through Steven R. Lytle, archivist.

2. Lawrence B. Goodheart, *Mad Yankees: The Hartford Retreat for the Insane and Nineteenth-Century Psychiatry* (Amherst and Boston: University of Massachusetts Press, 2003).

3. Exhibit at the Institute of Living, photographed by the author in 2011.

4. Francis J. Braceland, M.D., *The Institute of Living: The Hartford Retreat, 1822–1972* (Hartford, CN: Wiley, 1972).

5. Ibid., 108.

6. This book was in Henry's library, inventoried in 1882 when E.B. Spaulding rented the house on Rue des Carrières.

7. "From Quackery to Bacteriology: The Emergence of Modern Medicine in 19th Century America," text for an exhibition at Ward M. Canada Center, University of Toledo, 1994. The application of electric current to the head for the treatment of mania, dementia, and melancholia came into vogue in the last half of the nineteenth century. The body was believed to operate like a large magnet, with positive and negative charges. Electricity applied to areas where the charges were out of balance would allegedly cure the patient.

8. Howard Markel, *An Anatomy of Addiction* (New York: Pantheon Books, 2011).

9. Winthrop B. Hallock, M.D., "Accommodation for the Insane on the Cottage Plan," *New York Medical Journal*, January 1874.

10. In Connecticut, the author, after successfully extracting Henry's 1881–82 patient record from the Hartford Institute, sought similar information about his treatment at Hallock Hall. I visited the Holy Apostles College and Seminary, which presently occupies the site of what was Cromwell Hall. The librarian there has no records of patients when the place was a hospital for the mentally ill. There turned out to be a reason. Lois and Richard Donahue of the Cromwell Historical Society advised me that Hallock Hall's records were destroyed in the 1960s when the place became a seminary.

11. *Cromwell Hall, Established in 1877 in Cromwell, Connecticut.* Photocopy of brochure obtained from the library of Holy Apostles College & Seminary, which now occupies the former Hallock property.

Chapter 24

1. The original petition of Dame Mary Jane Dawson to the Superior Court was signed by her and recorded May 30, 1882, in Montreal. Document in the Archives Nationales de Quebec.
2. Interdiction of Henry Fry. Questions submitted to Louis Joseph Cyprien Fiset, John Henry Ross Burroughs, and Archibald Campbell, joint Prothonotary in the Province of Quebec Superior Court, District of Quebec, June 2, 1882.
3. Testimony of Winthrop B. Hallock, M.D., before the Honorable Judge, Superior Court, June 2, 1882.
4. Statement of Mary Dawson Fry's assets on the death of her husband, Henry Fry, notarized by Ronzo H. Clerk in the city of Montreal, October 26, 1896. Mary proudly declared in 1896 that she administered and managed her husband's property to the best of her ability, reinvesting capital while using the interest and dividends for her own expenses and Henry's.
5. While the Census defined a widow as a woman whose husband has died, an informal use of the word was to describe a woman whose husband was frequently away or absent.
6. That Henry Fry's activities from the summer of 1882 until 1889 can only be a matter of conjecture is not due to a lack of dogged research. When did he move to Quebec's Eastern Townships? I visited the library of the Brome County Historical Society where Arlene Royea was most helpful in finding information about Dr. George Slack, but alas nothing about Henry Fry. In Cowansville, part of which was once Sweetsburg, where Henry died in 1896, I worked with Michel Racicot of the Société d'Histoire. I am grateful to him and historian Gilbert Beaulieu for detecting the first official record of Henry's presence in the Eastern Townships in the 1991 Census, showing him to

be living with a family of Joseph Massicotte in a house very near to Dr. Slack, who was caring for him in 1896 when he died.

7. Bibliothèque et Archives nationales du Québec, 1245198. Subject Dr. George Frederick Slack, Biographical and Profession information, email from Liz Avison to John Fry, December 31, 2010.

8. Documented in the papers of Mary Dawson Fry after the death of Henry Fry in 1896.

9. Information provided to the author by James J. Terleph of Katonah, New York, certified psychoanalytic psychotherapist with the National Association of for the Advancement of Psychoanalysis, and licensed New York State psychoanalyst.

10. Lucy Fry Webster, *A Short Biography of Henry Fry Sr.*: "In or around 1880 it is understood that Henry Senior has a nervous breakdown and retired to the home of a Dr. George F. Slack in Farnham, Quebec, where he remained for approximately ten years."

11. 1891 Census of Canada, District of Missisquoi, Ville de Farnham, April 7, 1891. Henry Fry's religion is given as *"Église d'Angleterre"* (Church of England), information completely inconsistent with Henry's long and intense attachment to the Baptist Church.

Chapter 25

1. Tribute to David Marsh, written by Henry Fry, "One Who Loved Him," July 1889, Quebec.

2. In the 1891 Census of Canada (see chapter 24, note 11, of this book), under "Infirmities," Henry is listed as "Unsound of Mind," defined "to include all those unfortunates who are plainly deprived of reason." The enumerator or census taker was not required to make an attempt to distinguish what type of malady caused the individual's condition (email January 8, 2012, from Eileen Marcil to John Fry).

3. Henry Fry, *Essays*.

4. Ibid.

5. Donald Creighton, *John A. Macdonald: The Old Chieftain* (Toronto: Macmillan, 1955), 547.

6. Henry Fry, *Essays*.

7. Donald Creighton, *The Old Chieftain*. The White dinner in Montreal, 206.
8. Henry Fry, *Essays*.
9. Ibid.
10. James Ferrabee and Michael St. B. Harrison, *Staying Connected: How MacDougall Family Traditions Built a Business over 160 Years* (Montreal: McGill-Queen's University Press, 2009), 63.
11. Henry Fry, *Essays*.
12. Henry Fry, *Notes on England*.

Chapter 26

1. Henry Fry, *Essays*, 22.
2. Henry Fry. *Reminiscences*, 16.
3. Henry Fry, *History of North Atlantic Steam Navigation*.
4. Henry Harrisse, *The Discovery of North America by John Cabot: The Alleged Date and Landfall, Also the Ship's Name, The Matthew, A Forgery of Chatterton?* (London: B.F. Stevens, Publisher, 1897); Samuel E. Dawson, *The Voyages of the Cabots: Latest Phases of the Controversy* (Ottawa, Toronto, London: 1897).
5. Henry Fry, *History of North Atlantic Steam Navigation*, 74, 144, 166, 216, 284.
6. Ibid., 276.
7. Henry Fry, photocopy of typeset statement "The Fast Atlantic Steamship Service," September 14, 1894, Sweetsburg, Quebec, with handwritten notation, "Wilfrid Laurier Esq. M.P. with Mr. Fry's compliments."

Chapter 27

1. It is not known with certainty who took the picture, nor where it was made. Notman lists Henry Fry as having been photographed in 1891, but no negative or print exists, and Notman's listing may be for a photo of Henry Fry Jr.

2. A set of silverware is in the author's possession.

3. Google Sweetsburg Fenian Congressional Edition. Letter no. 26, C.G.B. Drummond U.S. Vice-Consul to William H. Seward, Secretary of State, January 3, 1867.

4. According to the Brome County Historical Society, Belmont was a retirement or convalescent home in the late 1800s, owned and operated by Montrealers, one of whom was Robertson: "Fry himself may have been instrumental in setting it up. It had some connection with the YMCA." Today the building houses the Bar Yamaska, with drink and food service.

5. Henry Fry, "Shipbuilding in Quebec," *The Canadian Magazine* 5, no. 1 (May 1895): 3.

6. "Lloyd's in England and Canada," *The Gazette*, Montreal, June 28, 1895.

7. "North Atlantic Steam Navigation," *The Gazette*, Montreal, January 28, 1896.

8. The undertakers were Thomas Slogett of Cowansville and George Armstrong of Montreal. Documents assembled under the direction of Rouzo H. Clerk, Notary Public, signed October 26, 1896, in Montreal under number 1979.

9. Lucy Fry Webster, *A Short Biography of Henry Fry Sr.*

10. Rod McLeod, *Quebec Heritage News*, Autumn 2010, 13.

11. "Canadian Forger Sentenced," Montreal, November 27, *New York Times*, November 28, 1896.

12. Email to the author from Eileen Marcil, March 19, 2003. Ms. Marcil on the phone interviewed Mary Elizabeth Craig, a granddaughter of Edward Carey Fry, who recalled that her mother told her that Henry Fry ruined Edward Carey Fry. Because of Henry, her grandmother, Elisabeth Marsh Fry (the daughter of Baptist minister David Marsh) had to live very frugally. When Marcil asked Ms. Craig the cause, she said it was something that had happened in England, but she didn't know more.

13. Eileen Marcil, Henry Fry timeline, "Sale of Sillery Cove. Succession of H. Fry, per notary Jacques Auger, for Henry Fry Jr. and Arthur Dawson Fry of Montreal, to Richard Reid Dobell for Dobell, Beckett & Co. All of Fry's interest in cove known as Fry's and Bowen's Cove,

Sillery, cadastral lots 267 and 269, measuring 45 arpents 75 perches from the ridge of the hill to 1wm, bordering Sharples, Wainwright & Co. on the s.w. — all deep water lots, ways, paths, passages, commodities, advantages, easements and appurtenances whatsoever appertaining and the wharves, piers, houses, tenements and other buildings without reserve. Dobell to settle all accounts with Government and Quebec Harbour Commissioners."

14. S.E. Dawson, *The Prose Writers of Canada: An Address Delivered Before the Teachers of the City and District of Montreal* (Montreal: E.M. Renouf, 1901), 20.

15. Montreal Museum of Fine Arts, Cornelius Krieghoff, *Indian Family in the Forest*, 1851, oil on canvas, 44.7 x 66.6 cm, Mary Fry Dawson bequest, inv. 1954.1105.

16. Lucy Fry Webster, *A Short Biography of Henry Fry Sr.*

Conclusion

1. Eileen Marcil, *The Charley-Man*, 212, 384; also, Eileen Marcil, emails of May 9, 2009.

2. Henry Fry, "Shipbuilding in Quebec," *The Canadian Magazine*, May 1895.

Bibliography

Baldwin, Alice Sharples. *High, Wide and Handsome*. Montreal: Price Patterson Ltd., 1981.

Bernier, J.E. *A Narrative of 60 Years at Sea, from the Logs and Yarns of Captain J.E. Bernier*. Ottawa: Le Droit, 1939.

Bernstein, William J. *A Splendid Exchange: How Trade Shaped the World*. New York: Atlantic Monthly Press, 2008.

Blair, Louisa. *The Anglos: The Hidden Face of Quebec City, Volume II, Since 1850*. Quebec: Commission de la capitale nationale du Quebec, 2005.

Callbeck, Lorne C. *My Island, My People*. Charlottetown: The Prince Edward Island Heritage Foundation, 1979.

Calvin, D.D. *A Saga of the St. Lawrence: Timber and Shipping Through Three Generations*. Toronto: Ryerson Press, 1945.

Creighton, Donald. *John A. Macdonald: The Old Chieftain*. Toronto: Macmillan, 1955.

Dawson, Samuel. *Handbook of the Dominion of Canada*. Montreal: Dawson Brothers, 1884.

Dawson, Samuel Edward. *The Prose Writers of Canada: Address to the American Library Association*. Montreal: E.M. Renouf, 1901.

Defebaugh, James Elliott. *History of the Lumber Industry of America*. Vol. I. Chicago: The American Lumberman, 1906.

Dufferin and Ava, Marchioness of. *My Canadian Journal, 1872–78*. London, John Murray, 1891.

Fingard, Judith. *Jack in Port*. Toronto: University of Toronto Press, 1982.

Fry, Christopher. *Can You Find Me: A Family History*. Oxford University Press, 1978.

Fry, Henry. *A Biographical Sketch of Sir N.F. Belleau*. Quebec: A. Coté & Co., 1894.

_____. *Essays on Free Trade and Protection, British Statesmen, Lloyd's, Cycles in Trade, Commercial Union and Reciprocity*. Papers donated to the Thomas Fisher Rare Book Library, University of Toronto, 1890.

_____. *The History of North Atlantic Steam Navigation*. London: Sampson Low, Marston and Company Limited, 1896.

_____. *Lloyd's: Its Origin, History and Methods*. Quebec: Dawson & Co., 1895.

_____. *Notes on England, Wales, Scotland, Ireland and Paris, for a Young Canadian. Handwritten with Sketches of Typical Sailing Steamships*, 1891.

_____. *Reminiscences of a Retired Ship Owner*. Handwritten with illustrations, dedicated "To my eldest and beloved son, Henry Fry, Jr." 1891. Book in possession of the author.

Gale, George. *Historic Tales of Old Quebec*. Quebec: Telegraph Printing Company, 1923.

Goodheart, Lawrence B. *Mad Yankees: The Hartford Retreat for the Insane and Nineteenth-Century Psychiatry*. Amherst and Boston: University of Massachusetts Press, 2003.

Greenhill, Basil, and Ann Giffard. *Westcountrymen in Prince Edward's Isle*. Halifax: Formac Publishing, 2003.

Harrisse, Henry. *John Cabot: The Discoverer of North America and Sebastian His Son*. London: Benjamin Franklin Stevens, 1896.

Hawkins, Alfred. *Hawkens's Picture of Quebec with Historical Recollections*. Quebec: printed for the Proprietor of Nelson & Cowan, 1834.

Holloway, Richard. *Looking in the Distance*. Edinburgh, New York: Canongate Press, 2004.

Leclerc, Jean. *Les Pilotes du Saint-Laurent, 1762–1960*. Sainte-Foy: Les Editions GID et Jean Leclerc, 2004.

Lower, Arthur M. *Great Britain's Woodyard: British America and the Timber Trade*. Montreal and London: McGill-Queen's University Press, 1973.

Mackenzie, Kenneth S. "Canadian Shipbuilding and Imperial Legislation: Part I." *Seaports and the Shipping World*, November 1987.

_____. "The Canadian Timber Trade, 1871–76." *Seaports and the Shipping World*, April 1987.

_____. "1888, Ship Loading." *Seaports and the Shipping World*, July 1989.

_____. "Incompetent Captains." *Seaports and the Shipping World*, August 1987.

_____. "Jack Ashore." *Seaports and the Shipping World*, July 1987.

_____. "Peter Mitchell: The Search for a Canadian Lloyd's: Part I and II." *Seaports and the Shipping World*, December 1987 and January 1988.

_____. "The Pilotage Question to 1873." *Seaports and the Shipping World*, September 1987.

_____. "The Quebec City Graving Dock." *Seaports and the Shipping World*, January 1987.

_____. "Retrospective, 1853–1886." *Seaports and the Shipping World*, May 1989.

_____. "Retrospective Montreal Businessman." *Seaports and the Shipping World*, August 1989.

_____. "Ship Laborers, Plimsoll." *Seaports and the Shipping World*, August 1989.

MacPherson, Mrs. Daniel. *Old Memories, Amusing and Historical* (printed for the author, circa 1890).

_____. "The St. Lawrence Timber Trade to 1902." *Seaports and the Shipping World*, May 1987.

_____. "Wooden Men and Iron Ships." *Seaports and the Shipping World*, June 1987.

Mann, Susan. *The Dream of Nation*. Carleton Library Series. Montreal and Kingston: McGill-Queen's University Press, 1982.

Marcil, Eileen. *The Charley-Man: A History of Wooden Shipbuilding at Quebec, 1763–1893*. Kingston, ON: Quarry Press, 1995.

Morgan, Joan Elson. *Castle of Quebec*. J.M. Dent & Sons (Canada) Limited, 1949.

Morison, Samuel Eliot. *The European Discovery of America*. New York: Oxford University Press, 1971.

Ouellet, Fernand. *Economic and Social History of Quebec, 1760–1850*. Ottawa: Carleton University, Gage Publishing, 1980.

Roche, Mazo de la. *Quebec: Historic Seaport.* Garden City, NY: Doubleday, Doran & Company, Inc., 1944.

Wade, Mason. *The French-Canadian Outlook.* New York: Viking Press, 1947.

Wallace, Frederick William. *Wooden Ships and Iron Men.* London and Toronto: Hodder and Stoughton, Ltd., circa 1920s.

_____. *In the Wake of the Wind-Ships.* Toronto: The Musson Book Company Ltd., 1927.

Wood, William, ed. *The Storied Province of Quebec*, 4 vols. Toronto: Dominion Publishing Company, 1931.

Acknowledgements

Authors customarily say of their books that they "would not have been possible without …," politely nodding approval to people whose aid they enlisted in its research and writing. But *A Mind at Sea* is a book that literarily could not have been written without the close involvement of one person, Eileen Marcil. The foremost historian of Quebec's phenomenal age of shipping and shipyards, Marcil is the author *The Charley-Man: A History of Wooden Shipbuilding at Quebec, 1763–1893*, published in 1995, and no one possesses a greater knowledge of the subject.

In the course of writing *Charley-Man*, Marcil came to realize that one of the most significant yet overlooked figures in the river port city's history, and in the commerce of the lower St. Lawrence, was Henry Fry, who arrived in Quebec from Bristol, England, in 1854, just as wooden shipbuilding was reaching a crescendo. Marcil compiled hundreds of notes about Fry's influence, and intended to write about his life. When other writing and lectures, as well as age, intervened, she generously supplied me with all of her research so that I could write the biography that she so desired would see the light of day. Her research is the foundation of this book. And she did more. Over the four years that I took to write *A Mind at Sea*, I repeatedly called on her to ferret out information that eluded me, and to remedy my shortcomings as a maritime historian.

Near to completion of the manuscript, I happily discovered another maritime historian willing to help me. Kenneth S. Mackenzie found numerous occasions to write about Henry Fry in his work for *Seaports and the Shipping World* magazine, published between 1985 and 1992. A member of the Canadian Nautical Research Society, Mackenzie agreed to read my manuscript, and suggested additions and made vital corrections.

Maritime researcher Gilbert R. Bossé of Métis-sur-Mer furnished me with supplementary information about Henry Fry's shipping activities on the Lower St. Lawrence River, including his pilotage disputes. Cacouna historian Georges Pelletier discovered for me documents relating to Henry's property purchase and construction of the family's summer cottage.

Both Eileen Marcil and myself thank Dr. Pierre Louis Lapointe, Reference Archivist, for his help in locating records at the Bibliothèque et Archives nationales du Québec. Jean-Francois Caron aided me in researching Henry's reconstruction of the Wolfe-Montcalm monument, as did Gaston Déry concerning the models of the sailing ship *Cosmo* made by Edmond Lecouvie in Quebec. Thanks also to the Blair family, and to the Literary and Historical Society of Quebec in Morrin Centre.

I ran into numerous dead ends in attempting to uncover details of the final ten years of Henry Fry's life in Quebec's Eastern Townships, or Estrie. What success I did realize I owe to the assistance from Michel Racicot of the Cowansville Historical Society. Judy Antle and the Missisquoi Historical Society were helpful as well. I received encouragement from Rod MacLeod, the editor of *Quebec Heritage News*, who published two long excerpts from *A Mind At Sea*.

Pulling back the curtains on Henry Fry's devastating mental breakdown of the period roughly 1878 to 1888 was a painful personal experience, and one that consumed many days of hard-digging research. The breakthrough came when, with clearance from living descendants of Henry Fry, Stephen Lytle, archivist of the Institute of Living and the Hartford Hospital in Hartford, Connecticut, was able to release to me the record of my great-grandfather's treatment at the Hartford Retreat for the Insane.

Regarding his treatment at Cromwell Hall in Connecticut, I was assisted by the present owner of the property, Holy Apostles College and Seminary, by the Cromwell-Belden Public Library, and by the Harvey Cushing/John Hay Whitney Medical Library at Yale.

Psychiatrists George Naumburg and Larry Goldblatt, and psycho-analyst James Terleph guided me to a modern scientific interpretation of Henry's illness.

The genealogy of the Fry family and its place in Somerset history were supplied by the late Norman Davies of Newcastle, England; Frances Knight, historian of Winscombe; and Maria Forbes, genealogist and historian of Maxmills Barton. I utilized as much information as I could from a brief biography of Henry Fry written by his granddaughter, the late Lucy Fry Webster of Nova Scotia. Of inestimable help to me was Liz Avison, a great-granddaughter of Henry Fry and librarian emerita of the University of Toronto. Along with Dick Avison and other Fry family members, she assisted me in locating photographs and, with the help of Russ Strathdee, created a website to help promote interest in the book.

I am indebted to Doug Abdelnour of Bedford Photo-Graphic for the hours he spent enhancing century-old illustrations. Also to Nora Hague and the staff at Montreal's McCord Museum, where the Notman photos are archived, and to William Alexander for his help with picture research.

I would like to thank the Chawkers Foundation whose generous grant helped to underwrite publication of *A Mind at Sea*, and to the Townshippers Foundation, which acted as the charitable intermediary for the grant.

I am grateful to my German-born and educated wife, Marlies, whose observant perspective on early drafts was helpful in making my work more intelligible to readers unfamiliar with Quebec history.

Thanks to Alex Paterson and to Michael Ballantyne and My-Trang Nguyen in Montreal, and New York editor and playwright Gay Walley (a former Montrealer), for their suggestions and encouragement, and especially to Allison Hirst, Beth Bruder, and Kirk Howard at my publisher, Dundurn. Having spent more than half a century as an editor of magazines, newspapers, and books, I appreciate the professionalism of everyone at Dundurn who made the editing and production of this biography move resolutely to its final publication.

John Fry
snowfry@verizon.net
http://johnfry.net